Praise for *Glass Hou*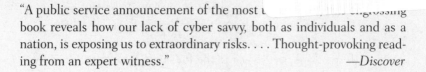

"A public service announcement of the most ........................ engrossing book reveals how our lack of cyber savvy, both as individuals and as a nation, is exposing us to extraordinary risks. . . . Thought-provoking reading from an expert witness."                                                                    —*Discover*

"The author's background as a former anti-trust prosecutor is on impressive display as he mounts his case with meticulous attention to detail."
                                                                                                    —*Kirkus Reviews*

"Brenner offers a comprehensive recipe for shoring up network security in both government and private sectors."                                        —*Booklist*

"This alarming account by an expert is worthy of serious attention from policy makers and average readers alike."                        —*Publishers Weekly*

"[*Glass Houses*] offers an expert's keen insight into the netherworld of cyberrisk. Rich in facts, stories, and analysis, the book is a clarion call for more effective cyberpolicies and practices in both the government and private sector. America should take heed."
    —Ambassador Henry A. Crumpton, author of *The Art of Intelligence*

"If you have a responsibility for protecting intellectual property, trade secrets, and other instruments of successful business; if you are responsible for protecting national information and technology interests then you have a responsibility to read this book. Bring a change of underwear."
                        —Vint Cerf, Chief Internet Evangelist at Google

"Cybercrime, espionage, and warfare are among the great challenges of this century, but as Joel Brenner argues, we are woefully ill-prepared to meet them. Drawing on history, law, economics, common sense, and his rare experience in counterintelligence, Brenner deftly describes the problems and offers a series of very practical solutions. This book is both well written and convincing."
                        —Joseph Nye, author of *Soft Power* and *The Future of Power*
                            and University Distinguished Service Professor at
                            the Harvard Kennedy School of Government

PENGUIN BOOKS

# GLASS HOUSES

Joel Brenner is the former senior counsel at the National Security Agency, where he advised on legal and policy issues relating to network security. Previously, he served as the national counterintelligence executive in the office of the director of National Intelligence and as the NSA's inspector general. He is a graduate of the University of Wisconsin–Madison (BA), the London School of Economics (PhD), and Harvard Law School (JD). Brenner currently practices law in Washington, D.C., specializing in privacy, data security, and related issues.

# GLASS HOUSES

*Privacy, Secrecy, and Cyber Insecurity*

*in a Transparent World*

## JOEL BRENNER

PENGUIN BOOKS

Previously published as *America the Vulnerable*

PENGUIN BOOKS
Published by the Penguin Group
Penguin Group (USA), 375 Hudson Street,
New York, New York 10014, USA

USA | Canada | UK | Ireland | Australia | New Zealand | India | South Africa | China
Penguin Books Ltd, Registered Offices: 80 Strand, London WC2R 0RL, England
For more information about the Penguin Group visit penguin.com

First published in the United States of America as *America the Vulnerable* by The Penguin Press,
a member of Penguin Group (USA) Inc., 2011
This edition with a new preface published in Penguin Books 2013

Portions of Chapter 10 appeared in "Privacy and Security: Why Isn't Cyberspace More Secure?"
by Joel Brenner, *Communications of the ACM,* November 2010.

THE LIBRARY OF CONGRESS HAS CATALOGED THE HARDCOVER EDITION AS FOLLOWS:
Brenner, Joel.
America the vulnerable : inside the new threat matrix of digital
espionage, crime, and warfare / Joel Brenner.
p. cm.
Includes bibliographical references and index.
ISBN 978-1-59420-313-8 (hc.)
ISBN 978-0-14-312211-1 (pbk.)
1. Computer crimes—United States—Prevention. 2. Internet in
espionage—United States. 3. National security—United States. I. Title.
HV6773.2.B74 2011
364.16'80973—dc23
2011019801

Printed in the United States of America
3  5  7  9  10  8  6  4  2

DESIGNED BY AMANDA DEWEY

*For Victoria*

# CONTENTS

# PREFACE TO THE
# PAPERBACK EDITION

RETURNING TO THE private sector after service in two intelligence agencies, I find myself advising companies about security and counterintelligence threats that hardly existed a decade earlier. Security measures that used to be relevant only to a few government agencies, the military, and defense contractors are now urgently required by most businesses. Counterintelligence questions—Who's stealing my information? Why do they want it? What will they do next?—face every organization with secrets to keep. Companies are bleeding the intellectual property and technology that create jobs and wealth and on which our future prosperity depends—even if a dismaying number of corporate executives prefer to ignore what's happening. And the government, even as it over-classifies all sorts of anodyne information, struggles to stop leaks of its most legitimately held secrets. Meanwhile, personal information continues to be for sale on the criminal market by the boatload. As my title indicates, we are living in a glass house, or a series of glass houses: at home, at work, and in public places. These pages explain in lively and nontechnical terms how and why this has happened—and what could happen next.

The state-sponsored theft of Western intellectual property urgently requires a more robust response from governments as well as companies. In February 2013, a private cyberforensics firm called Mandiant revealed irrefutable evidence that China's People's Liberation Army has been systematically stealing a wide range of technology from scores of Western companies. This wasn't news to our intelligence agencies, or indeed to anyone who'd been paying attention, but never before has such detailed proof been laid before the public. Those who claim the threat has been hyped must now confront the evidence.

China is the worst offender but it is hardly alone. Russia and Iran are also large-scale practitioners of state-sponsored espionage against private companies, and the Iranians aim at disruption as well as theft. In August 2012, the information systems of Saudi Aramco, a leading oil producer, were attacked from Iran. About thirty thousand computers were wiped clean of all data and had to be junked. Later that month, RasGas in Quattar suffered a similar attack. As I write these words, many American banks are under relentless attack from computers from Iran—almost certainly by cut-outs for Iranian intelligence services. These attacks have thus far taken the form of distributed denial of service attacks—the computer equivalent of engineered traffic jams—but at a level of intensity never seen before. The attacks disrupt service and cost millions to defend against. If attackers can wipe all content from thirty thousand computers at a Saudi oil company, they could also do it to many Western companies—or perhaps to your bank. Our financial system is based on information. It's simply a system of accounts—records of who owes what to whom—and that system is electronic. If big pieces of it were wiped out or corrupted, the resulting economic wreck would be felt around the world and would make the economic consequences of 9/11 look trivial. Like our electric grid, which has also been infected with advanced persistent computer viruses, financial systems are critical to the country, and they are vulnerable.

This struggle for the security of essential institutions and infrastructure, like the struggle for the privacy of your personal information and the security of commercial trade secrets, is evolving as you open this book.

*Washington, D.C.*
*April 2013*

# INTRODUCTION

—

**HOW DID THE** Chinese manage to remotely download up to twenty tera-bytes of information from the Defense Department—equal to about 20 percent of all the data in the Library of Congress? And why don't we know exactly what they took? How did WikiLeaks get its hands on classified diplomatic cables, and why hasn't the U.S. government been able to shut it down? How did the specifications for the avionics and armor on the president's helicopter end up in Tehran, and what has that got to do with the theft of Supreme Court Justice Stephen Breyer's private data from his investment adviser? The answers to these ques-tions reveal alarming threats to our personal, corporate, and national security that come from a new type of espionage and from the sudden transparency that electronic connectivity has brought to all aspects of our lives. Your difficulties with electronic privacy, the electronic theft of America's cutting-edge technology, and the government's loss of state secrets are a lot more alike than you know.

I spent most of the first decade of the twenty-first century work-ing at the heart of the U.S. government's efforts to thwart spying and terrorism against us, first as inspector general of the National Secu-rity Agency, and then as chief of counterintelligence for the director of National Intelligence. As I carried out these assignments, I saw plenty of the old-fashioned kind of espionage, but I also witnessed the dramatic rise of a new kind of spying that exploits digital technology itself, and the fact that we have all come to rely so thoroughly on that technology.

During my tenure in government I came to understand how steeply new technology has tipped the balance in favor of those—from freelance hackers to Russian mobsters to terrorists to states like China and Iran—who want to learn the secrets we keep, whether for national, corporate, or personal security. Much of my understanding arose from classified work that I cannot discuss here or anywhere. But I can share the insights I gleaned about this new form of espionage: how it works; what the biggest and most vulnerable targets are; who does it best; as well as what it means for the future of warfare, intelligence, market competition, and society at large. I also came to understand what we can—and cannot—do to counter this flood of espionage.

The truth I saw was brutal and intense: Electronic thieves are stripping us blind. I'm not just talking about the pirating of DVDs and movies in Asia or somebody ripping off your Social Security number. That's bad enough, but it's worse than that. Technologies that cost millions or billions to develop are being bled out of our corporate laboratories via the Internet; or they're slipping out after hours on thumb drives, walking onto airplanes bound for foreign ports, and reentering the country as finished products developed by foreign entrepreneurs. In effect, we're buying back our own technology. Other Western firms, meanwhile, are bleeding trade secrets, engineering designs, know-how, and other intellectual property through electronic leakage. In the public sector, sensitive diplomatic cables are suddenly splashed across the headlines worldwide. The same organizations that broadcast those cables gleefully distribute lists of critical infrastructure—airports, bridges, chemical plants—that are the most vulnerable to attack. And as I describe in the pages that follow, we're losing strategically sensitive data about aircraft and ship design, radars, and other defense technology, as well as information about auto manufacturing, engineering designs, and other commercial innovations. This theft contributes to the tidal flow of capital from West to East that threatens our prosperity, and it could in wartime cost many American lives.

This kind of theft is targeted and systematic. The U.S. Navy spent about $5 billion to develop a quiet electric drive for its submarines and ships so they'd be silent and hard to track.[1] Chinese spies stole it. The navy spent billions more to develop new radar for their top-of-the-line Aegis Cruiser. Chinese spies stole that, too. The electronic intelligence services of the Chinese and the Russians are working us over—taking advantage of our porous networks and indifference to security to steal billions of dollars' worth of military and commercial secrets. Some of our allies, like the French and the Israelis, have tried it too.

Pentagon information systems have been under attack since at least 1998. In August 2006, Major General William Lord of the air force let the public in on the secret when he mentioned that massive heist of up to twenty terabytes. To carry this volume of documents in paper form, you'd need a line of moving vans stretching from the Pentagon to the Chinese freighters docked in Baltimore harbor fifty miles away. If the Chinese tried to do that, we'd have the National Guard out in fifteen minutes. But when they did it electronically, hardly anyone noticed. As it happens, the data were stolen from the Pentagon's unclassified networks, but those networks hold lots of sensitive information—including the names and private identifying information of every man and woman in the U.S. armed forces.

It would be a serious mistake to think that the difference between classified and unclassified is the difference between important and unimportant, or sensitive and nonsensitive. Lots of information is sensitive but not classified, especially when it relates to technology and personnel. According to the air force's General Lord, when the Chinese pulled off this heist, they were "looking for your identity so they can get into the network as you."[2] General Lord did not reveal what is perhaps even more troubling: We don't know exactly what data were taken because the Defense Department doesn't bother to encrypt this kind of data. They thought it was too much trouble. But the Chinese, on their way out the electronic door, did encrypt it. Too much trouble? They didn't think so.

According to the Government Accountability Office, the number of unauthorized accesses or installations of malicious software on U.S. government computers increased by 650 percent since 2006.[3] The trend is disquieting, and the official data almost certainly undercounts the problem.

And this trend is hardly limited to the public sector. To give just one example of the magnitude of threat aimed at private companies: A sophisticated team of hackers broke into a Royal Bank of Scotland payroll system in late 2008 and stole information that let them counterfeit credit balances on ATM cards. They then mounted a coordinated attack on 139 ATMs in the United States, Canada, Russia, and China that netted about $9 million in thirty minutes. If this were a traditional bank robbery, it would rank as one of the largest in history. Chinese and Russian cyberoperators have made advanced, persistent intrusions into the networks of other banks too—to what end, we don't yet know. This kind of intrusion infects a system with malicious code that's difficult—sometimes even impossible—to wipe out, because it continually changes to evade detection. It opens electronic "trapdoors" so that outsiders can bypass the system's security, and if one door is nailed shut, the code automatically opens another one. We don't even know who's doing this. This point will come up again and again throughout this book, because our inability to figure out who's responsible for illegal behavior on our electronic networks is a fundamental reason why we can't safeguard our personal data, corporate intellectual property, or national defense secrets.

Nor can we ensure the safety of the infrastructure without which our world would collapse: electricity grids, financial systems, air-traffic control, and other networks. All these systems run electronically; all run on the same public telecommunications backbone; and increasingly all run on commercial, off-the-shelf hardware and software that can be bought anywhere in the world. Many of these systems have already been penetrated by criminal gangs or foreign intelligence services—sometimes to steal, sometimes to reconnoiter for uncertain purposes—using offensive tools that are often more effective than our defenses. All of these systems could become targets for disruption in wartime or even during a lower-grade conflict like a diplomatic standoff.

These are all things I learned during my four and a half years as inspector general of the nation's electronic intelligence service, the National Security Agency, and my subsequent three years as head of U.S. counterintelligence. In the latter job I was responsible for strategy and policy coordination among the CIA, FBI, Defense Department, and other government departments and agencies. Counterintelligence is the business of dealing with foreign intelligence activities against our own intelligence services, military, and national security infrastructure. This business used to be concerned almost entirely with foreign spies, and that remains its core mission. But electronic espionage has increased exponentially since the mid-1990s, so counterintelligence has become deeply concerned with what's happening on—and to—the nation's electronic networks.

**ONE MORNING ABOUT** five months after 9/11, I was perched on a sofa in a large office on the top floor of a glass-enclosed building called OPS 2B, in Fort George G. Meade, Maryland, thirty miles north of Washington, answering questions from then Lieutenant General Michael V. Hayden, the director of the National Security Agency, and his then deputy William Black. They were interviewing me for the position of the NSA's inspector general. This is a nonpolitical, top-secret job at the top level of the intelligence community's version of the civil service. The IG is in charge of internal investigations, and he audits and inspects the agency's operations for fraud, abuse, and just plain inefficiency. Along with the head of security, he's one of the two people in any agency—especially an intelligence agency—you do not want darkening your doorway. Like most people, I'd rather be liked than disliked, but if you need to be liked, this job is not for you. By my early thirties, however, having been an antitrust prosecutor, I was already used to lawyers for price fixers and monopolists accusing me of single-handedly destroying the U.S. economy. I knew what I'd be in for if I got the job.

A cordial man in his late fifties, Mike Hayden was unassuming even with three stars on each shoulder of his blue air force uniform. Hayden had run signals intelligence, or SIGINT, for the air force, and before that had flown countless hours in the windowless fuselage of unmarked airplanes, wearing earphones and collecting radio signals in Eastern Europe. He had also been deputy chief of staff to the four-star commander in Korea. But he was not a techie. Hayden had been the star pupil of the nuns and priests in an Irish Catholic neighborhood in Pittsburgh and had driven a taxi to work his way through Duquesne University, where he studied history, not engineering or computer science. He was ambitious, but he never forgot his Pittsburgh roots.

Black was a different type altogether. If you looked at an organization chart of the NSA at the time, all the solid lines ran predictably to Hayden, the NSA director, or DIRNSA, and the dotted lines ran all over, but the invisible lines ran to a table in Bill Black's next-door office, where this bald, blunt character in cowboy boots summoned subordinates, pulled bureaucratic levers, and worked the phones. On the wall over his left shoulder he had hung a drawing of Wyatt Earp, so when you sat at his table you were staring down the barrel of Earp's Buntline Special. Bill was a bureaucratic operator, and many feared him. I liked him. He grew up on a ranch in New Mexico, and in the late stages of the cold war ran what was then called A Group. A Group was the NSA's main game: It was in charge of collecting signal intelligence against the Soviet Union. A dark master of electronic intelligence, Bill knew every intelligence satellite in the sky and what it did, and every success and every blunder in the history of the NSA, which he loved deeply. He knew the wheels within the wheels. He also had a well-earned reputation as a tough SOB who wasn't afraid to make decisions. (In government, anybody who isn't afraid to make decisions is regarded as an SOB.) After 9/11, Hayden brought Black back from retirement, and the two of them were determined to steer the NSA out of the doldrums, budget slashing, and decline of the 1990s. They wanted an outsider as IG, someone not afraid to tell them the truth.

And so began my near nine-year journey into the belly of the intelligence beast, first at the NSA and then running counterintelligence for the director of National Intelligence, where my biggest headache was cyberespionage in a world where everything was becoming electronically connected to everything else. In those positions I had a hair-raising view of the incessant conflicts being waged in cyberspace—conflicts short of war but involving concerted attempts to penetrate our nation's information systems and critical infrastructure. Some of these conflicts could indeed turn into war, but the tendency to treat them as such is likely to lead us astray. In American law and politics, "war" and "peace" are presented as a binary toggle switch: We're either enjoying peace or waging war. In this view, in which the world is drawn with straight lines and right angles, peace and struggle cannot coexist. But the world is not so easily compartmentalized, and as I argue in this book, we are now in a period, typical in international affairs, in which conflict and symbiosis, struggle and trade, exist side by side in a condition that is neither war nor peace, and which is both promising and dangerous.

Personal and organizational secrets all live on the same electronic systems. Gaming and social media technologies once thought to be solely for personal and entertainment uses are now at the front edge of many business applications. Boundaries of many kinds are eroding—legally, behaviorally, electronically—in all aspects of our lives: between the public and private behaviors of ordinary people, for example, in the dress, speech, and decorum appropriate to the street, the office, or houses of worship; between what the government does and what privately owned companies do; and, not least, between nation-states and nonstate actors. Large corporations have police, military, and intelligence capabilities that are hardly distinguishable from those of most governments. Organizations like al-Qaeda, Lebanese Hezbollah, and the Russian mob operate across international borders with ease and have budgets that exceed those of many nation-states. Meanwhile, some of those nation-states are hardly more than lines on a map. Technical capabilities that a decade or two ago could be found only in advanced military aircraft—GPS, for example—now come standard in your rental car and can be bought at RadioShack for a few bucks. Computing capacity greater than governments could muster during the cold war now resides in mobile devices that fit in a pocket. The original iPhone, released in 2007, weighed a hundred times less than a portable computer from 1982, was five hundred times smaller, cost ten times less, and ran a hundred times faster.[4] There are now 5.3 *billion* handsets in use around the world, and three fourths of them are in the developing world.[5]

In the postindustrial West we think technology advances in the order in which it was invented—usually by us. Plumbing came before wired telephones and radio, which came before airplanes, which came before penicillin, which came before television, and so on. But this isn't the way the rest of the world experiences modernity. Thirty years ago, approaching Lahore's airport in a Pakistan International Airlines Boeing 727, I watched out the window as a stick-wielding peasant prodded a buffalo tethered to a water wheel—a scene from biblical times. Ten years ago, in rural Yunnan Province, China, I stopped for lunch at a roadside restaurant where the ducks on the menu were slaughtered out back. The only toilet was an open-air hole in the ground, and a local businessman was squatting over it while talking on a cell phone. Technology in the developing world is moving fast—but not in the order we take for granted. People in the developing world may not have all the modern conveniences we do, but they do have the same digital technology and programming skills we do. And many of them have the skills to pick our electronic pockets.

The boundary between national and economic security is also eroding—has eroded, in fact, almost completely. When it comes to national security the boundary between public and corporate secrets has also more or less vanished. The current U.S. National Security Strategy—that's the president's statement to Congress about the nation's principal security concerns—contains sixty-eight references to economic issues.[6] The boundary between military and economic secrets remains firm in the law of Western nations, but the law is always trying to catch up with life. The technology our military relies on is mostly developed in the private sector, and most of the research it's based on is carried out in universities and private companies. The know-how of our engineering firms, the drugs that our pharmaceutical companies spend billions to develop, the trade secrets of our aerospace industry—these are the bases of our national welfare. Much of our infrastructure is also privately owned and subject to attack. Terrorists pilot jetliners indiscriminately into private office buildings as well as into the headquarters of government departments and blow up passenger trains in Russia and under the streets of London. As a result, the infrastructure, the technologies, and the information that governments must protect extend well beyond government property.

The Office of the National Counterintelligence Executive, which I headed from 2006 to 2009, is charged with protecting America's secrets. Our responsibilities required us not only to understand and thwart the systematic efforts of foreign intelligence services to insert spies into our government, but also to prevent foreign spies from working in the bowels of private industry and the nation's laboratories. But human spies are no longer the whole game. If someone can steal secrets electronically from your office from Shanghai or Moscow, perhaps they don't need a human spy. Or perhaps the spy's job is no longer stealing secrets but subverting your network to allow the secrets to bleed out over the Internet. In a networked world, I quickly saw that counterintelligence must contend with the penetrations of the public and private electronic networks that are the backbone of our communications, the storehouses of our technology, and the nervous system of our economy and government. These networks, I regret to say, are porous and insecure, vulnerable not only to casual hackers but even more so to professional electronic thieves and powerful foreign intelligence services. But we want seamless, effortless interconnectivity and the productivity that comes with it—who doesn't? And so our vulnerabilities multiply as we continue to privilege convenience over security.

Meanwhile, the world is speeding up. We experience this acceleration in the pace of our daily lives, in product cycles and fashion trends, in the instantaneous dissemination of information, in the awesome and continual increases in the capacity of our electronic systems, in the speed at which our products and ideas are copied and pirated. Businesses know that their ability to profit from their own innovation depends on their ability to get their products to market faster than ever and to exploit them more quickly than ever—before they become obsolete or unfashionable, or are ripped off by an overseas pirate with low overhead and no R&D costs. Value appears and disappears with bewildering speed. Who today remembers the computing juggernauts Wang Laboratories or Digital Equipment Corporation? Financial giants like Bear Stearns, Lehman Brothers, and Washington Mutual vanished overnight.

The value of intelligence is also transitory. This is especially true of SIGINT—the electronic stuff. It's useful only if you can act on it in time, and the time for action is getting shorter and shorter. Information from an African country about an impending attack on an airliner at Kennedy Airport is useless if you can't put it in the hands of security officials at the airport right away. With tactical military intelligence—that is, on-the-spot information about unfolding situations—commanders must be able to feed it into their decision cycles, which grow shorter and shorter.

This kind of acceleration is ubiquitous in our society. For example, if the price of a security on Wall Street is momentarily $0.005 more or less than the price of the same security in London or Frankfurt or Singapore, a trader whose electronic systems are agile enough to act on that difference can make millions in less than a second. So both the public and the private sectors are bowing to unrelenting pressure to enhance the connectivity that both increases productivity and decreases security, to shorten decision cycles, and to move information faster and more widely. That pressure also creates a dilemma, because the more widely and quickly you make information available, the more trouble you have protecting it. Regardless of whether that information is a classified diplomatic cable, valuable engineering drawings, or your own medical records, when you put it on an electronic network to which thousands of people have access, it is no longer really secret—or private. The name for this condition is transparency, and it is a fundamental condition of contemporary life, for good and ill.

In this book I hope to show that the difficulties of protecting your privacy and mine and the difficulties of keeping secrets in an intelligence agency or corporate office are remarkably alike. Secrecy is to companies and governments as privacy is to individuals. Both rise or fall on the same technologies and cultural proclivities, and at the moment both are falling precipitously.

In 1949, the architect Philip Johnson built himself a remarkable house on an eleven-acre Connecticut estate of woods and meadow: a transparent glass rectangle with a completely open floor plan, and without shades or curtains. Even the sleeping area was completely exposed to the outside. Johnson did make one concession to privacy in his glass house: He enclosed the bathroom, whose walls were the only interior structure to extend from floor to ceiling. Nearby he constructed a more conventional house, called Brick House, for weekend guests. But transparency was not an unalloyed virtue, even for a modernist architect, and soon Johnson sought police protection to ward off trespassers, and he nailed up a sign pleading: THIS HOUSE IS *NOW OCCUPIED*. PLEASE RESPECT THE PRIVACY OF THE OWNER. This measure apparently did not meet with great success, because Johnson eventually moved into Brick House and used Glass House chiefly for entertaining. Even modernist architects need places of refuge. Johnson's transparent dwelling is now an icon of twentieth-century architecture—and a fitting image of our current predicament in which relentless transparency threatens our security and our privacy.

I begin this book by examining the threats to our personal security, all of which are more dire than we generally realize. Then I expand the focus to the welter of threats facing the larger-scale enterprises and institutions that together form our society: companies, financial markets, infrastructure, the military, and intelligence. Throughout the book, as I widen our view, we'll see that the same principles—the same dangers—apply at all levels, from the personal to the national. In all cases, the views I express are my own, not the U.S. government's. Our world is becoming a collection of glass houses that provide only the illusion of shelter. Finally, I'll draw on my experience to offer suggestions for how all of us—individuals, companies, and the government itself—can shore up these ever more fragile and transparent structures.

# 1

# ELECTRONICALLY UNDRESSED

**YOU'VE PROBABLY DECIDED** that in order to save a buck on a bunch of grapes, you'll let the supermarket compile data about your eating habits, and that in order to avoid a long line at the tollbooth, you'll let some contractor for the state know how often and at what times of day you cross that bridge or drive on that highway. Maybe you even pay for a cup of coffee with a credit card. We are what we eat—and what we buy, and who we know, and where we live, and what we look at, and where we go. All of us—not just young people—give this information away freely because it's convenient and often enjoyable to do so. Forty-five percent of Facebook users are twenty-six years old or older, and the fastest-growing segment of that group is women over fifty-five.[1] Older people may not use Twitter, but they do use credit cards, pay tolls automatically on the interstate, bank online, and buy cars equipped with GPS.

In the last twenty years the ready availability of inexpensive, in-creasingly powerful, and ever-smaller networked computers has revo-lutionized how—and how fast—we create, process, store, and transmit information. These developments have changed our lives so pervasively, and accelerated the speed of change in our lives so sharply, that it's hard to recall what the world was like before we were so happily and relentlessly connected. We think of letters written on paper as relics of a bygone era, but even dial-up modems or waiting thirty seconds for a Web page to load now seems quaint. In 2010 a six-year-old watching a 1980s movie asked her father, "Why is the phone attached to the wall?" If you can answer this question, you're getting old. Manual typewriters, carbon paper, party-line telephones—these are incomprehensible phrases to the majority of people now living.

Computing power has doubled every year and a half since the mid-1960s.[2] To grasp what this means, consider that in 1978 it cost about nine hundred dollars to fly from New York to Paris, and the flight took seven hours. If airline travel had accelerated at the same rate as computing power, you could now make the trip for about a penny, in less than a second.[3] Our machines have sped up—today's game processors can do at least a *billion* operations per second—but we haven't. We can't keep up with our own machines. So our machines have begun to talk to one another, making decisions for us, exchanging information about us. They apply the brakes in our cars when we're too slow to do it, land huge aircraft unassisted, trade enormous volumes of securities, adjust the flow of electricity on the grid, and share data about us that we think of as private. And these machines are everywhere. The "personal digital assistant" in your pocket is more powerful than the 1960s IBM mainframe computer that occupied an entire room.

The movement of technology between government and the private sector is not a one-way street. Just as GPS has migrated from fighter planes to your car, so has technology moved from your living room to the front lines of conventional and cyber warfare. Most of the government's computing systems are developed in the private sector now, and gaming consoles have directly influenced the design of instrumentation for weapons systems. The Cyber Crimes Center in the Department of Homeland Security has even dumped the eight-thousand-dollar consoles it once used to crack the passwords of seized computers—then replaced them with Sony's PlayStation 3s for "brute force" password attacks that run through every conceivable password until they find the right one.[4] The difference between electronic toys and business applications is vanishing.

The border between commerce and government wasn't always so porous. In the beginning the Internet and its precursors were federally funded links between universities and government researchers, and it was *illegal* to use them for commercial purposes. Congress didn't change that law until 1992.[5] Even so, many university users were furious at the thought that an educational tool would be polluted by commerce, and as recently as the mid-1990s the Internet was still essentially a research tool and the plaything of a few. In 1995, the idea of buying and selling on the Internet aroused more suspicion than enthusiasm, but by January 2008 there were 1.3 *billion* Internet users.[6] By 2011 the number of users had climbed to nearly 2 billion, and many of them were buying and selling online.[7] No wonder that by 2009 information technology stocks had become the single largest sector in the U.S. economy.[8] By 2015, the number of Internet hosts is expected to exceed the planet's human population.[9] Mobile data traffic is doubling every year, and all that data leaves a trail.

Going from rummaging in a file drawer to searching electronic data and images was dramatic; so was clicking a mouse instead of traveling to the library. In these cases, however, we were *fetching* things we wanted; new technology merely allowed us to fetch faster. Now data comes to us unbidden, based on choices we made in the past, who our electronic friends are, and where we live. Or it comes based on where we *are,* like a coupon for a latte that shows up on our mobile phone when we walk past the coffee shop.[10] We now live in a sea of ambient data. Or rather, each of us increasingly lives in his or her own customized virtual sea of ambient data. And wherever we swim in that sea, each of us leaves electronic evidence of where we've been and strong indicators of where we are likely to go next—of which we are often unaware.

## The Data Market

Data is a commodity, and the market for it is measured in billions of dollars—trillions if we include electronic banking and credit card issuers. Reed Elsevier PLC, one of the world's biggest data aggregation companies, has reported a steady 10 percent annual growth of online traffic since 1999.[11] Reed Elsevier owns LexisNexis, the largest source of online legal and periodical information. It also owns ChoicePoint, which does background and public records searches; it's the outfit that checks the accuracy of the résumé you sent to a prospective employer or graduate school.[12] These companies and others like them make fortunes based on information that has always been publicly available. They aggregate that information, sort it, reformat it, and make it instantaneously available to public- and private-sector users willing to pay for it. Other firms occupy other niches: financial data for investors; medical records for hospitals, doctors, and insurance companies; credit scoring for any business that gives you credit; and of course banks and credit card issuers. Master-Card alone made $5.5 billion in net revenue by managing $567 billion in charges, transactions, and settlements worldwide.[13]

Aggregated data tell a merchant what goods to stock and how to target advertising. Do you like fish but avoid red meat? Fine, we'll send you an ad when we have a fish special, but we won't waste our money sending you ads for roast beef. You prefer SUVs to convertibles, or casual clothing to suits, or certain kinds of movies or music? Great— we won't waste our money or your time telling you about products you won't buy anyway. This is good for the merchant; arguably it's good for you, too. Aggregated data is also good for insurance companies, because without it they can't calculate premiums for groups of people that represent different levels of risk. Whether that's good for you depends on which risk pool the insurance companies put you in—and whether the data is accurate.

A single set of fingerprints probably has no value, but a bank of such prints helps the police identify criminals; DNA databases do the same. The federal DNA database holds 4.6 million profiles, or 1.5 percent of the U.S. population—mostly convicted criminals. Across the ocean, two thirds of Britons favor a law that would require *everyone's* DNA to be stored.[14] And if you visit central London you're being photographed every time you walk down the street or enter the Underground, and if you drive, your license plate is being photographed wherever you go. The better the database, the more crimes will be solved. Whether that benefit is worth the privacy loss is another question. But however you feel about that, the benefit of aggregated data in solving crime is beyond dispute.

Data are valuable in all these cases because the aggregator can link an identity with a history or a pattern of behavior. But aggregated data also have enormous social importance even without links to individuals. Without that information, public health officials don't know what diseases need more or less attention and resources, and predicting what kind of flu will strike next year would be even harder than it is. Having this data in real time, or near real time (as opposed to getting it a month or a year later), is also valuable, because it can warn that a new epidemic is breaking out right now, when we may be able to prevent or slow down its spread, and this is true whether the epidemic is natural or the result of a terrorist attack. Add personally identifying information back in, and you add more value. It helps find victims and, in some cases, the source of infection or attack.

The amount of information available about you is startling: your date of birth, driving record, medical history, credit rating, shopping patterns (including where you shop and what you buy), mortgage and property records, political contributions, vacation patterns (including the route you drive), whether you drive, telephone numbers (even if unlisted), the names of your spouse and children and business partners, your grades in school, your criminal record (if you have one)—and much else besides. In order to get that information about you, someone used to have to stand in line in several different buildings, not necessarily in the same city, just to request it, and he probably had to wait around or come back a second time to pick it up. Now, with several mouse clicks, the information is often available to anyone anywhere in the world who wants it.[15] Your medical records are supposed to be under lock and key, but who keeps them? Your doctor, to start with, but so does the software provider that your doctor pays to store those records, and the doctor's outside laboratory, and the insurance company that covers you, and their database administrator, who may work for someone else. Information you may think is confidential, sensitive, and private is sent to many different places *automatically*, sometimes in different countries, and each leg of its transmission over public communications networks represents a potential vulnerability. There is rarely such a thing as a single, unique record anymore. There are multiple copies of every record, stored in multiple places, in databases whose level of security is a mystery to most users, and sometimes even to company officials.

### *"We never don't know anything about someone"*

How did all this data become so readily available? Because you and I have given it away. In many cases we've had little choice about it—not if we want a mortgage or lease, a marriage or driver's license, or health insurance; not if we want to enter the hospital, send our children to school, contribute to a political candidate, or buy a snack on the many airlines that no longer accept cash in flight.[16] In other cases we don't even know it's happening. If you click on the credit card page of Capital One Financial's Web site, for example, thousands of lines of code representing information about your education and income level and residence will be sucked up by the company in a fraction of a second. Your machine is talking to their machine, and in that fraction of a second your machine is working for them, not you. And so aggregated data snowballs. As Capital One's data contractor quipped, "We never don't know anything about someone."[17] That contractor probably doesn't think he's in the personal espionage business, but he is.

But do we care that we're being spied upon? Is this new type of commercial spy collecting secrets—or simply gathering information we freely spread around? Many people find it comforting that someone else knows where they are at all times. Mobile phone companies and location services for your car, like OnStar, advertise their ability to do just that for you. Your mobile phone or PDA makes a constant record of where it goes. Mobile devices in the United States generate about 600 *billion* events per day.[18] These events don't just include the calls, text messages, and Internet connections you know you're making. They also include the silent "pings" between each cell phone and a nearby tower whether you're using the phone or not. They are the heartbeat of cell phone service and typically occur every few minutes. Each ping is tagged with geospatial location information,[19] and if you have GPS or use Wi-Fi that record is very precise—less than eleven yards. If not, the record is still pretty accurate, because the cell towers that handle your calls are constantly pinging your phone and pinpointing your location to within about a block. According to Jeff Jonas, a data expert at IBM, this information will soon warn us about events that haven't even occurred yet. Your free Gmail account, he surmises, will advise you "that your buddy Ken is going to be 15 minutes late to the pool hall this coming Thursday, unless he leaves work 15 minutes early . . . which he has done only twice in seven years."[20] With enough information about your past movements, scientists can predict your movements with about 94 percent accuracy. Or forecast traffic congestion. By examining patterns of communication and movement, they can detect flu symptoms before you know you're getting sick. The emotional content of Twitter lets researchers predict the moves of the Dow Jones index with about 88 percent accuracy.[21] Jonas also points out that the police could use the same kind of information to watch crowds form and disperse—a powerful tool for crowd control. Or for discouraging political expression. As of mid-2011, law enforcement officials in most jurisdictions can get geolocation data from mobile carriers simply by issuing a subpoena. Most jurisdictions don't require a warrant signed by a judge—at least not unless the surveillance is long-term or involves movements inside a dwelling.[22]

And so, little by little, we find ourselves living in a glass house. Last year's novelty is this year's necessity; your friends wonder why you don't have one. The price of last month's expensive electronic luxury just fell by half. Your kid wants one for her birthday. It's not simply adults who are being watched and marketed to, identified, and classified. Sure, we give up some privacy with each little step, but we get something back: convenience, peace of mind, whatever. We may be electronically naked, but we demand it. This is the world we now live in, and let's face it: *We find that world irresistible.*[23]

THIS IRRESISTIBLE WORLD in which we are all numbered and accounted for crept up on us largely unnoticed, but its roots are old. Americans and Western Europeans have been counting, classifying, and identifying ourselves for several hundred years, but the initial steps were slow. The first modern European census was taken in Prussia (naturally) in 1719; the United States took its first census in 1790; Britain and France[24] followed in 1801. Indeed, representative democracy required counting in order to achieve fairness in taxation and legislative representation.[25] And then, in the last quarter of the nineteenth century, two things happened that dramatically accelerated this business of identifying everybody. First, the state pension was born in Germany, and therefore the state was required to know who was owed money and at what age. Keeping increasingly exacting records was one essential result. National identity cards began to appear. Second, in big cities like London, Paris, and Buenos Aires, the police began to wonder, Who is this man we have arrested *really*? Haven't we arrested him before?

Enter Alphonse Bertillon, a low-ranking functionary in the Paris *sûreté* who in 1882 showed that he could reliably reidentify anyone by measuring his or her head and body and making a careful record of tattoos, scars, and other quirks. Bertillonage was the beginning of systematic biometrics but it was soon superseded by fingerprinting, which quickly became the identification method of choice for law enforcement agencies worldwide. We fingerprint not only those charged with crimes, but also everyone in the military, everyone who applies for a security clearance, and welfare recipients. In the UK and in some parts of continental Europe, the fingerprinting of schoolchildren is widespread, and it is used in place of library cards.[26] There are now fingerprint scanners, fingerprint door locks, safes with fingerprint locks, fingerprint time clocks, and fingerprint kits for your favorite niece or nephew.[27] These devices are not being foisted on people; there's a market for them. Fingerprinting is so ubiquitous that it has become a metaphor for any system of positive identification, like "DNA fingerprinting."

The credit markets we take for granted are another aspect of this irresistible world. We could hardly live without them. Pioneered in the United States during the Great Depression,[28] these markets require instant, accurate information about potential borrowers. Without them a home buyer could not "prequalify" for a mortgage on the phone or get instant credit to buy a refrigerator, as we now do as a matter of course. Before that, creditors didn't lend to people they didn't know, or they took property as security, like a pawnshop.

The overlapping and ever-expanding appetite of government and commerce to keep tabs on us—and our own appetite for keeping tabs on one another—means that it's virtually impossible to elude our own autobiographical trail of purchasing habits, property ownership, employment history, credit scores, educational records, and in my case, a security clearance record a mile long. If you live in India, everyone's personal data record will be a mile long, because the government there has launched a project to assign a unique twelve-digit identification number to every one of its 1.2 billion inhabitants, and to link that number to their fingerprints and iris scans. The idea is to ensure that welfare payments reach the right people and to permit India's vast impoverished population to gain access to online banking and other services.[29] Critics worry that the information will not be guarded adequately. They should also worry that aggregating data to prevent fraud also enables fraud, because gathering huge quantities of data in one place means it can all be stolen from one place.

Meanwhile, the shelf life of all this data gets longer and longer, because the cost of storing it has fallen like a stone. In 1990 a one-terabyte storage drive would have cost $1 million to buy. (A terabyte is a billion bytes of eight 1s and 0s, or a thousand times more than a gigabyte. Sixty-four terabytes is half the size of a big university library.) Now you can buy that drive for under $100. *The price has fallen ten thousand times*. Information about us doesn't disappear with time. It can be saved forever, cheaply, in lots of places. That's worrisome, but we also find it appealing. For about $175 you can buy a USB stick—also called a flash drive or a thumb drive—with sixty-four gigabytes (or "gigs") of memory. That's thirty-two million pages of text dangling at the end of a key chain. As we will see later, the ease of transporting huge amounts of data has dramatically changed the espionage trade.

**FOLLOWING A SUDDEN** explosion of Internet-enabled crime and the growing sense that our personal lives were exposed to strangers, Americans and Europeans began to search for ways to protect ourselves. Chiefly we have sought to regulate "personally identifiable information."[30] The European Community defines this somewhat more broadly (and vaguely) than do U.S. laws, but the phrase generally means data such as your postal and e-mail addresses and Social Security and credit card numbers, which can readily be associated with you. Companies like to tell you how carefully they protect this kind of information. But are these efforts effective?

The answer depends on the objective. The rules have undoubtedly forced companies and government agencies to tighten their handling of information about their own customers and employees. Whether they have had any effect in reducing fraud is doubtful, however, because the amount of personal information legally available is burgeoning, and the black market in such information is vast, as we'll see in the next chapter. But if the objective is to protect your anonymity, these laws have little effect—and may soon have none at all. That's because each of us can now be easily identified without reference to any of the usual categories of personally identifiable information. Strip it away—that's called "anonymizing" it—and data aggregators can put it back almost instantly.

Let's suppose I know your zip code and gender. If twenty thousand people live in your zip code, I can eliminate ten thousand of them by gender. Add in your age, and I can reduce the number much further. If I know what kind of car you drive, I can identify you with near certainty. Researchers at Stanford University were able to reidentify people by their Netflix viewing habits simply by comparing the company's carefully anonymized viewer ratings with publicly posted ratings on other Web sites that rated the same movies. Essentially, they showed the emptiness of the promises that Netflix and others make that you can do, watch, or buy whatever you like anonymously on their Web sites. Information scientists says they need only thirty-three "bits" of information—mundane things like your zip code or the make of your car—to identify you, and the information may have nothing to do with the legal definition of personally identifiable information. There are two possibilities for each bit (each bit must be a 1 or a 0), and $2^{33}$ is a very large number—more than 8.6 billion, which is more than the Earth's human population.[31] A firm called PeekYou has filed a patent application for a "computerized distributed personal information aggregator" that matches real names with pseudonyms used on blogs and social network sites like Facebook and Twitter.[32] It's becoming almost impossible to be anonymous anymore.

Many of us are uncomfortable with the proliferation and transparency of personal data, and some would like Congress to pass laws to stop it. But the law is chasing reality, not shaping it. (This is another theme we'll see cropping up repeatedly throughout this book.) The law is not fundamentally altering the direction or speed of our society's movement toward the instant, universal availability of massive amounts of information that can be sliced, diced, and analyzed in microseconds—nor can it. You will have such data if you want it; your friends, enemies, and bank will have it too, and the government will either have it or be allowed to get it under certain legally defined conditions. We will write some rules that make access somewhat more difficult, but those rules won't be able to hold back an overwhelming tide.

There are aspects of this that I find wonderful; others strike me as distasteful or worse. It has led to massive increases in productivity and wealth. It has also created vulnerabilities of staggering proportions—vulnerabilities that now generate billions of dollars in criminal revenue, are exploitable and exploited by foreign intelligence and military services as well as by criminals, and that—if not better understood and mitigated—put our communications, our economy, and even our military at risk of failure. For both good and ill, this is what's happening. This is the glass house we live in.

# A PRIMER ON CYBERCRIME

**JUST AS THE RAIN FALLS** on the unjust and just alike, so aggregated data have value for thieves and swindlers as well as for law-abiding merchants and public health officials. Organized gangs of international criminals have moved eagerly into cybercrime, and often use it to fund other nefarious enterprises, because it makes more money than even the illegal drug trade.[1] Profits are high because crime on the Internet is cheap; e-mail is essentially free. The chance of scamming any particular individual for data is poor, but the chance of scamming one in a thousand is much better, and if I can get my hands on a million sets of records, my chances of running a successful scam become really good. This is why electronic crooks are systematically stealing large batches of data from places such as the University of Virginia, the Catholic Diocese of Des Moines, Citibank and the Royal Bank of Scotland, hospitals across the country, the Pentagon, the General Dynamics Corporation, and a slew of other agencies and companies.[2] In 2010 Verizon, a telecommunications company that tracks this market, reported that over nine hundred million sensitive data records had been stolen from

Americans in the previous six years.[3] And an ominous new trend has emerged: The rate of theft by corporate insiders, who are in a better position to steal valuable information than are external hackers, has gone up.[4] In 2010, the incidence of electronically stolen data surpassed that of physical theft for the first time.[5]

The Internet crime business has become international. An identity thief in Tulsa, Toulouse, or Tunbridge Wells can buy stolen credit card numbers from a gang in Moscow that freely advertises its wares. He can e-mail those numbers to a counterfeit credit card shop in Guangzhou that produces cards that are indistinguishable from the real thing. And if that shop doesn't make driver's licenses—he'll want a fake ID before he goes shopping—he can get one from another counterfeiting shop in Minsk, in Belarus.

If you're a victim, you pay for this kind of theft directly in loused-up credit, months of aggravation, and possibly money you'll never recover. And all of us pay indirectly through higher prices. For example, our banks prefer not to talk about their losses from credit card fraud, because they don't want to scare us away from doing business on the Internet, which is highly profitable. That's why in the United States you pay nothing when someone makes a fraudulent purchase on your card, not even the fifty dollars the issuer could legally charge. Instead, banks prefer to make up the losses by charging you for transactions that used to be free or cheaper than they are now.

The cost of becoming an Internet thief is low—and getting lower. You can download user-friendly hacking tools for free. The cutting-edge tools cost money, but not much considering the potential rate of return. They are stealthy, innovative, and customized for the kind of information they target.[6] If you want one that searches out engineering drawings, for example, you can buy it. If you want one that searches instead for personal identification numbers (PINs) and bank data, it's available.

Thieves who know how to steal your data but may not know how to exploit it can sell it to a third party who does.[7] And so, when an Indian hacker broke into the European computer systems of the Best

Western International hotel group in 2008 and scraped up the credit card information of about eight million customers, he immediately sold it to an underground network run by the Russian mafia, who knew exactly how to misuse it.[8] It would be comforting to think that hoteliers have learned since then to protect themselves, but that's doubtful.[9] In 2010 HEI Hotels & Resorts, which manages hotels for Hilton, Marriott, Sheraton, and others, reported that thieves had gotten away with the credit card data of several thousand guests, apparently by doctoring the swipe machines at check-in counters.[10] That kind of operation requires a combination of network skills and close-up physical penetration—the sort of operation that only a few years ago would have been associated exclusively with a state intelligence service.

In the last few years the flood of stolen credit card data has been so vast that its value has recently sunk to junk levels on the black market. According to Verizon, market saturation drove the price down "from between $10 and $16 per record in mid-2007 to less than $0.50 per record" by late 2008.[11] But even this bit of good news has a dark side: Instead of ripping off credit card numbers, the smart criminals have begun focusing on PINs and cash. When credit card numbers are stolen, consumers rarely pay for any resulting fraud. This is one reason why anxiety over identity theft hasn't translated into consumer demand for more secure communications or more careful online behavior. But when a criminal steals the PIN to your account, he grabs your cash. And if you want your bank to refund the money you lost, the burden is on you to prove the withdrawal was fraudulent, which is often impossible.

Let's look at who these criminals are, and how they rip us off.

## "Most of the Money Was Sent to Russia"

When the feds finally took it down, the criminal organization known as Shadowcrew had as many as four thousand members and had operations in Russia, Ukraine, Hong Kong, Estonia, and Latvia, as well as in the United States. National boundaries pose no difficulty for international cybercrime. This organization had a virtual private network, or VPN, for secure communications. It had an efficient internal auction system for stolen credit information, known as dumps, which they stored on servers in Latvia and Ukraine. Its members obtained blank credit and debit cards from China. With an embosser, printer, heat foil press, and magstripe writer, they turned out counterfeit cards that no cashier could spot, complete with holograms. And they were hierarchically organized. Administrators decided who could or could not join, rewarded loyalty, and punished disloyalty.[12]

Shadowcrew hijacked at least 1.5 million stolen numbers, resulting in actual losses of more than $4 million to companies. People who do this are known as carders, but Shadowcrew didn't just do credit cards. It was a full-service operation that also counterfeited passports; driver's licenses; birth certificates; and Social Security, college IDs, and health insurance cards—all subject to quality control "to ensure," as the indictment put it, "that only the highest quality illicit merchandise and services" were being sold to its members. This gang even had a presale system for verifying whether retail vendors would accept stolen numbers. They did this by hacking into a seller's computer network and electronically swiping it to see if it was still good. This was precertified merchandise—like taking a car for a test-drive before you decide whether it is worth stealing.

Busting Shadowcrew was a big victory for the feds—their biggest cybercrime takedown ever to that point. The indictment happened to mention that one of the nineteen defendants, Andrew Mantovani, aka BlahBlahBlhSTFU, had cofounded Shadowcrew in August 2002. But a careful reader would notice that no other cofounder was identified. One of them turned out to be a guy with the screen name of Cumba-Johnny. His real name was Albert Gonzalez. As a kid, Albert had a knack for computers. By age fourteen he had hacked into NASA. By age twenty-three, when the Secret Service took his mug shot, Gonzalez was running Shadowcrew's VPN, giving him an exclusive window into the activities of every Shadowcrew member around the world. But the feds didn't indict Gonzalez. They flipped him, making him a key witness and guide through the cyberunderworld.

Gonzalez's former confederates had no idea, of course. With continuing access to the Shadowcrew VPN, Gonzalez knew his way around the organization like no one else, and he was trusted. Outsiders don't just walk into a criminal organization and start doing business, but if Gonzalez vouched for you, you were in. And so began Operation Firewall, an eighteen-month investigation in which federal agents posed as buyers of stolen information.[13] What the feds didn't know, however, was that CumbaJohnny, aka soupnazi, aka segvec, aka j4juar17, was also running parallel, compartmented operations—different sets of cronies running different fraud schemes who knew nothing of one another. While Gonzalez was ratting out his Shadowcrew pals, he was running two other major scams, each larger than Shadowcrew. And not incidentally, he was playing the Secret Service agents for suckers.

About nine months after the Secret Service took down Shadowcrew, Gonzalez and a different set of confederates, including a couple of Russians, began hacking into the networks of the Marshalls department store chain. They'd sit with their laptops and powerful antennas in a van in the parking lot of a big-box mall. These stores were using wireless networks that transmitted unencrypted data by radio waves— hence the antennas. Within minutes they'd be in the store's network and using a "sniffer" program to seek out the most sensitive data. Their software would gather it up and encrypt and compress it, after which the software would "phone home" and slowly bleed the data out—not too fast, because large volumes of moving data attract attention. With this technique they stole about four hundred thousand credit card numbers from BJ's Wholesale Club and about a million from DSW. Then they went after the TJX Companies, Marshalls's parent company. TJX also owns T.J.Maxx, and in the next fifteen months, Gonzalez and his cronies swiped 45.6 million credit and debit card numbers from the company, which later paid out more than $130 million to settle claims with banks and customers.[14]

When a Gonzalez gang broke into 7-Eleven's network, they got about $2 million cash from twenty-two hundred Citibank ATMs in the stores. They also got another $5 million in fraudulent withdrawals tied to prepaid iWire cards. According to the *Financial Times*, "Most of the money was sent to Russia."[15]

If you thought security standards were keeping up with the electronic thieves, you were wrong—but you wouldn't be in bad company. Hannaford, the supermarket chain, discovered that its systems had been hacked on the same day that its system was declared compliant with the Payment Card Industry Security Standards Council's Data Security Standards. This heist netted 4.2 million credit and debit card numbers, resulting in at least eighteen hundred fraud cases. Gonzalez was behind that one, too.

In earlier cases of retail data theft, merchants—including T.J.Maxx—were criticized for transmitting customer credit and identity information through unencrypted wireless networks, which can be hacked by a moderately competent high school student. Hannaford was more careful, transmitting its point-of-sale data over fiber-optic cable. But the Gonzalez gang apparently hacked into Hannaford's server and used it to remotely install malware (poisoned software) in the hardwired swipe machines at every checkout counter. Once you control point-of-sale devices, you've hit gold. The malware grabbed the data before Hannaford encrypted it, and then sent it out it to servers in far-flung locations controlled by the gang. This is called exfiltration.

The Hannaford incident illustrates an important principle: *If you can do something with software, someone else can undo it with software, and often they can undo it remotely.* In software, a "lock" on information is just a figure of speech. It consists of an electronic instruction expressed in 1s and 0s. If you can get into the system, you can change the lock—or just open it—by changing the 1s and 0s.

Eventually the Secret Service figured all this out. They figured out Gonzalez's other electronic heists, too: Dave & Buster's, OfficeMax, Boston Market, Barnes & Noble, and Sports Authority—some of the largest retailers in the country. Gonzalez is now locked up, and this is not a figure of speech. In 2010 a federal judge sentenced him to twenty years in prison, by far the longest sentence ever imposed for such a case.[16]

Breaking Shadowcrew has had no effect on the rate of economic loss from this kind of crime.[17] Other criminals have cracked Walmart,[18] Montgomery Ward,[19] and many other companies. Data aggregators such as ChoicePoint have been prime targets. Individuals are also under attack. Every week criminal hackers churn out 57,000 new Web addresses onto which they load computer viruses and other malware in the hope that you or I will click on them and give up the log-in credentials for our accounts with eBay, Western Union, Visa, and other financial sites, such as those of banks.[20] Shadowcrew had nothing to do with the electronic heists from the Royal Bank of Scotland or Citibank, each of which appears to have netted tens of millions of dollars.[21] These jobs were pulled off by a professional Russian gang, probably the Russian Business Network, or RBN. The Internet security firm VeriSign calls RBN "the baddest of the bad"; it is based in St. Petersburg but reportedly has servers in Panama, Turkey, Malaysia, Singapore, China, the United States, and Canada. Like other criminal organizations, RBN may have links to figures in the Russian government.[22]

This kind of malware is increasingly spread on social networking sites such as Twitter, Facebook, YouTube, and Flickr.[23] Criminals go where the action is. Their next major target set will be cloud-based services. A "cloud" means you have a keyboard and a screen, but the real computing—including word processing and spreadsheet manipulation—is scattered across multiple servers in multiple locations. Cloud-based services offer efficiencies, but their security characteristics are not yet fully trusted by many businesses. As they become more widely accepted and used, they will become targets of crime.

There will also be more indictments, but not many. The problem is international, and it's out of control.

According to Microsoft, 97 percent of all e-mail is unwanted; most of it is spam, and much of it has malicious attachments.[24] In Britain more than 420,000 spam e-mails are sent *every hour*.[25] Like their American cousins, British gangs have subverted point-of-sale devices in retail shops by physically adding extra circuitry in ways that were extremely difficult to detect. The data taken at the point-of-sale were then used to steal from bank accounts and make purchases on a random basis, and only in relatively small sums, so the scam went on for months before it was discovered. In at least one case the money then ricocheted between foreign bank accounts until it ended up in Pakistan.[26] A few years ago only a foreign intelligence service or a very sophisticated crime syndicate could pull off a scheme this complex. Now it's a business model for small-time hoodlums. The Secret Service, the FBI, Britain's Serious Organised Crime Agency (known as SOCA), and European law enforcement authorities are all capable and diligent in dealing with cybercrime.[27] They just can't keep up.

Consider the numbers. The Internet Crime Complaint Center referred 72,940 crime complaints to law enforcement officials in 2008, mostly involving fraud. The total fraud loss was about $264 million.[28] Yet, with all the thousands of reported abuses in the United States in 2008, only fifteen resulted in arrests or prosecutions,[29] and only nineteen in 2007.[30] The truth is that in most heists we have no idea who the thieves really are. And we don't know because the Internet is one big masquerade ball. You can hide behind aliases, you can hide behind proxy servers, and you can surreptitiously enslave other computers without their owners' knowledge—and then use their computers to do your dirty work. This is a cruel irony: If you want to shield yourself against information theft or hide your own identity as you go about your business, it's extremely difficult. But if you want to hide your identity in order to attack a person or an institution, it's unnervingly easy. Assuming you're in the United States or a small number of industrial democracies, the law enforcement authorities can eventually find out who you are, but that's expensive and time-consuming. As a practical matter, the volume of crime is so great that no one will bother to find you unless you're a huge player, like Albert Gonzalez.

The Internet was not built for security, nor was it built to be the commercial and financial backbone of an advanced, postindustrial economy. But that's how we use it. We've taken an open system based on anonymity and meant for a small, trusted community of government officials and university scientists, and we've turned it into the backbone of our national commerce and much of our national and military communications. Few people, even among business and government leaders, realize how gravely vulnerable this situation makes us.[31] The prosecutions of Shadowcrew and the other Gonzalez conspiracies were major victories, but those cases took years of effort and millions of dollars to develop. If you doubled, tripled, or even quadrupled the number of prosecutions—which in light of the required resources would be impossible—there would still be an overwhelming mismatch between the number of cybercrimes and the number of prosecutions. Law enforcement is an essential tool for dealing with cybercrime, but law enforcement alone cannot bring it down to a tolerable level.

We got a taste of the difficulty of the situation in late 2010, when the FBI, together with its UK and continental counterparts, announced that it had rolled up more than a hundred people in raids on a criminal ring that specialized in the ZeuS Trojan virus. Once you let it inside your computer by clicking on an attachment that carries it, it sneaks around to find your banking information, then logs in and makes transfers. That's how this gang sucked more than $700,000 from a county school district in Pennsylvania in late 2009. And by the time the district and the bank figured it out, more than $440,000 had already disappeared abroad. These arrests were a big deal, enabled by unparalleled international cooperation. Unfortunately, the cooperation didn't extend to the countries like Ukraine where the operation's masterminds were located. All the people nabbed in the West were low-level money mules, merely the willing funnels who agreed to let their accounts be used to siphon the money out of the country in exchange for a chunk of the cash. Much later, Ukranian police arrested five people who were the supposed masterminds behind the operation; their case is pending. Meanwhile, ZeuS remains still readily available on the Internet, and new strains of malware appear faster than one every second, and we can't train cybersleuths fast enough.[32]

**AS A SOCIETY** we tolerate a level of lawlessness and anonymity on the Internet that we would never tolerate in the brick-and-mortar world. Perhaps the root of the problem is that we don't quite know how to think about something that has taken over our lives in what seems like the blink of an eye. Indeed, most of us don't even know what that something *is*. To an engineer the Internet is a vast network of computers connected by wires, switches, and wireless devices that exchange information through an agreed-upon system, or protocol. Called TCP/IP (or Transmission Control Protocol/Internet Protocol), it dictates how bytes of information should be structured so they can be read and understood and how senders and receivers of information all over the world can identify each other. To some people, a computer is an amazing tool for communicating and finding things out. It helps them do what they used to do but much faster and more thoroughly. These people want the Internet to be easy to use, and safe. As a rule they don't care much about how fast it is, but they want it to be free.

Other users have experienced the power of the Internet in transforming the way they do businesses—to take orders, ship goods, target advertising, and so on. These people want the Internet to be fast and secure. If they're in financial services, they want it to be *very* secure. And they're willing to pay for that security.

For still others—mainly but not entirely younger generations of Internet users—a computer is a portal into another zone of existence, an entrance into a palace of virtual places where they can chat, play games, put on masks, and make and break rules—in short, *a place to have experiences*. These are the terms on which tens of millions of users understand virtual Internet space. It conditions how they experience the world. Making rules for technology that serves as the mechanism for commerce and pleasure, politics and play is no easy task. At the end of this book I'm going to propose some steps to help us get there, but for now let's examine what's happening to technologies that we all depend on but which are creating serious insecurities for you, your employer, and your country.

## The Art of the Scam

With no warning your bank manager calls and says your account is overdrawn. Stunned, you demand to know how this could have happened. "Well," says the bank manager, "we got instructions using your PIN number to wire your entire balance to a bank in Ukraine—so we did." You're furious and want the bank to reimburse you for honoring fraudulent wire instructions. But the bank points out that the instructions came with your password and reminds you that your account agreement, which you never read, exonerates the bank from acting on instructions received in that manner. When the ZeuS gang siphoned $700,000 from the account of that school district in Pennsylvania, that's how they did it. Other cyberthieves cracked the account of the town of Poughkeepsie, New York, at TD Bank and transferred $378,000 to accounts in Ukraine. In another case, $800,000 was looted from a Texas company and ended up in accounts in Romania and Italy.[33]

Here's how that works. First, an electronic fraud artist copies the format codes used by the real Web site of the bank (or of another merchant). That allows him to create another Web site that looks *exactly* like the real one. Then he starts sending mass e-mails that look like they came from your bank. These e-mails might say that there's a problem with your account or announce that you've just won an award. To solve the problem or collect the reward, the e-mail directs you to click on a link. When you do, you're automatically routed to the fake Web site. But unless you pay close attention to the Web address[34] at the top of the page (it will be different from that of your bank), you probably won't detect any differences between the fake and real Web sites until after you log in. Even then you won't figure it out unless you try to follow one of the links to your account, or to customer service, or to whatever, because those links will be dead ends. If the criminals are particularly clever, they'll also keep you from figuring this out by quickly sending you an error message after you log in. The message might say "System temporarily down. Try again in a few minutes." That way you're not likely to know you've been scammed. Or it will automatically redirect you to the legitimate Web site, and you'll be none the wiser. Meanwhile, you've given up your customer ID and password. By clicking on the site you may also have unknowingly downloaded an "executable" malware file to your computer. An executable file (which often ends in ".exe") runs, or executes, preset directions that tell it what to do without your involvement. When your computer boots up, for example, it runs an executable file. Depending on its sophistication, the malware may then reconnoiter your system in search of particular kinds of files (like the password to your brokerage account) that are likely to be valuable, package them up, and automatically send the information back to the thieves.

Many schemes are based on a technique called "phishing" because, like fishing, it involves a lure or baited hook and requires the fish to "bite." When the e-mail is socially engineered to a specific person or narrow audience—for example, by appearing to come from a friend or coworker or boss—it's called "spear phishing." You open the e-mail because it looks like it's from someone you know, and in an instant you've downloaded poisoned code. Even the most careful person can be trapped by a well-executed spear-phishing campaign, and the credulous elderly, using a computer chiefly to chat with their grand-children, are especially vulnerable to this kind of fraud. You don't have to be gullible to fall for some of the more sophisticated schemes, how-ever; you just have to be less than perfectly careful, as all of us are. Indeed, most electronic crimes don't involve gullible old ladies. In 2008 more than half the victims were men, mostly between the ages of thirty and fifty. The median loss was $931. On average men lost more than women but today the average is evening out.[35]

We users unwittingly introduce vulnerabilities into computer systems all the time. For example, have you ever used file-sharing software such as Kazaa, BearShare, Morpheus, or FastTrack? Even if you haven't, your kids or your coworkers probably have. These are peer-to-peer, or "P2P," sharing systems that let you stream in your favor-ite movies, music, and other large data files. Lots of people use them at home, blithely putting information onto P2P networks unaware that this is little short of publicly broadcasting their most private informa-tion. Researchers investigating these networks recently turned up tax returns, medical records, financial information—all freely available to anyone with file-sharing software. They also turned up information about an Iraqi student who offered to help U.S. forces in Iraq and then had to go into hiding for fear of being killed.[36]

Many people also install personal P2P software on systems where they work—including, unfortunately, a contract worker at the Pentagon.[37] This kind of software links computers directly rather than through an Internet service provider (ISP) like AOL or Verizon, and like most people who install this stuff, this Pentagon worker had no idea that unless P2P is configured correctly, it basically lets down the drawbridge into your entire system—or your employer's entire system. Millions of government and private documents containing sensitive and sometimes classified information began floating around on file-sharing networks as a result of what this worker did. The documents included Defense Department security system audits, IP addresses and passwords, information on how the military was using radio frequencies to defeat roadside bombs in Iraq, terrorist threat assessments for three U.S. cities, and a lot more.

Most of us have no idea when we're playing with electronic fire, and P2P software is a flamethrower. In July 2008 an employee at a Washington-area investment firm set up P2P file sharing on the LimeWire network so he could trade music or movies from the office. The result was the unwitting compromise of the birth dates and Social Security numbers of about two thousand investment clients, including Supreme Court Justice Stephen Breyer. The breach wasn't discovered for six months—and then only by accident.[38] These stories tell us something, if we're willing to listen: *Security doesn't work when it's left in the hands of the customer or user.* We shouldn't expect ordinary people, few of whom are trained computer experts, to understand the vulnerabilities of the systems they work on. The institutions responsible for those systems should have made sure that nobody could set up open P2P networks on them. When convenience butts heads with security, convenience wins. This is true even among security professionals.[39] If these people won't follow their own rules, others won't follow them either. In short, *if security is not built into our systems, our systems won't be secure.*

**THE KEY WEAPON** in the cybercriminal's arsenal is the "botnet," or bot (slang for networked robots), which is a tool for enslaving multiple computers of unwitting victims. You start by hacking victims' computers. This isn't hard if you already have personal identifying information for a million people, which, as we've seen, is widely available and dirt cheap. It's even easier if you have password-cracking software, which is also cheap, but you don't really need it. If only one computer user in a thousand uses "password" as her password, and if you have a million names, you can crack a thousand computers. If another one in a thousand users uses "12345" as his password, you can crack another thousand. And so on. Once you're in, you can remotely instruct your newly enlisted legion of computer slaves to download your malware, which you have either developed yourself (if you're a pro) or purchased on the thriving black market.

At some point the botnet malware beacons out through the Internet and says, in effect, "Master, here I am. I await your command." The instructions may arrive quickly or not for some time, or they may be built in. They may tell the enslaved computers to start sending spam to the computer owner's address list. This is a valuable service for pornographers, vendors of illicit drugs, and other sleazy types. Criminals can buy botnet services the way you can buy time in a beachfront condo for your next holiday. Or the first generation of slaves may be instructed to recruit more slaves by installing malware on the machine of anyone who clicks a link in the next wave of spam. Bots therefore grow exponentially. At the beginning of the year it took me to write this book, the largest botnet had about ten thousand enslaved machines. Before I'd finished, the number was over one million.[40]

Botnets can also put people out of business, at least temporarily, by shutting down their systems. The bots do this by instructing the enslaved computers to send vast numbers of messages to a particular address. The content of the messages doesn't matter; the point is to flood somebody's system so completely that it shuts down. This is called a "distributed denial-of-service," or DDOS, attack, and it's a fairly elementary form of delinquency. Supporters of WikiLeaks, for instance, used DDOS attacks against its perceived enemies, such as PayPal and MasterCard. These companies were targeted as enemies of free speech because they stopped doing business with WikiLeaks after that group broadcast stolen classified information and published a list of the nation's critical infrastructure.[41] With much greater effect, Russian hackers used DDOS attacks against Estonia in 2007, shutting down government ministries and banks for days after the Estonians announced plans to move a World War II memorial to their Russian "liberators." The following year, in a foretaste of the use of a network onslaught in conjunction with a conventional armed attack, the

Russians employed DDOS attacks when they invaded Georgia. They temporarily brought down Georgia's communication networks just as Russian troops were moving in, making it difficult for the leadership to understand what was happening or to coordinate a response. We'll discuss cyberwarfare in chapters 6 and 7.

Botnets propagate themselves over a cascading series of computers and servers in different countries. That way, when investigators trace the proximate source of the attack, the culprit appears to be an enslaved computer owned by an innocent and unwitting person like you or me. Good forensic cyberinvestigators can follow the trail further, but it usually leads overseas, often to a country with weak law enforcement, like Russia or Ukraine. China, meanwhile, is stepping up its enforcement—but only if the victims are Chinese—because the Chinese government doesn't care if their nationals are committing crimes overseas. Or else the money ends up in a country with no laws at all against cybercrimes, like many nations in Africa and Latin America. Forensic investigations require effort, time, and lots of resources. The FBI, the Secret Service, and their European equivalents are good at it, but unlike the bots themselves, these investigations are not efficient. In some cases law enforcement officials can shut down the IP address used for the botnet's command and control, but then the botmaster just sets up another one. Once again, the good guys simply can't keep up.

**NETWORK INSECURITY ISN'T** just the threat of identity theft for individuals. As we will see in the next chapter, it has also become a serious corporate problem. Big companies as well as consumers have been severely hurt by cybercrime where it hurts most—in their stock prices. Corporate officers and directors who don't understand this danger and defend against it are assuming unnecessary risk. Here's a cautionary tale.

In December 2008, Albert Gonzalez and yet another bunch of his cyberthugs were launching an attack on the networks of one of those companies that make the world go round but few people have heard of, Heartland Payment Systems. Heartland processes bank card payments for merchants. You may not know it, but you cannot use your credit or debit card without putting your credit information into the hands of Heartland or another company like it. These businesses are an essential cog in the credit and debit card clearing process, and Heartland is one of the biggest, processing one hundred million transactions per month for more than 250,000 merchants.[42] The company maintains millions of credit and debit card numbers on its network, but the first phase of the attack was aimed simply at Heartland's payroll-manager application software, which holds personal information about the company's own employees. Heartland's network security people put this fire out in about a month and figured they had solved the problem. But they didn't know that the attack had also implanted hidden malware in the company's payment-processing system—the heart of its business. During 2008, Gonzalez and his cronies stole about 130 million credit and debit card numbers from Heartland. The company didn't figure this out for about a year. On January 20, 2009, Heartland publicly disclosed the theft,[43] and immediately its stock began to tank. From over $15 per share on January 19, it fell to $3.78 by March 9. A year later it had still not fully recovered. A business built on network security had been exposed as deeply insecure. Heartland has reserved about $100 million to deal with this intrusion, and the figure could go much higher.[44]

## Putting an End to Anarchy

As we saw in the first chapter, the Internet was designed for a relatively small, trusted community of mainly American university researchers and government officials to share their work and ideas, and commercial uses were actually outlawed until 1992. For its original purpose the Internet is cheap and extremely efficient. When you want to send an e-mail or check out somebody's Web site, you call up an e-address, and essentially you get an electronic handshake that says "Okay, we're connected, no questions asked." This is good. You can review unpopular or controversial material without anyone looking over your shoulder. You can go electronic window-shopping for free and visit many merchants in less time than it takes to drive to one brick-and-mortar store. If you like, you can visit politically or socially controversial Web sites or electronically bad neighborhoods, like Web sites devoted to data scraping or porn, and do it incognito. Or you can simply chat with others while in disguise—a pastime with a long and elaborate history but until now not so easily done. "Man is least himself when he talks in his own person," Oscar Wilde observed. "Give him a mask, and he will tell you the truth."[45] Now that ordinary people have the ability to do this, proposing that they give it up would be foolish and futile—though the mask of anonymity is often penetrable. Giving it up would also be expensive and, in some contexts, pointless, or worse. Being able to visit hundreds of thousands of commercial Web sites cheaply is good for business and good for customers.

But is that little electronic handshake good enough when you want to pay your mortgage or make a bank deposit? Today this simple handshake is the economic underpinning of the Internet and thus the economy of the entire developed world. Without the Internet our financial systems would collapse and our commerce would slow to a crawl. Yet the risk to that commerce is growing. The risk to our military communications, which ride on the same public backbone that you and I use, is also growing. Reducing this risk will require great care, because Internet security involves not only how—and how freely—we converse and express ourselves but also how and whether things work.

In every aspect of our lives other than in cyberspace, we expect liberty under law: On the sidewalk we expect to go where we please— free from assault. On the highway we drive unmolested—provided we obey the traffic laws. We also expect that the road signs won't intentionally mislead us. In public parks we value the freedom to linger, rest, and converse—provided we permit others to do the same. In the marketplace we expect to buy, sell, and trade—but we also expect fraud to be stopped and punished. In short, we demand a balance between liberty and order, and while we may disagree at the margin on how to strike that balance, no one in the West contests the basic principle that liberty goes hand in hand with accountability when what we do harms others.[46]

If I am found loitering after hours with a crowbar in the alley behind the jewelry store, a police officer has the right to stop me, frisk me, and ask me questions.[47] I can't be arrested, because I haven't committed a crime, but I can be stopped. If I use the crowbar to smash a window or pry open a trapdoor on the roof, I can be handcuffed and arrested. There's a graduated threshold for the state's ability to interfere with my liberty. We could do this in cyberspace, too.

The stakes are high, and the danger goes far beyond the theft of personal information.

# 3

## BLEEDING WEALTH

**FOREIGN INTELLIGENCE AGENCIES** have been penetrating American corporate networks and stealing technology electronically since the 1990s, but we have been slow to catch on. That began to change in January 2010, when Google went public with news of massive attacks on its networks and blamed the Chinese government.[1] In retaliation, Google announced that it would stop filtering and blocking searches that the Chinese government deemed politically sensitive. This kind of censorship was a condition the government of China required in exchange for allowing the company to conduct business there. Partly as a result of this threat, and partly because Google wasn't eager to advertise that its source code has been filched,[2] the company treated the episode as a story about censorship. The White House also adopted this line, and most of the media went along.[3] Freedom of expression is a bedrock issue in our relations with China, which would like nothing better than to lock down the Internet and regain government control over what its people can know and write. Once inside the company's networks, Chinese operators could determine who was running politically sensitive searches, and through Google they "routinely accessed" the accounts of "dozens of U.S.-, China-, and Europe-based Gmail users who are advocates of human rights in China."[4] That's serious. But the Google incident was not entirely, and perhaps not even chiefly, a story about Internet freedom.

When it launched Google.cn in 2006 (".cn" is the designation for the China domain name), the company had acknowledged that China would require it to censor "sensitive information" from its search results. Google nevertheless intended to be in the Middle Kingdom "for the long haul" and announced its intention to make "significant and growing investments" there. Google invested billions in the Chinese market *after* it had accepted these limitations on freedom of expression as a condition of doing business there. Why would the company jeopardize its investment in the largest national market on Earth over that issue? Yet Google publicly went ballistic over the 2010 incident. Something else was also going on.

Operation Aurora didn't just hit Google. It was a coordinated attack on the intellectual property[5] of several *thousand* companies[6] in the United States and Europe—including Morgan Stanley, Yahoo, Symantec, Adobe, Northrop Grumman, Dow Chemical, and many others.[7] Intellectual property is the stuff that makes Google and other firms tick. The caper was enabled by an expertly targeted phishing expedition that must have involved months of research and reconnoitering inside the Google servers on the roles and habits of company executives, careful target selection based on probable access to proprietary data, and an analysis of each target's network of acquaintances. The attackers then generated fake e-mails that seemed to come from another executive whom the target knew, so the target clicked on it, clicked again on a hot link or an attachment—and *presto!* the attackers were in. They then exploited a previously unknown vulnerability in Microsoft's Internet Explorer to install customized malware that opened a stealth connection to a pirate server. At that point the attackers owned the system and could explore it at leisure. Their operational security was excellent. They encrypted their malicious code at a very high level to make it undetectable by ordinary filters—the kind of encryption you'd expect from a foreign intelligence service but not from commercial criminals. A McAfee executive said, with grudging admiration, "Like an army of mules withdrawing funds from an ATM, this malware enabled the attackers to quietly suck the crown jewels out of many companies while people were off enjoying their December holidays."[8]

This is why Google flew off the handle: The keys to Google's magic, in the form of source code—or at least some of it—had been swiped, *and* the company was being used unwittingly not merely as a filtering tool but also for surveillance.[9] Not only that, but if you can get to the source code, you can change it to give the attackers long-term, persistent access to Google and its customers. Google should now assume that the Chinese authorities are permanently inside its systems.

So who did it? We can cavil about whether the right verb is "directed" or "oversaw" or "authorized," but the operation was approved at high levels of the government of the People's Republic of China. According to sources available to U.S. diplomats, Li Changchun, a member of the Politburo Standing Committee and therefore a top dog,[10] did what lots of people do: He looked himself up on Google.cn. And what he found upset him: Chinese people were writing unpleasant things about him, which other Chinese people could find on Google. This should not have been too surprising for a man who was the country's senior propaganda official, nor was his response surprising. Li decided it was time to reassert control over China's information space. So he directed (or oversaw, or authorized) a payback operation.[11]

This is one of the many stories from classified State Department cables that are now floating freely around the world thanks to Wiki-Leaks, but while the details were new to the public, the Chinese government's involvement in the operation should not have surprised anyone who had been paying attention.

Promptly after the attack, Google sleuths easily traced the attack to a server in Taiwan and took over that server. From there they quickly saw that the attack came from the mainland, and they could identify some of the other companies that had been whacked.[12] At that point State Department spokesman P. J. Crowley asserted, "We will be issuing a formal démarche to the Chinese government in Beijing on this issue in the coming days, probably early next week."[13] (A démarche is diplomatic jargon for a formal complaint.) A few days later the case got even stronger when an American software analyst reverse engineered the malware and discovered that it contained code from a Chinese language technical paper that had been published exclusively on Chinese language Web sites.[14] But the démarche never came. Meanwhile, the Chinese became indignant. All this business about a free Internet, said a prominent academic at Beijing's Tsinghua University, was nothing but a calculated "U.S. tactic to preserve its hegemonic domination."[15] By mid-February, however, the *New York Times* was reporting that the attacks on Google and other U.S. companies had been traced to specific computers at two Chinese educational institutions. One of them was Shanghai Jiao Tong University, a world-class computer programming school; the other was Lanxiang Vocational School, which trains computer scientists for the People's Liberation Army. Lanxiang's computer network is operated by a company with close ties to Baidu, a homegrown search engine that competes directly with Google in China.[16]

About a week after the Google story broke, the plot was revealed to be even thicker, when Mark Clayton of the *Christian Science Monitor* exposed systematic, long-term electronic espionage against Marathon Oil, ExxonMobil, and ConocoPhillips in which thieves got away with a huge trawl of real-time "'bid data' detailing the quantity, value, and location of oil discoveries worldwide." Bid data are among an energy company's most closely guarded secrets. This information costs tens of millions of dollars to obtain, using expensive exploration techniques. Energy companies use it to make huge bets on which fields will produce oil and gas, and of what quality and quantity. In these three cases, however, Chinese intelligence operators had hidden in the networks for months and gotten the data free from three of the world's biggest oil companies. These were orchestrated, highly professional attacks, using custom-tailored malware that no antivirus software could filter because no antivirus software maker had seen it before. As in the Google affair, the attackers had used an elaborate phishing expedition that involved advance reconnoitering, good target selection, and social network analysis of company executives. The companies had no idea what was going on until the FBI alerted them months later. Where did the stolen information go? According to the *Monitor*, at least some of it flowed "to a computer in China." More recently the computer security firm McAfee traced all these attacks to a single site in China.[17]

Still, the United States issued no démarche. There may have been several reasons for second thoughts in the White House and State Department, but one key reason must have been the difficulty and uncertainty of attributing cyberattacks. As we've seen, the Internet is built for anonymity. Until recently I couldn't place a nasty phone call to my neighbor and make it look like the call came from someplace else (alas, this too is changing). Caller ID screens and phone company records almost always told the truth—and nobody thought that was an invasion of privacy any more than having a license plate on your car. Even those who blocked their own phone numbers from view assumed—and appreciated the fact—that incoming calls really did originate from the number that flashes on the screen. That's why we've been largely successful in blocking telephone spam.[18] Moreover, a caller can place only one call at a time, and if I want to block calls from someone who won't disclose his or her own number, it's easy to do. This is not true on the Internet. I can send a single message to thousands, even millions of people. My service provider doesn't guarantee that any or all of them will arrive, but it does let me throw a message into a vast network of networks. Nor is the originating computer's IP address (those strings of numbers that correspond, say, to an e-mail address or to a name like www.store.com) a single, unchanging identifier like a phone number. Most IP addresses are dynamic. They change. And if you know how, you can change them very, very fast, over and over again, so tracing can be difficult. On top of that, the Internet's naming and addressing protocols are fairly easy to spoof.

By mid-May the State Department had excellent information from human sources about who authorized the assault on Google, but it could not take that information to the Chinese government without burning its sources.

Definitive forensic proof of where a cyberoperation originated— this is called attribution—can be difficult to obtain. To attribute a cyberattack you first have to find out what hardware it came from. To do that, forensic investigators must trace the path of the intrusion back to the server that handled it last. But as we saw in the last chapter, almost invariably that server was merely the last of several through which the attackers passed in order to hide. But let's assume that with international cooperation and some delay, we get beyond that problem and trace the attack all the way back to the computer that generated it. Unfortunately, identifying a computer and its location doesn't mean we know who was behind the attack. Further painstaking analysis may answer that question, possibly with the aid of human intelligence, but the people behind the attack are usually in a country with weak law enforcement. That country may not even have laws that prohibit that kind of behavior.[19] If their authorities cooperate, we may be able to shut down the botmaster's Web site, and that's worth doing, because it raises the thieves' cost of doing business. But it won't shut them down for long. It costs them money to move elsewhere, set up a new Web site, and notify their confederates—but they do.

Or perhaps the attack came from a booth in an Internet café in Riga or Hyderabad or Houston. Who was at the keyboard? Extensive and time-consuming forensic analysis of the operator's habits may point to a particular operator and a screen name or alias. But who is that person *really*? Whom does she work for? We could be dealing with a clever loner, a malicious member of a private hackers' club, or a shill for a foreign intelligence agency. When it comes to Chinese cyber-militias and Russian gangs, this is a significant difficulty. Governments play dumb.

The State Department could insist that nations are responsible for acts of war originating within their territories,[20] but were the attacks on Google and the oil companies acts of war? That's doubtful. Nor does the United States or any other nation wish to declare war simply in order to defend its networks. Besides, if you're unsure who mounted the attacks, whom do you declare war against? The laws of war aside, we could also take the diplomatic position that the Chinese government is responsible for cybermischief originating in its territory. But that would prove a two-edged sword. Which country originates the most cyberattacks world-wide? If you include ordinary hacking, crime, and sport, it's the United States.[21] The Chinese can't control all of their Internet cowboys and bandits any more than the U.S. government can control theirs.[22]

One way forensic sleuths attribute attacks is to figure out who wrote the malware. But that line of investigation brings its own frus-trations. In the Google case, for example, the malware seems to have been written by a diverse and unorganized group of Chinese security professionals, consultants, and contractors who operated largely in the open and did not necessarily know how their code would be used.[23] Programs, including malware programs, are usually written by teams of engineers, often from different countries. To complicate matters even further, a third country's foreign intelligence service could spoof an attack to make it look like it came from China.

The difficulty of attributing a particular cyberattack coming out of China does not mean that China and its government are unwitting dupes. In the Google case there is no room for serious doubt that the PRC government was behind it. As a general matter, American and European companies and governments are under constant, withering cyberattacks from China, and these attacks reflect government policy, denials notwithstanding. The wave of attacks emanating from China is too relentless, the connections to Chinese institutions too pervasive, and the relationships of certain targets to Chinese governmental interests are too close to admit of any other conclusion. There are also cases in which U.S. intelligence has been able, beyond a reasonable doubt, to attribute attacks to identifiable Chinese attackers, and we know the relationship of those attackers to the Chinese government. These people are not amateurs. They're big-game hunters who know what they're after. And once inside a system they need be in no hurry. They can exfiltrate what they want when they want. Typically they work during daytime hours—that is, daytime in China.[24]

CHINESE THEORY AND practice do not recognize a clear line between governmental and nongovernmental functions, or between government and society. For example, the China National Aero-Technology Import & Export Corporation, or CATIC, is part of a complex, state-owned conglomerate of profit-making companies with an annual export-import volume of $24 billion. It markets, sells, and buys civilian and military aircraft.[25] In American terms, CATIC functions like a combination of the marketing and sales departments of Boeing and Lockheed Martin plus the Export-Import Bank—plus parts of the Commerce and Defense departments. Comparing CATIC to a private U.S. company would be therefore highly misleading. In 2001 CATIC pleaded guilty to making false statements in order to procure a U.S. export license for specialized equipment used for airframe fabrication. According to the license, CATIC was going to use the equipment for civilian purposes. According to the indictment, however, it intentionally diverted the equipment for military use, in direct violation of U.S. criminal law.[26] Neither the case nor the company can be understood in terms of our Western distinction between public and private, or official and unofficial, functions. CATIC was operating as a privatized government ministry.

China's legions of cyberoperators also straddle the line we draw between official and unofficial. According to press reports, a classified

FBI account states that the People's Liberation Army (PLA) of China has developed a cadre of 30,000 cyberspies, who are supplemented by more than 150,000 "private sector" cyberexperts "whose mission is to steal American military and technological secrets and cause mischief in government and financial services."[27] In effect, China has fostered a vast electronic militia, a sort of cyber National Guard on virtual active duty every day of the year. Just as CATIC was pursuing Chinese government policy in connection with the illegal export of U.S. airframe equipment, the electronic pirates who attacked Google and the oil companies were pursuing official policy whether or not they were on their government's payroll. In some cases we know these militias have close relations with government officials and operate under official sanction. In those instances they operate like seventeenth-century privateers, who were freelance sea captains with crown commissions to attack enemy shipping. Sir Francis Drake, the most famous of them, was a pirate to the Spanish, but to the English a hero. In China, cyber-privateers are heroes. In this respect China enjoys a benefit long lost to Western governments: The educated elite in China are nationalistic and have high confidence in their government.[28] When a Los Angeles law firm sued the Chinese government and nine Chinese companies over a state-sponsored "censorware" called Green Dam Youth Escort, the law firm quickly became the victim of a phishing attack that infiltrated its server. According to the firm, the attack "appears" to have come from China.[29] Did the Chinese army or security services do it? Not likely. They didn't have to. The Russian government also uses cyberoperators that it keeps at arm's length, but in Russia the surrogates are criminal gangs with deep ties to intelligence and security services.

## The New Espionage Game

All nations, including the United States,[30] spy on their adversaries, and even strategic allies sometimes target one another's state secrets. They do it because they want security and do not want to be surprised. And some nations do it because they want to catch up with an adversary that has an overwhelming technical or scientific advantage. But unlike China—and to a lesser extent Russia, France, and Israel—the United States does not use its intelligence services to support its national industrial base.[31] The French services have even bugged the seats in Air France's first-class cabins to spy on U.S. executives.[32] Espionage is a constant. In the last ten years, however, it has changed in two fundamental ways. First, it is no longer a game played only with human spies and electronic bugs in government offices. Ferreting out human penetration remains a daunting challenge for the FBI, the CIA, and the military. But running spies is risky and expensive. If you can steal terabytes of sensitive information electronically, from the comfort of a computer terminal thousands of miles away, perhaps you don't need a spy. Or perhaps your spy's job is no longer stealing information but planting malicious software from the inside to enable a remote cyberthief to snatch information later. In that case, your ideal mole may no longer be the minister's private secretary but rather the ministry's chief technical officer.

The second recent change in espionage is the rapid expansion of the target set into the private sector, particularly into companies that are *not* working for the Defense Department or their ministerial equivalents. Foreign intelligence services are not only pilfering intelligence from our military and our government; they're robbing us of the technology that creates jobs, wealth, and power. China is not the world's most skillful cyberoperator—at least, not yet. The Russians, the French, the British, and the Israelis have more advanced cybercapabilities, at least in some respects. So does the United States. But the Chinese are catching up quickly, and their attacks are relentless, determined, and persistent. Chinese attackers are not smash-and-grab criminals, pilfering personal bank accounts and running up fraudulent credit card charges. Their line of work is hard-core cyberespionage, and their targets are the technology, designs, and trade secrets of private companies, many of which have no direct connection to traditional notions of national security. Who's winning this battle? They are. And that has profound implications for your children and grandchildren and the world they will inherit, and for the place of the United States in the world.

Economic espionage has been on the upswing since the mid-1990s, following the end of the cold war.[33] In response to that development, Congress passed the Economic Espionage Act of 1996,[34] which sought to deter this kind of spying through prosecution.[35] As a deterrent it has yielded some successes but has certainly not stemmed the tide of technological losses. More than ever Western companies as well as governments are high-priority targets of foreign intelligence operations, especially companies that know how to create and market advanced technologies, pharmaceuticals, and industrial designs. These firms export to the world. They take brainpower and raw inputs and create value, jobs, and a standard of living that the rest of the world envies. Advanced industrial designs, business plans, and test data are called intellectual property, and they are the private sector's equivalent of top secret. Like secret State Department cables and the PIN for your bank account, corporate secrets no longer exist on a few pieces of paper locked in a safe. They're arrangements of 1s and 0s that live in vast electronic databases, and they move at the speed of light over electronic networks. We are losing these secrets over the same vulnerable networks that threaten your personal privacy.

Commercial espionage has long been practiced by freelancers bent on personal gain.[36] In the early 1990s, the purchasing chief for GM's European operations jumped ship to Volkswagen and allegedly took with him GM's cost-cutting secrets. (Yes, they had some.) He was never convicted, but German prosecutors tied him to a huge stash of secret GM documents, and VW settled with GM for $100 million and a commitment to buy $1 billion in auto parts.[37] In 1997, Steven Davis betrayed Gillette's design for a battery-powered safety razor to a competitor. That kind of theft still goes on,[38] and we deal with it more or less satisfactorily through criminal and civil litigation. What is new, however, is the amount of information that a corporate insider can steal with a few keystrokes, or by sticking a thumb drive into a USB port. And many of the thieves are taking what they steal overseas. In late 2010, for example, the U.S. software firm Oracle won a $1.3 billion judgment against the German software firm SAP for what amounted to a systematic industrial espionage scheme that involved repeated and unauthorized access to Oracle's proprietary, password-protected Web site. SAP was able to compile an illegal library of its competitor's copyrighted software code.[39] At about the same time, a former employee of Bristol-Myers Squibb, the pharmaceutical firm, pleaded guilty to stealing trade secrets from his employer, which he planned to take to India to start his own venture. Unfortunately for him, his "investor" was an FBI agent.[40]

Less than two weeks later, Xiang Dong (aka Mike) Yu, a product engineer for Ford, pleaded guilty to stealing about four thousand Ford documents with sensitive design specifications for engines, transmissions, power supplies, and so on. He copied the information onto an external drive and took it straight to his new employer, the Beijing Automotive Company, which competes directly with Ford. Most of the information Yu stole had nothing to do with his job, but he was able to download it anyway. This case is an almost exact parallel of the hemorrhaging of classified State Department cables to WikiLeaks, allegedly by an army private in Iraq. There, too, the soldier was able to download to external media information that was totally unrelated to his job. Neither the government nor most companies have understood the danger of giving all their employees access to all their information, regardless of an employee's roles and responsibilities.

There's more economic thievery from the United States than most Americans realize. In March 2011, a former vice president of Goldman Sachs, Sergey Aleynikov, was sentenced to an eight-year prison term for stealing the secret algorithms (the mathematical formulas) the firm used to run its automated securities trading operation. Brokerages and investment banks use these trading programs to buy and sell securities very fast, taking advantage of price changes or differences in prices among markets. Aleynikov reportedly encrypted and uploaded the program, or at least part of it, to a server in Europe, then decamped for a new employer.[41] In March 2009, two Tennessee engineers were indicted for stealing trade secrets from Goodyear Tire & Rubber on behalf on a Chinese tire manufacturer. According to a recent study, electronic media were involved in all ten recent cases involving foreign economic espionage that led to indictments.[42] In every case the defendant stole either to form a competing business abroad (overwhelmingly in China) or to take intellectual property to a new employer in a competing business abroad (usually in China). Losses in two of the cases could reach several hundred million dollars.

If the companies involved in these cases had been an intelligence agency, the press would call the cases counterintelligence failures and, indeed, that is what they are.

### "There's tons and tons of stuff going to China"

Radiation-hardened, programmable semiconductors are used in satellites to withstand the high doses of solar radiation that would quickly burn out ordinary chips. They're made in the United States, but you can't buy them at RadioShack or Best Buy. These chips cost thousands of dollars apiece, and they appear on something called the United States Munitions List, together with a lot of advanced weaponry, precision radars, state-of-the-art cryptography, and other items whose uncontrolled export would be dangerous to our national security. Items on this list are controlled by International Traffic in Arms Regulations, known as ITAR, and it is a crime to export them without a license.[43] Which doesn't stop some people from trying.

In early 2010, an engineer in the Seattle area, a Chinese national named Lian Yang who did contract work for Microsoft, began making inquiries about programmable semiconductors.[44] An acquaintance put him in touch with a "confidential source," as the FBI calls him, who might be able to help out. They met on March 9, 2010, and Yang explained to this source that he wasn't a spy, and he certainly didn't want to deal in restricted goods, but he was interested in acquiring part number XQR2V3000-4CG717V from a company called Xilinx. How many? Three hundred. So Mr. Yang's source began checking around, only to learn that the buyer would be required to produce an "end-user certificate," which states precisely what the goods will be used for, by whom, and in what country. So on March 19 he reported back to Mr. Yang, who advised him that the parts were intended for China Space Technology's next generation "spaceship program." This was apparently a reference to a state-owned enterprise, Xian Space Star Technology (Group) Corporation, which specializes in the research and development of satellite load systems.[45] On March 31, however, Mr. Yang's source explained to him that the parts were radiation-hardened, programmable semiconductors, and they were on the munitions list. No problem, said Mr. Yang, and on the same day he e-mailed his source an end-user certificate that listed a Hong Kong firm as the end user and said the parts were for "China's new generation of passenger jet."

The two men met on April 1 at a restaurant in Bellevue, a Seattle suburb, to discuss splitting the profits, but on April 13 the confidential source gave Mr. Yang the bad news: Since these parts were on the munitions list, the company could not sell them for an end user in China. Weeks passed. Mr. Yang's Chinese contacts grew impatient and began to push. On August 15, Mr. Yang's confidential source sent him an e-mail. He was getting nowhere, he wrote, because the parts are restricted by ITAR. However, he happened to have a promising new contact. "I am certain he will be able to arrange for us to obtain and buy the parts in large quantities," the confidential source said, "and on a regular basis, and have the items delivered for us here. What we do with them is up to us."

Ten days later Mr. Yang and his contact had a heart-to-heart in a

Seattle restaurant. "You know," the source said, "what we're doing is illegal, for all intents and purposes. So, we have to be really careful."

"Yeah," said Mr. Yang.

The source's contacts in the industry were careful too. They wanted to meet Mr. Yang in person.

So the four men met in a restaurant on September 14—Mr. Yang, his confidential buddy, and two men who seemed to know the business very well. These semiconductors, one of the men explained, basically come in two flavors. One's hardened and controlled by law, one's commercial and not controlled. If Mr. Yang's partners in China could use the commercial grade, well, "everybody is safe and there's no issue." Yang rejected the commercial grade. His partners were "very firm" on that. They want the radiation-hardened version, he said, and "they want it badly." Mr. Yang said he didn't know how the parts would be used, but said they'd be going to China. They mulled it over. It would be dangerous. Did Mr. Yang understand what would happen if they got caught? The industry man answered his own question: "We're going to jail."

"Yeah," said Mr. Yang. "That, that's like, that's exactly why my first concern is safety."

Yang met the two men from the industry again on October 1, this time in San Francisco, to discuss how to move the goods to China. "The product will stay here in the States until it is safe, absolutely safe, to ship to China," Yang said. Then his stateside associates would figure out "how to repackage it, erase the serial number," and ship it over as something else. Really? Sure, said Yang. "There's tons and tons of stuff going to China."

On October 7, a wire for sixty thousand dollars came in from a Hong Kong account in the name of "Ardent Solar, LLC." Obviously a fake company, a cutout.

On October 15, Yang flew to China. On November 2 he flew back.

On the day delivery was to occur, November 5, one of the men e-mailed Yang. For some reason, he wrote, the State Department had not yet approved the transaction. There would be a delay. A phone call followed. Mr. Yang was told not to worry; it's just paperwork.

But of course Mr. Yang did worry. Finally, anxious weeks later, on November 30, the men agreed to meet Yang in Seattle on December 3 and deliver the goods. Yang would bring the final twenty thousand dollars in cash. That same day Yang e-mailed his bogus purchase order. It misidentified the supplier and falsely claimed the goods were "commercial" grade. Under "prepared and approved by," the document said YANG.

On December 3, 2010, the day delivery was to be made, the FBI arrested Yang for violation of the Arms Control Act. Yang's original confidential source was an FBI informer. His two industry contacts were FBI agents. They had taped every meeting.

This is what a good counterintelligence investigation looks like, but there's so much thievery going on, it's impossible to keep up.[46]

A few months earlier, in July 2010, the FBI arrested Huang Kexue, formerly a Dow Chemical employee, for sharing Dow's research with scientists in China and then obtaining a grant from a Chinese state-run foundation to start a rival business there. Former engineers from Ford, General Motors, and the DuPont Company were also arrested during 2010 for stealing intellectual property, but the Huang case is different. He was charged with economic espionage rather than with an export violation, and he was charged with acting directly on behalf of the Chinese government.[47] That link is difficult to prove beyond a reasonable doubt and so is rarely charged, even in a case like Yang's. Whether the goods are illegally exported (perhaps to be reverse engineered), however, or whether the specifications and drawings for the goods are stolen, may make no economic difference. In both cases we bleed technology.

Chinese economic spying is not confined to the United States, and much of it is electronic. Both the British and German governments have publicly complained about it,[48] and the British Security Service known as MI5 has warned British businesses that Chinese agents are eavesdropping and stealing secrets from British firms and compromising executives through blackmail. They do this in part through "lavish hospitality" at trade fairs and exhibitions[49]—the sort of hospitality you might not tell your wife about. The Chinese are also generous with "gifts"—cameras and thumb drives, for example. Connect the camera or thumb drive to your computer, and you're infected with a program that lets electronic spies into your company's system. Electronically transmitted diseases work like sexually transmitted diseases: When you insert a thumb drive into your USB port, you're exposing your computer to every electronic disease your thumb drive has ever been exposed to.

The Chinese have other even subtler methods of stealing our know-how. Several years ago, while serving as the national counterintelligence executive, I sat with colleagues discussing how we would plan an espionage attack against an American business. And then a lightbulb went on: the law firms! Of course: A company's outside intellectual property lawyers have its technical secrets, and their corporate law colleagues are privy to strategic business plans. And lawyers don't like taking instructions from anybody, particularly their less well paid underlings who are responsible for network security. They're impatient. In some firms the rainmakers have nixed even simple steps, like requiring a password on mobile devices that connect with the firm's servers. They couldn't be bothered. Privileged with secrets, highly paid, often arrogant and usually impatient, lawyers are the perfect targets. I cannot disclose *what* I know, because it's classified, but I can disclose *that* I know that my surmise was soon justified. U.S. law firms have been penetrated both here and abroad. Firms with offices in China or Russia are particularly vulnerable, because the foreign security services are likely to own the people who handle the firms' physical and electronic security. These services are not interested in stealing brilliant legal briefs; they want information about the firm's clients. Every law firm with offices on several continents holds privileged and sensitive electronic documents worth millions of dollars to a foreign service, ranging from investment plans to negotiating and business strategies, and much more.[50]

**OUR ADVERSARIES UNDERSTAND** that the strategic security of the West is bound up with our economic security. Our science, technology, and ability to rapidly turn ideas to commercial use are what generate our wealth, fund our defense, and make us powerful. A strong military is only one of the elements of national power. In the 1940s, every industrial nation knew how to build ships and tanks and airplanes, and ours weren't always the best. At the beginning of World War II, to take only one example, the Mitsubishi A6M Zero had a longer range and was more maneuverable than any Allied fighter.[51] But World War II was an industrial war of massed armies supported by mass production. The Allies won because the United States could produce more armaments well enough, in larger quantities, and faster than anybody else. Today a postindustrial world order is being created—not by ships and tanks and airplanes but by a changing economic dynamic. This order depends heavily on the balance of trade, which in turn depends on a nation's ability to nurture science, to turn that science into applied technology, and to quickly turn that technology into products that people want to buy—products that may or may not have military applications. On the whole the United States has done this better than any other nation in history. The day when virtually all advanced technology resides in the United States may be over, but it is still the case that more of the world's advanced technology resides here than anywhere else. And it's worth stealing. At least one former French official has been uncharacteristically candid on this point. According to Claude Silberzahn, who headed France's External Security Directorate from 1989 to 1993, "It is true that for decades, the French state regulated the markets to some extent with its left hand while its right hand used the secret services to procure information for its own firms."[52] And most of that technology is in the private sector.

The Chinese also went to school on the cold war. They saw what happened when a rigid, command economy on Lenin's model took on the most dynamic market economy in history: The USSR collapsed. They also went to school on our two Gulf wars and saw what happened when mechanized armor on the 1940s model went to war with the most technologically advanced armed forces in history: Saddam's army collapsed. Chinese, Russian, and other military observers also studied NATO's war in Kosovo, when Serbian hackers disrupted U.S. command-and-control networks, and both sides used the Internet in a fierce public relations battle.[53] It dawned on the Chinese (and anyone else who was paying attention) that our military was commanded and controlled electronically—through porous public networks that were easily hacked. This was its weak point. And so the Chinese, the Russians, and others have gone to work on our networks, which are privately owned.

Another reason foreign intelligence services target our private sector is that many of our classified military secrets also reside there. About $400 billion of the Pentagon annual budget of about $700 billion is spent on contracts.[54] Companies like Boeing, Lockheed Martin, General Dynamics, and Northrop Grumman now do much of the national defense work that used to be done within the government. These companies don't just make tanks and airplanes anymore. Along with big consulting firms like Booz Allen Hamilton, SAIC, and others, they're called "systems integrators." They take complex defense and intelligence subsystems and make them function together—and not just for the Defense Department. In a real sense, they make the government work. This wasn't true in 1945. Today we rely heavily on private companies because they are agile and creative, and they attract much of our most experienced and well-educated talent, because they pay well. Without these companies our national defense effort would shrivel. Republicans and Democrats may disagree at the margin about how much work the government should contract out, but there is no disagreement that the government must rely heavily on these firms. If anything, our government is likely to become more reliant, not less, on the private sector in the future. This means that ever more national defense secrets can be stolen from the private sector. Government communications live on a privately owned telecommunications backbone. Not just telephones. Voice, video, and data signals have converged. All these modes of communication travel across the same fiber-optic cables, the same microwave signals, and the same satellite links. If you can penetrate our telecommunications carriers or the companies that make their equipment, you may be able to penetrate government and other private systems, too.

About 108 foreign intelligence services target the United States, and many of them collect information against economic targets. Collection by Russia and Cuba is back up to cold war levels. Against economic targets, however, the heaviest foreign human spying comes from Iran and China. The 2008 Economic Espionage Report examined twenty-three such cases: nine involved Iran (which chiefly targets nuclear technology), eight involved China, and two involved India. No other nation was involved in more than one case.[55] Prosecutions represent only the visible fraction of all commercial espionage, however.

Criminal gangs have also figured out that there's more money to be made from stolen intellectual property than from credit card numbers. In February 2010, the computer security firm NetWitness exposed a gigantic botnet that had infected at least seventy-five thousand computers at twenty-five hundred companies and governments around the world, including the pharmaceutical giant Merck & Co., Paramount Pictures, and Juniper Networks, a U.S. manufacturer of electronic routers.[56] The attack used ZeuS malware, which until then had not been seen except in connection with identity theft. Now it was being used to steal log-in credentials for corporate electronic financial systems.

Counterintelligence used to be the stuff of government spies and nation-states; it was the concern of the FBI, the CIA, and the military. It is now a concern for every organization that lives on electronic networks and has secrets to keep. Information is liquid, and liquid leaks.

You can sneak a whole library onto a thumb drive in your pocket, and nobody's the wiser. We expect to access data from everywhere, and we carry around massive quantities of it. This genie cannot be put back in the bottle. Technological expectations accelerate; they do not go backward. (You bought a laptop because it was portable. Then you bought a BlackBerry and a thumb drive because the laptop was too heavy.) Information also moves at the speed of light on our networks, and when it's gone, it's gone forever. You could surround a system with a watertight membrane and make it leakproof, but then you couldn't use it. If you want e-mail, you have to punch a hole in the system's membrane. Downloads? That's another hole. WiFi? That's a third hole, and a particularly risky one. And so on. No system can be widely usable and watertight at the same time. And so our corporate national wealth, like our personal data, is leaking. The Google story, the oil company thefts, and similar cases now coming to light are merely the visible edge of the massive theft of Western intellectual property. As for the electronic penetrations, they're mostly invisible. To put it plainly: Corporate America lives in a glass house—just like the rest of us.

## China's Long View

China had the world's largest economy for eighteen of the past twenty centuries.[57] The two exceptions were those of America's youth and rise to power. The Declaration of Independence and Adam Smith's *The Wealth of Nations,* the twin pillars of political and economic liberalism, were published in 1776. At the same time that our textile industry was being mechanized, inventions were being patented at an unprecedented pace, and coal was being mined with the aid of machinery. The transfer of wealth from the East and South to the North and West was underway, and that transfer would literally pick up steam as the Industrial Revolution accelerated. Along with Western Europe, we bought raw materials cheaply, added value to them through capital and manufacturing know-how, and resold them at a profit in Asia, Africa, and Latin America. There was also a dark side to the amassing of such wealth. By the late eighteenth century, the colonization of these continents was underway, and so was the slave trade.

While 1776 marks the beginning of the American national story, for China it merely marks the beginning of an ignominious, two-century aberration in a national history that goes back more than four thousand years. The West was not created rich and the East poor. In 1776 a farmer in China had an annual income that was about the same as that of a farmer in Britain.[58] But this was about to change. By 1820, China's share of world output had peaked at about a third.[59] By 1870, the United States, Germany, the UK, and France accounted for nearly 79 percent of the world's manufacturing production. India accounted for 11 percent. No other Asian country, including China, even shows up in the tables.[60] Living standards evolved accordingly.

The British had been trading heavily with China, their principal source of tea, since 1800, but it was a one-way trade. China controlled foreign trade rigidly and required its manufactured goods to be paid for in hard currency, usually sterling. Its government was not interested in European goods, but it did want European money for Chinese goods, so money was flowing from West to East. The British therefore needed to find something the Chinese were willing to buy, and around 1816 they found it: opium. The British grew opium poppies in India. In Bengal, the British actually suppressed native textile manufacturing, which competed with their home industries, and expanded the cultivation of opium poppies. The British quickly became the world's largest dope dealers.

Like drug trafficking today, the nineteenth-century opium trade from British Bengal to China grew like a virulent disease. By the 1830s China's Qing rulers had seen enough of the social and economic effects of widespread addiction and decided to close their ports to the drug. To the British this was a violation of the principles of free trade, and Whitehall sent the Royal Navy and Marines to argue London's point of view. China's military was no match and suffered the first of a string of humiliating defeats. In the Opium Wars of 1839–42 and 1856–60, the British forced China to reopen its ports to opium. China fought the original "war against drugs," and they lost. The result was the carving up of China's trading ports into European concessions governed by European law. The Chinese have not forgotten this humiliation and the attendant economic dislocation.

Just as we have a national story, so do they. A thousand years ago, when Europe was in a Dark Age at the western end of the Asian landmass, China had a highly developed literature, graphic and plastic arts, and philosophy. So did India. China had also developed an administrative apparatus second to none. By the eighth century the Chinese had invented gunpowder. By the tenth century they had invented the compass and were becoming a maritime power. Until the fifteenth century China had the world's highest per capita income and was the world's technology leader. If you think this is "just history," you're mistaken. Chinese leaders know these things in their bones. When the U.S. treasury secretary complains to the Chinese premier that his country creates an unfair trade advantage by pegging its currency at artificially low levels, this history cannot be far from the premier's mind. Like India, China does not regard Western domination as normal, and it does not suffer from an inferiority complex. China's chief national strategic objectives are to lift its population out of poverty and reestablish its place in the international order. Those objectives do not make China our enemy. But they do mean we must learn to think about the Chinese in subtler terms than the convenient black-and-white simplicities of ally and foe.

## Struggle Without War

China has demonstrated the ability and intention to dominate its neighbors, and it has mounted a full-court press to steal from us whatever intellectual property it can. At the same time, we are so deeply enmeshed with China economically that neither partner could extricate itself without creating immense suffering for itself, the other, and the rest of the world. Our relationship with China is difficult, rewarding, profitable, and full of real and potential conflict, and it is destined to remain so for many years. It is also very different from our relationship with the Soviet Union during the cold war.

After World War II we didn't trade with the Soviet Union, Soviet bloc nationals rarely were allowed beyond the Iron Curtain, and Westerners couldn't readily travel in the other direction. Today, in contrast, China is a major trading partner, we invest heavily and travel freely there, and Chinese nationals travel freely in the West. Diplomatically, the U.S.–China relationship is sometimes mutually supportive and sometimes adversarial. Economically, the relationship is both competitive and mutually supportive, even symbiotic. Try telling an American or European businessman who's making a 50 percent return on his direct investment in China that it's hostile territory, and he'll think you're crazy. But the same businessman may not understand that the Chinese have made his cyberenvironment entirely hostile and are picking his pockets of know-how and technology. When he goes to Shanghai or Guangzhou, his hotel room may be searched, his laptop and mobile devices *will* be compromised, and his networks back home are almost certainly under attack.

This kind of ambiguity is difficult for Americans to digest. We are direct and aboveboard, and we like to think others are like us—or would be if given half a chance. Throughout most of its history America was largely isolated from the world and could indulge in the idealistic notion that friends were always friends and enemies were always enemies, and that the distinction between them was clear. In the aftermath of World War II, the international order seemed for a time to actually conform to this Manichean worldview, if only superficially. As one of our finest scholars of statecraft, the late Adda Bozeman, put it, we suffer from a Western misconception in our law, religion, and policy that "peace" and "war" are opposites that cannot occur at the same time.[61] "Our ideology," she wrote, has led us to the befuddling but "controlling conviction that 'war' and 'peace' are always absolutely polarized, mutually exclusive, strictly factual conditions, and that total peace must naturally take over when the fighting stops."[62] In the 1990s this naiveté led the United States to gut its intelligence services. Whether a nation capable of such guileless simplicity can remain a world leader in the twenty-first century remains to be seen. But the cold war was over, and according to prevalent opinion, the need for intelligence had more or less vanished. Bozeman contrasted this artless trust with the culture of Indian statecraft, in which trust in espionage "reaches back to the *Rig Veda*, where the spies of the god Varuna are pictured seated around him while the deity holds court over the cosmic universe—much as angels are often rendered in the Christian religious tradition."[63] In our law and political theory conflict is open and declared and occurs between nation-states. Indeed, in the minds of many for whom World War II remains the paradigmatic conflict, war is not "real" unless it involves complete mobilization. Many Americans cling to this view, even though war has not been declared on the planet since 1945, while there have been hundreds of organized, violent, and militarized struggles in the interim.

China challenges this mind-set as well as our place in the world order. Disengagement from China—let alone war—would be a worldwide disaster. Yet conflict *is* the reality, even in the midst of a mutually advantageous relationship. For the foreseeable future our relationship with China will continue to involve constant struggle for unilateral advantage, even as we seek common ground and mutual advantage. Sometimes this struggle will occur in ways that are open and visible and sometimes in ways that are clandestine or covert. There are mutual advantages to be had and zero-sum disadvantages to be avoided. The struggle is diplomatic, economic, and ideological, and it involves radically different visions of individual liberty and social order.

That struggle also involves economic espionage in which we are targets far more often than thieves. There are two reasons for this.

First, the developed world has a deep interest in a global order that protects and defends intellectual property rights. Upholding this interest, and persuading developing countries to uphold this interest, is far more important to us than any advantage that would accrue from state-sponsored violations of our own legal norms on behalf of a domestic company. Our position as the scientific, technological, and business leader is not ours by right, however; that lead can be lost abruptly and, once lost, may not be recovered.[64]

Second, China doesn't have much to steal, while the United States is the prime target of economic espionage, with Europe not far behind. It is likely to be two decades or longer before China amasses scientific and technological know-how that rivals our own. In the meantime its leaders are determined to close the gap, and their success has been awesome. During the most rapid economic growth in U.S. history, American living standards doubled about once every thirty years. In China, for the past thirty years, the standard of living has doubled about every ten years.[65] Never before have so many millions been lifted from poverty in so short a time.

**WESTERN COMPANIES ARE** largely unprepared to deal with either the Chinese challenge or the hostile and anarchic cyberenvironment they live in. To be sure, there are exceptions. Several large financial services firms have superb reputations for electronic security. So do many companies in the gaming sector. But much of the corporate world fails to confront this threat, either because they don't understand it or because their leadership isn't convinced that cybersecurity is worth the investment. Before a CEO approves a strategic investment, he or she wants to know what the return on that investment will be. If the company spends $10 million to improve its electronic security, how much will it get back? If we don't spend it, what is the risk? These questions are difficult to answer. Companies did a pretty good job of it where personal data was concerned: They just added up the fines, legal fees, and cost of providing credit counseling to those customers whose personal information had been stolen. The resulting cost was hefty, but it didn't represent a strategic risk to the business. Or so they thought. Then came the Heartland Payment Systems debacle in 2009, when the company's stock tanked after it disclosed that its credit-card clearing system had been hacked. Still, that was a case involving the theft of other people's personal secrets, not their own corporate ones. Companies must now reassess their risk postures and ask: What would happen if our basic designs, our formulas, or our codes were compromised? What would happen if our networks were taken down or corrupted? These are strategic risks, and organizations must do what well-managed organizations always do with risk: Buy it down.

The cybertheft of Google's source code and of bid data from the oil companies didn't change the corporate stakes as much as they exposed what the stakes have been for more than a decade. Identity theft is a minor league game in comparison. Our companies are under constant, withering attack. After the Google heist, *companies* started asking the government for help in defending themselves against *nations*. This was unprecedented. We are now in uncharted territory; the boundary between state actors and private actors has become much blurrier, and the boundary between economic security and national security has completely disappeared.

# 4

## DEGRADING DEFENSE

**THE AMERICAN MILITARY-INDUSTRIAL** complex is the world's fattest espionage target. While the scope and intensity of economic espionage have assumed startling proportions, the "traditional" espionage assault on our national defense establishment dwarfs anything we have ever before experienced. This assault is constant, it is relentless, and it is coming from all points on the compass in ways both old and new. As I previously indicated, about 108 foreign intelligence services target the United States. The number of Russian intelligence officers in the United States, which fell sharply at the end of the cold war, is actually greater than it was when the Soviet Union collapsed. The Russian services are adept at both human and technical intelligence, and they now target both economic and military secrets. The other top-tier intelligence threats come from China and Iran. The Cuban services, trained by the KGB, are also highly skilled and disciplined at human intelligence, but Cuba is not a strategic threat to the United States. Since the late 1990s, however, the overall threat has become both more intense and more complex, for reasons that should now be obvious: Stealing information electronically is cheap, easy, and low risk.

What are foreign services after? They want to know how to get into our systems and remain there undetected. They want information about plans, weapons, and people—the identities, roles, and responsibilities of everyone who works in an organization. That information identifies who has access to the other kinds of information they really want. In the case of the Chinese, we know what they want because they have told us in writing.

# Red Flower of North America

In the mid-1960s, when all of China was a poor and chaotic tyranny, a modest, compulsively hardworking engineer named Chi Mak was given permission to leave the mainland and move to Hong Kong, which was British, free, and rich. For a time he worked in a tailor shop, but by the 1970s he was working for the Hongkong Electric Company and, in his off-hours, keeping copious notes on the hull numbers and other details of U.S. Navy ships coming in and out of Hong Kong.[1] In 1978 he emigrated to the United States, where the defense contractor Rockwell employed him as a stress analyst for the space shuttle. Air- and spacecraft are subject to enormous stresses in flight. Understanding those stresses, knowing how to test for them, and figuring out how to withstand them are what stress analysts do. We're good at this, while the Chinese have a lot to learn. By 1979 Chi Mak was supplying stress and testing information to Chinese officials. Meanwhile, living a modest married life in a California suburb, he made friends, worked hard, and earned the respect of his colleagues. He became an American citizen and gained a secret-level clearance. According to the government, he also took masses of classified and unclassified documents home, some of which he shipped back to China, much to the satisfaction of his handlers. No one asked him to "hurt" the United States, of course.

His handlers merely wanted him to "help" China. From time to time he was invited to return to China to lecture on specified aspects of his work, such as "F-15 Jet Fighters," "Helicopter structure design," and "Fight lift," and he did—secretly. All the while, he communicated with his handlers in code, using the name Red Flower. When Boeing acquired Rockwell the pattern continued. Chi Mak was reliable—so reliable that his handlers sometimes used him as a conduit for information from other spies, with code names like Chrysanthemum. That was bad tradecraft, because when the FBI rolled up one spy it had a direct link to others. But it was convenient, and, as we've already seen, people will often break rules for the sake of convenience.

The Chinese were specific about what they wanted and gave Chi Mak written task lists that went far beyond his original area of expertise. They were after the technology that makes the U.S. Navy the world's best fleet as well as its biggest. China's interest in our navy is not surprising. An armed conflict between the United States and China would likely be a naval confrontation, and naval modernization is one of China's highest priorities.[2] Topping the task list was the Quiet Electric Drive propulsion system that would allow our warships to run with less noise than a Lexus sedan—and make them extremely difficult to track. By that time Chi Mak was working for L3 Power Paragon and was the lead engineer on the quiet drive project.[3] His task list, which he had shredded but which the FBI had painstakingly put back together, also included sixteen other topics, including information about the DD(X) (the next generation of U.S. Navy destroyers), aircraft carrier electronics, submarine torpedoes, electromagnetic artillery systems, and so on. This technology cost American taxpayers tens of billions of dollars and many years to develop. But the People's Republic of China didn't pay us for it. The PRC now has warships that look remarkably like ours. Their new ships also have radars as good as those on the DD(X), but with one difference: They know the characteristics of our radars, but they have modified their own in ways we must guess at.

Chi Mak spied for about twenty-five years. The FBI arrested him and his wife in 2005 just as they were yanking his brother Tai Mak and Tai's wife, Fuk Li, out of the security line at Los Angeles's airport before they could board a midnight flight to Hong Kong. A PRC counter-surveillance team was at the airport to watch them board. The Chinese knew they were coming, because Tai Mak had left a telephone message: "I work for the Red Flower of North America and will be traveling to the PRC on October 28th and will be bringing the assistant."

Tai Mak and his wife were arrested carrying a CD-ROM disk stuffed with encrypted secrets in disguised file formats that were further hidden under innocent-looking music files. A typical CD-ROM disk holds about 740 megabytes of data. In paper terms, this is about three fourths of a pickup truck full of printed pages. Not long afterward the FBI rolled up an entire network of spies whose lines of communication ran through Chi Mak.[4] He is the first spy (that we know of) through whom we lost critical military secrets and who was not a government employee. He will not be the last. If further proof were required, the case thus illustrates how thoroughly the functional boundary between the private sector and the government has dissolved.

Chi Mak is in prison for twenty-four years—but not for espionage. The basic espionage statute criminalizes giving or selling national defense information to someone not entitled to receive it "to the injury of the United States or to the advantage of any foreign nation."[5] The Justice Department will not prosecute under this statute unless the information transmitted is classified, however, and although Chi Mak had access to classified information, the government could not prove that he actually sent classified information to China. He was therefore convicted of *economic* espionage, under a different statute.[6] His brother Tai was sentenced to ten years for conspiracy to commit export violations, and Chi's wife Rebecca was sentenced to three years for acting as an unregistered agent of the PRC. Their son Billy, also part of the conspiracy, was sentenced to the time he had served while awaiting trial. All three were to be deported upon the conclusion of their sentences.[7]

I am not proposing that we expand our classification system. If we sometimes classify too little, we often classify too much. But when it comes to research, our classification system creates a rigid dichotomy between basic science and developmental research, with no intermediate category. It assumes a kind of on/off switch, a point at which all of a sudden laboratory work ceases to be pure science and becomes the less glorious business of developing something practical. Identifying technologies with practical applications, military or not, is difficult, especially in the early stages. Venture capitalists spend their fortunes and professional lives trying to do it, and the best of them lose their bets three or four times out of five. As technologies move closer to practical applications, however, the odds shorten. Take lasers, for example. Research on lasers is an inquiry into how certain kinds of light behave. In its early stages we don't classify that research, even if it's sponsored by the Defense Department, nor should we. There is a somewhat arbitrary point, however, at which it becomes apparent that certain lasers are likely to be weaponized. That process involves both science and engineering. At a still later stage there are no scientific questions to answer, just engineering challenges. Our classification process is not sophisticated enough to recognize the middle ground, where we can identify technologies that are likely to be classified in the near future. We should not only become more nimble at protecting R&D in that middle ground, we should also be scrupulous about whom we permit to do the work. As a nation we are not good at this.

The Chinese intelligence services meanwhile have made an art of exploiting the seam between the classified and the preclassified, where technologies begin to emerge from basic science but which, under our rules, are not yet military R&D. This is the sweet spot to an espionage strategist as well as to a venture capitalist, and this is an area where the Chinese services spend a great deal of effort. In essence, the PRC is leveraging the Pentagon's R&D budget in support of its own war-making capability.

The Chinese also specialize in illegally exporting dual-use technology and military equipment that is on our Munitions List. In 2009, for example, an ethnic Chinese U.S. citizen pleaded guilty to violating the Arms Export Control Act by sending a low-temperature fueling system that would be used by the People's Liberation Army. Jian Wei Ding and Kok Tong Lim pleaded guilty in the same year to conspiring to illegally export high-modulus carbon fiber to China and other countries.[8] Of the twenty-three arrests and convictions for industrial espionage in 2008, eight involved China, nine involved Iran. No other country was close behind. The list of technologies involved included hard-core military equipment, such as infrared assault-rifle scopes, military aircraft components, missile technology, and others that show the convergence of military and civilian technologies, such as engineering software, telecommunications equipment and technology, and certain kinds of amplifiers.[9]

Chinese espionage methods are unusually varied. In contrast to the Russians, who are highly professional, the PRC often enlists amateurs from among a huge pool of sympathizers. In 2008 there were about 3.2 million ethnic Chinese living in the United States, heavily concentrated in a few large cities. About half of them were born in China.[10] They are among our best-educated and most productive residents. Additionally, there were about 600,000 visa applicants from the Chinese mainland alone in 2009, of which 98,500 were for students. These numbers are rising at an annual rate of 16 to 20 percent.[11] In the 2009–10 academic year, there were about 128,000 Chinese students studying here.[12] About a million Chinese tourists visited the United States in 2010.[13] These figures are a sign of American strength, not weakness. The huge presence of ethnic Chinese in North America nevertheless represents a rich recruiting ground for Chinese intelligence services, and they exploit it. In the most startling example, an employee of Rockwell (later Boeing) named Dongfan "Greg" Chung volunteered himself. "I don't know what I can do for the country," meaning China, he wrote to a professor in the PRC. "Having been a Chinese compatriot for over thirty years and being proud of the achievements by the people's efforts for the motherland, I am regretful for not contributing anything."[14] Later he became part of the Chi Mak spy ring and contributed quite a bit before he was arrested and convicted.

The motivations for espionage are varied.[15] In some cases they are ideological, as with Chi and Chung.[16] The more common motivations, however, are money, ego gratification, and the resentments that come from thwarted ambition. Kuo Tai-shen, a Taiwanese businessman, was recruited recently to milk secrets from a midlevel Pentagon employee named Gregg Bergersen, who knew he was violating the law but thought he was helping Taiwan rather than the PRC. By feeding information to Kuo, Bergersen was greasing the skids for the kind of lucrative postretirement contract he saw others getting but which had eluded him. He thought he was reeling in a Taiwanese high-roller client, when in fact he was a pigeon in a PRC trap. The FBI caught Bergersen on tape exchanging classified information with Kuo for cash.[17] Now they're both in prison.

The rationale for espionage, as the novelist Alan Furst remarked, is a matter of MICE: "the m stands for money, the i for ideology, the c for coercion, and the e for egotism."[18] The Chinese have not omitted coercion. Several years ago a PRC agent in the United States made on offer to an ethnic Chinese executive of a major U.S. corporation. But the target was loyal to his adopted country and his company; he turned it down. Some time passed. Then they approached him again. This time the pitch was different: Look, the agent essentially said, your mother back in China is old and sick. She should be in the hospital. Unfortunately our hospitals are crowded, and she's not near the front of the queue. Would you like to reconsider our offer?[19]

Counterintelligence officials work these cases night and day and can talk about very few of them. It would be a mistake to believe there are no others we have not caught. Many red flowers are growing in North America.

# Cyberattacks on the Pentagon

I began this book with the story of how Chinese hackers broke into Pentagon systems and carted off ten to twenty terabytes of data—so much information that, had it been on paper, they would have needed miles and miles of moving vans lined up nose to tail to cart it away. That attack, known as Titan Rain, was part of a series that began in 2003. It targeted the Defense Information Systems Agency, the Redstone Arsenal, the Army Space and Strategic Defense Command, and several computer systems critical to military logistics.[20] Attacks like these persist, and their intensity is breathtaking. In 2007, there were 43,880 reported incidents of malicious cyberactivity against our Defense networks. In 2009, the figure was increasing at a 60 percent rate and was already at 43,785 by midyear. A large percentage of these attacks originate in China and are part of a series reportedly known as Byzantine Hades.[21] Defending against these attacks is extremely expensive. During one recent *six-month* period the U.S. military alone "spent more than $100 million . . . to remediate attacks on its networks."[22] The Office of the Secretary of Defense had to go off-line for more than a week in 2007 to protect itself from attacks coming from China and to clean up its systems.[23] The same kinds of attacks that occurred in 1998 were still happening in 2009, and they continue today.[24]

Penetrations of Defense networks follow the same paths we encountered when we examined commercial networks in the previous chapter. Peer-to-peer software, or P2P, is a major problem. It permits your computer to communicate with my computer directly, bypassing the Internet service provider (like AT&T, Comcast, or British Telecom) that funnels e-mail and other traffic between us. With P2P there's no funnel. Just as in a commercial context, unless P2P is configured just right, it drops the drawbridge into an information system. The *Washington*

*Post* disclosed in 2009 that personal information on "tens of thousands" of U.S. servicemen and -women, including Special Forces members and others working in war zones, had been downloaded and were found floating electronically in China and Pakistan. The army barred the unauthorized use of P2P in 2003, and the entire Defense Department followed suit in 2004.[25] But that merely serves to emphasize a point that cannot be stated too often: Policies regarding information systems that are not expressed technically are little more than blather. No one pays attention. *If you don't want people to be able to run unauthorized P2P on your system, you must design and build your system so that such software cannot be run—or that it pinpoints exactly where it is.*

Other penetrations exploit vulnerabilities in the same commercial software we all use—vulnerabilities that let an attacker inject malicious code right into a system. This is often done with a tactic called buffer overflow. A buffer is a region of computer memory where data is stored temporarily. Buffer overflow permits data that is too big for the buffer to overwrite adjacent software code. This can be done intentionally; it's an attack methodology. In my opinion, software companies could eliminate this vulnerability, but they haven't done it yet. Consumers and commercial buyers don't demand it, and the Pentagon hasn't been willing to pay for it.

Information that used to be top secret now leaks through an open fire hydrant. WikiLeaks gets the most attention in this department; we'll visit that topic in chapter 8. But WikiLeaks is not the worst offender. Starting in 2007 or before, and extending well into 2008, cyberintruders robbed Pentagon systems of terabytes of information on the electronics of our next-generation Joint Strike Fighter aircraft, the F-35. Electronic systems associated with the project repeatedly were broken into, sometimes exploiting P2P vulnerabilities. While flight control systems have supposedly been isolated from the Internet, the intruders appear to have obtained data about the plane's design, performance, and other electronic systems. We can't be sure of what they took, however, because while we didn't think it was worth the trouble to encrypt the data ourselves, the thieves did so on the way out.[26] Most of these penetrations originate in China. As the U.S.–China Economic and Security Review Commission put it, "A large body of both circumstantial and forensic evidence strongly indicates Chinese state involvement in such activities, whether through the direct actions of state entities or through the actions of third-party groups sponsored by the state."[27] Some of these penetrations are technologically shrewd, but often they target the weakest link in any computer system—the user. Defense workers, including in the military, are just as impatient with security practices and just as susceptible to phishing attacks as everybody else. Like workers everywhere, they are also adept at subverting security rules and mechanisms designed to keep their systems healthy. As we've seen repeatedly, when convenience butts heads with security, convenience wins—even in war zones.

**IN APRIL 2006,** an enterprising reporter from the *Los Angeles Times* paid $40 to an Afghan kid for a secondhand thumb drive in the bazaar outside Bagram Airfield in Afghanistan, home to thousands of U.S. and allied troops. He decided to see what was on it. What he found were the names, photos, and contact information for Afghans willing to inform on the Taliban and al-Qaeda. He also found secret documents detailing "escape routes into Pakistan and the location of a suspected safe house there, and the payment of $50 bounties for each Taliban or Al Qaeda fighter apprehended based on the source's intelligence."[28] When it falls into the wrong hands, this kind of information gets our friends killed. But there it was—on sale in the bazaar for $40. It was probably stolen; there's a thriving black market for stolen electronics around Bagram. How the device found its way to the bazaar is a trivial detail, however. These devices aren't going away, and some of them will always be lost or stolen. In war zones as well as downtown office buildings, information walks around. So of course this incident was hardly a one-off story. British researchers did an experiment in May 2009: They bought up a few hundred hard drives in the UK to see what was on them. Along with banking and medical records, confidential business plans, and so forth, they discovered the test launch procedures for a ground-to-air missile defense system designed by Lockheed Martin.[29] All this information had been thrown away like trash. Whether the context is military or civilian, when you replicate secrets and make them portable, they will be duplicated, ported, and lost. (In just this way Apple lost its top-secret next-generation iPhone in 2010 when one of its engineers left it in a bar.[30]) So while most organizations need to work more diligently to reduce information leakage, that's merely the easy, tactical lesson. There are also two strategic lessons.

First, organizations must learn to live in a world where less and less information can be kept secret, and where secret information will remain secret for less and less time.

Second, the technologies we *require* for efficiency not only threaten the security of information we don't want to share, they also open us up to electronic infections that can kill us. Good stuff flows out, nasty stuff flows in.

To illustrate that point, let's walk the thumb drive back into Bagram Airfield to understand how an adversary could penetrate our information systems by walking something in instead of sneaking something out. Remember the Afghan boy in the bazaar. He and other merchants and peddlers have lots of thumb drives. Some were stolen from American service personnel right on the base, but not all. Let's imagine his uncle bought a box of them, brand new, that fell off a truck in Kabul. Maybe Uncle knew a good price when he saw it, didn't ask any questions, and bought them for his nephew to sell. These little drives happen to be the same brand, even the same color, as those the American heathen have been buying lately on the base, at a higher price. Or perhaps this particular box of thumb drives wasn't stolen. Perhaps Russian military intelligence (the GRU) or Russian external intelligence (the SVR, successor to the KGB's First Chief Directorate) has been quietly seeding Kabul and Bagram with thumb drives specially poisoned with malware. And now, let's suppose the boy doesn't sell the drive to a reporter from the *Los Angeles Times* but instead to Corporal John Smith, U.S. Army, 902nd Military Intelligence Group, 910th Military Intelligence Brigade, now forward deployed from Ft. Meade, Maryland, to Bagram.

John's working the swing shift this week, 4:00 P.M. to midnight, so after amusing himself in the bazaar and eating a meal, he clocks in to the watch floor, where he mans four different computers with four different screens: an Internet connection, a connection to the Pentagon's unclassified system (the NIPRNET), a connection to the Pentagon's secret system (the SIPRNET), and a connection to the Pentagon's top-secret system (JWICS, pronounced "Jaywicks"). These systems are "air gapped." That means there is supposedly no way to move electronically from one of them to another. (There are in fact some exceptions, but they don't matter here.) John is connected to each of these systems through a PC under or next to his cramped little metal desk. That night he's remotely supporting an operation in Paktika Province, and the captain on the phone urgently asks him for any information he has on a certain informant from a particular village. Is the guy for real, or is he a double agent? Should we trust him? And exactly where is that village anyway? Give me five minutes, John tells the captain. I'll call you back. John runs a database check on the informant, but he has nothing on the village. The map on SIPRNET is old and the scale is too small. He checks the NIPRNET but finds nothing better. He tries variant spellings and still comes up empty. When he goes to the Internet, however, Google Earth has exactly what he needs. But how will he get that map to the captain, whose only connection is through SIPRNET?

By using his new thumb drive, that's how. Every PC on his desk has a USB port, and those ports make a mockery of the air gap. Corporal Smith isn't careless, and he isn't stupid. He knows the prohibition on moving information between air-gapped systems, but he's working hard and he can hear the anxiety in the captain's voice through the phone line. He's got an urgent problem to solve, and he knows how. So he downloads the map onto the thumb drive, then removes the thumb drive from the commercial PC and inserts it into the USB port on the SIPRNET box, uploading the map so he can shoot it out to the captain, who can see it for himself. He calls the captain back: Problem solved. A little later John pops the thumb drive back into his commercial PC to download a snapshot his wife has just sent of their eight-month-old daughter. Having once figured out a way through his thicket of systems, he will repeatedly use the thumb drive to move between them. He wonders how he ever managed without it.

John solved his problem, but here's what else he did.

Russian intelligence had doctored the thumb drive he bought in the bazaar with poison code called agent.btz.[31] They couldn't have known that he would buy that particular memory stick, but they produced lots of them, and the likelihood that one or more American military personnel would buy some of them was very high. The likelihood that one of the buyers would violate U.S. military policy by moving information between air-gapped systems was also very high. The Russians would have known this for the same reason that every corporate information security officer knows it: People don't obey rules that add inconvenience to their lives. Anybody whose job requires working on four different information systems will at some point have to move information between those systems in order to do his job responsibly, even if rules prohibit it. So Russian intelligence put together a low-cost operation with a high probability of generating lots of trouble for the American military, not to mention excellent information and high entertainment back in Moscow.

When John inserted the poisoned thumb drive into his commercial computer in order to download the Google map, it automatically uploaded malicious code that sent a beacon back to a Russian command post through the Internet. The beacon merely said "Here I am, ready to accept instructions." When he removed it and then inserted it in the USB port on his secret SIPRNET computer, the drive uploaded malicious code that began sniffing its way around. It was programmed to look for specific items of interest to Russian intelligence. It was also programmed to package these items for exfiltration upon command. But how could it get the information back to the clever Russian fellows who devised this trick? The Russians are not connected to SIPRNET.

Here again the key to the operation was not technological brilliance but human failure. It was quite likely that the owner of the thumb drive would repeat the maneuver between systems, and in fact that's what John did when he reinserted the drive into his commercial system to download the photo of his baby daughter and then later reinserted the drive into his SIPRNET computer. He had become the unwitting agent of Russian exfiltration, because the package of data the Russians wanted to exfiltrate was now downloaded onto the thumb drive, and he was then transferring it to the commercial computer, where it would speed out to the Russians over the Internet. Was John the only American serviceman to fall into this trap? Of course not. Pretty soon SIPRNET and NIPRNET were thoroughly corrupted. But neither Central Command nor any other U.S. joint command can operate without them.[32]

I invented Corporal Smith and virtually all the details in this account, but something very much like this must have happened.[33] I can't explain how the NSA devised and executed a skillful plan to clean this shrewd garbage out of Pentagon systems, but I can say that it hasn't been simple. Agent.btz is programmed to think. When it's threatened, it morphs. When one exfiltration path is thwarted, it finds others. It's another version of a Whac-A-Mole game. The agent.btz story is one of many reasons why I refer to SIPRNET as IPRNET. The S in SIPRNET stands for secret, and you'd have to be delusional to believe this system isn't penetrated. You'd also have to be crazy not to believe that the Pentagon's top-secret system, JWICS, isn't penetrated. Even the NSA now operates on the assumption that its systems are penetrated. "There's no such thing as 'secure' anymore," said my former colleague

Debora Plunkett, the director of the NSA's Information Assurance Directorate (that's the defensive side). "The most sophisticated adversaries are going to go unnoticed on our networks," she said. Systems must be built on that assumption.[34]

In November 2008, when Strategic Command belatedly became aware of the seriousness of the threat posed by agent.btz, it issued a blanket prohibition against all removable media, including thumb drives, on Defense systems.[35] The outcry was immediate and deafening, and STRATCOM reversed itself within about a week. Why? Because they realized what the Russians must also have known when they devised the operation: Our military personnel cannot do their jobs without moving information between systems that are supposedly insulated from one another. So STRATCOM withdrew the prohibition and instead issued a sort of "safe sex" order for removable media. Basically it said that before you let somebody stick their thumb drive into your USB port, you'd better know where that thumb drive came from and where else it has been. This order was better than nothing— but not by much. As one STRATCOM specialist put it, the Defense Department "cannot undo 20-plus years of tacitly utilizing the worst IT security practices in a reasonable amount of time, especially when many of these practices are embedded in enterprisewide processes." *Translation:* We can't do our job without these devices, and it's going to take time to fix this. The headline in *Wired* got it right: HACKERS, TROOPS REJOICE: PENTAGON LIFTS THUMB-DRIVE BAN.[36]

It's easy to make fun of the Defense Department or any other large organization trying to manage information across worldwide networks. But nobody does it perfectly, and many organizations do it very badly. Still, leaving aside the NSA and the CIA, no government agency has more at stake in protecting its security than the Pentagon and, in fact, no other agency is better at it. As other agencies and the White House dither, the Pentagon actually does things. They have begun to issue authorized removable media, prohibit the use of everything else, and distribute portable kits that can excise viruses from disks, thumb drives, and other removable media.[37] How well this program works remains to be seen.

The Russians aren't the only ones who know how to run operations like the thumb-drive caper. I explained in a previous chapter that the Chinese have been caught spreading infected thumb drives around British trade fairs. And the same trick has been tried in Washington, D.C. The Executive Office of U.S. Attorneys in 2008 advised that "two USB thumb drives" were discovered in one of their buildings. One was found in a men's restroom, another on a fax machine. "The drives contain malicious code that automatically and silently executes when the drive is plugged into a system. The code captures certain system information and transmits it out of [the Justice Department]."[38] How many of these drives were actually picked up and used? We have no idea.

If poisoned thumb drives haven't yet been found in your agency or company, chances are they will be. USB devices are used to spread about one in four computer worms.[39] The convergence of the cyberthreats faced by the military and civilian organs of government, and by public and private organizations, is nearly absolute. Exotic technologies that were once the exclusive province of state-sponsored intelligence agencies with massive resources are now available to everyone, everywhere, and they are cheap. At the same time, social networking sites that a few years ago were the province of hipsters and college kids have become official U.S. government channels of communication.

## Our Enemies Are Not Stupid

In 1996 an official evaluation of the U.S. military's unmanned aerial vehicles pointed out that, while certain UAVs were designed to transmit encrypted video images, the Predator UAV relied on *un*encrypted data links. That meant that anybody with modest technical skills could intercept the images from the satellite downlink. This could have significant consequences, ranging from signal interception to active jamming.[40] Nevertheless, the warning went unheeded. The weakness in the Predator's communications was no longer theoretical, but the military could remain deaf to it because, well, had anybody actually proven it was a problem? Had anybody been embarrassed by it? Besides, were our adversaries in places like Baghdad or Belgrade smart enough to figure this stuff out? Nobody seemed to think so.

In 2002, however, a British engineer whose hobby was scanning satellite downlinks stumbled across footage of NATO surveillance videos from Kosovo that were transmitted on an open commercial satellite channel. He warned the military. If he could watch NATO soldiers looking for infiltrators across the Kosovo border, so could the infiltrators they were tracking. You can watch it too—on CBS, which ran the story.[41] The military's first response was that the footage wasn't really sensitive, which was nonsense. Then they explained that our NATO partners didn't have the equipment to decrypt the signals if we encrypted them. That may have been true, but it simply meant that NATO was operating on antiquated assumptions about how the world works. Did anybody fix it? No.

A 2005 CIA memo reportedly said that officials in Saddam's government had been able to watch real-time video of U.S. military installations in Turkey, Kuwait, and Qatar before Iraq was invaded. Apparently they had "located and downloaded the unencrypted satellite feed from U.S. military UAVs."[42] Still, nothing changed.

Then, in the summer of 2009, some of our soldiers arrested a Shiite militant, confiscated his laptop, and found intercepted Predator video feeds. Surprise! Shortly afterward they found similar images on other confiscated laptops. Somebody was systematically intercepting and disseminating them from our drones. Militants were being *taught* to do this—probably by Iranian intelligence. They were watching us watching them. Unfortunately, we couldn't hear them laughing. When the *Wall Street Journal* exposed this tragicomedy in late 2009, it noted that the weakness in the Predator link had been understood since the Bosnian campaign (actually, it had been understood even earlier, in

1996), but "the Pentagon assumed local adversaries wouldn't know how to exploit it." In fact, local adversaries in Iraq were exploiting it with Russian software you could buy for $25.95 on the Internet.[43] We thought they were stupid; they weren't.

**HOW DO WE** explain this kind of behavior? The worst wrong answer is to assume it is unique to the U.S. Department of Defense. In fact, it's typical of people in large organizations who must make difficult budgetary decisions (retrofitting Predators with encryption devices is expensive) and who, like most of us, find it easy to ignore inconvenient facts. The United States may still have more advanced hardware than the rest of the world, but we are no longer years ahead of our major international rivals. Failing to understand this is smug, careless, lazy, and dangerous. Unfortunately, however, there are smug, careless, lazy, and dangerous people in every organization. They can be trained to some degree, but organizational entropy is a fact of life. As the management sage Peter Drucker put it, "The only things that evolve by themselves in an organization are disorder, friction and malperformance."[44] Things fall apart. But in a world where almost everything is connected to almost everything else, the effects of such entropy are far more dire than when Drucker made his observation decades ago, because a gap anywhere in a system can infect information everywhere in the system.

The people who run and use our most vital information systems must take this notion of infection to heart. That thumb drive in Bagram (and untold others like it) passed on malware that weakened the Pentagon's entire system, just as touching your mouth with a germ-laden finger can infect your entire body. It's also useful to think of an information system as akin to a hospital, different parts of which require different conditions. The public walks in and out: doctors, nurses, administrators, patients, visitors, and passersby. No one is sterile, and some carry deadly diseases, yet surgeons must nevertheless perform operations. In the operating room we rigorously control who and what can come in and out, what they can wear, and how they must be scrubbed. We maintain a far higher level of hygiene there than we do in the lobby. We apply an intermediate standard in the kitchen—higher than in the lobby, but not as high as in the operating room. The hospital's data center applies still another standard: There we care less about bacteria but more about temperature. Risk assessment and management occurs in all of these places constantly, yet we know that at some point, regardless of our precautions, although infection can be greatly reduced, it cannot be eliminated.

Our leaders must similarly accept that their information systems are compromised and must plan accordingly. This is harder than you might think. People don't readily accept inconvenient news if they can avoid it—especially if the danger is invisible. In my experience, convincing leaders that their systems are probably corrupted is like trying to explain the germ theory of disease to an illiterate. If they can't see it, they don't believe it. However, the evidence is now clear for anyone who chooses to see it. Military leaders, agency heads, and CEOs must require systems that are both more secure and more robust. They must also learn to fight and manage with corrupted systems, must know how to restore those systems in the regular course of business—*and must practice doing it.* If they don't, they not only risk losing the data that makes them powerful, valuable, and intelligent, they also risk that their operations will grind to a halt.

As we'll see in the next chapter, the emerging danger is no longer simply the loss of critical information. The newest threat targets our essential infrastructure—from air traffic control to financial markets to the electricity grid. Losing control over any of these systems would create widespread disruption and loss, and bring our society to a standstill.

# DANCING IN THE DARK

ON MARCH 4, 2007, an electricity generator from the Alaska grid began to vibrate, slowly at first, then faster and faster, until the delicately balanced turbines in the massive generator rumbled, shook furiously, and blew apart. And then the generator just shut down, hissing and belching smoke from its burned-out coupling. Explosives didn't destroy this hulk of equipment, though you might have thought so from the look of it, nor was it employee sabotage. The saboteurs were outsiders, miles away; their tools were a keyboard and a mouse. They evaded firewalls, took over the controls, and opened and closed breakers at will, all while manipulating the operator's screen to make it appear that nothing untoward was happening.[1]

Fortunately the generator had been removed from Alaska and carefully reconnected elsewhere so that blowing it up would not wreak havoc on the grid. It was a secret experiment carried out by clever researchers at the Idaho National Laboratory. They reportedly called their project AURORA,[2] and they blew the turbines apart by hacking into the digital devices that regulated power on the grid. When they got into the system, they simply instructed it to make rapid changes in the electricity cycles that powered the equipment: fast, slow, fast, slow. Then they just waited a second or two for the big diesel-electric generator to explode.

Neither the United States government nor private industry can defend the networks on which our economic and national security depend. This situation is getting worse, not better. The AURORA experiment demonstrated that a risk to information technology had become a risk to operational technology—but few companies in the power-generation business were listening. Electronic security, physical security, and operational security are no longer separate lines of work. Electronic security used to mean keeping your information secure and available. The guys who did it were the geeks in the computer closet tinkering with racks of equipment. Physical security, on the other hand, was all about "guns, gates, and guards," and the guys who did it were in-house cops. Except in intelligence agencies, where operational security permeates every part of the business, operational security in most firms was just an aspect of physical security: Protect the building and the people in it, and you can keep doing business. Both types, the guards and the geeks, were specialized support cadres that most executives could ignore most of the time.

Business executives and government officials who still think this way are asking for trouble. In the old days a burglar got into a building by throwing a brick through a window, taking a crowbar to the backdoor, or picking a lock. Burglaries got more complicated when separately wired alarms were added, but not much. Today, however, your entire perimeter of windows, doors, and gates, your heating and ventilation, and your information systems are managed and monitored from one or more central servers. So are your production line, your shipping, and your finance and accounting department. The guys in the computer closet now control everything you do. If an intruder can break into the right server electronically, he can remotely shut down production, send your goods to the wrong destination, and unlock your doors. Or shut off your HVAC system. Or steal your information and delete your log entries so he leaves no record of ever having been there. The company's private security guards are also electronically connected. Their job includes providing physical security for the chairman of the firm. If an electronic intruder could get access to the chairman's calendar, planning an assault or kidnapping would be much easier. Everything you do goes back to that computer closet. This is what the experts mean when they say that electronic and physical security have converged.[3] Virtually every significant industrial, military, and commercial operating system in advanced nations has become electronic over the last two decades. Manufacturing controls, military command and control, banking and financial systems—they're nearly all electronic, most of them are interconnected, and many of them are unreasonably vulnerable to operational failure. For example, in 1998 the onboard controller of a communications satellite known as Galaxy IV malfunctioned. As a result, 80 to 90 percent of the pagers in the United States stopped working. Hospitals couldn't reach doctors on call, emergency workers couldn't be reached, and credit cards didn't work at gas pumps.[4] This was an early warning about the operational risk that comes with relying upon information systems that have single points of failure—that is, when one part of a system fails, the whole system collapses. But it went unheeded.

More than ten years ago—in 2000—a disgruntled sewer system operator in Maroochy Shire, Australia, decided to settle a score. He worked for the company that installed a radio-controlled sewage system for the shire, but he wasn't getting along with his employer, and the shire refused to hire him. So he decided to get even with everybody. After filling his car with a laptop and radio equipment that he apparently stole from his employer, he drove around giving radio commands to the sewage equipment, causing the system to fail. Pumps didn't run, alarms didn't go off, and pumping stations couldn't communicate with the central computer. Millions of liters of raw sewage poured into local parks and waterways. This was another physical disruption engineered through an information system. According to an Australian environmental official, "Marine life died, the creek water turned black and the stench was unbearable for residents."[5] The results of the Maroochy Shire attack were bad enough, but if the disgruntled misfit had attacked the drinking water supply rather than the sewage system, people as well as marine life would have died. This was another warning about connecting industrial control systems to the Internet. Again, nobody paid attention.

## What, Me Worry?

The principal risk of insecure networks is no longer merely purloined information. For a company, the larger risk is now losing the ability to do business. For the nation, the risk threatens to cripple the infrastructure that makes America work—banks, dams, railway switches, electricity grids, stock exchanges—even the military. The AURORA generator was sabotaged using the same kind of computer I'm using to write this sentence. In both cases someone uses a keyboard, a mouse, or a touch screen to move electrons. That's true of the alarm and video surveillance systems in a nuclear plant, the physical access controls where you work, and a blowout preventer on an oil rig in the Gulf of Mexico. A night watchman, a security officer, and occasionally an engineer may check these controllers from time to time, but the continuous checking and controlling is done by a machine that talks to other machines. This combination of hardware and software is called an industrial control system, or an ICS. SCADA systems perform supervisory control and data acquisition over dispersed components. These systems constantly check temperature, pressure, inputs, outputs, and other variables, and they make systemic adjustments faster and better than a person could. They allow consistent, centralized control of devices dispersed over far-flung areas. And they must be highly reliable. On the electricity grid, we expect these systems to work right 99.99999 percent of the time[6]—a far higher standard than any information technology, or IT, system can meet. The latter were designed to create and store information. In contrast, industrial control systems were designed to manage physical assets, and because they were isolated from the Internet, they were not designed with cybersecurity in mind. Few of them are encrypted. They were assumed to be used under tight physical security and accessible to only a few trusted insiders.

That's changing—fast. In the name of efficiency—for the short term—the owners and operators of our electric grid are connecting their industrial control systems directly or indirectly to the Internet, and they are putting the nation's economic security at unreasonable risk. As security expert Joe Weiss has written, companies feel they should be connected "from the plant to the boardroom." Weiss is still waiting for somebody to explain "why somebody in the boardroom needs to open a valve in a plant or control a breaker in a substation."[7] The problem isn't connectivity itself. Connectivity is what enables wholesale competition in power transmission—it gives users the same access to transmission information as the utility. That allows users to compare prices and get our power from whoever can provide it at the best price.[8] Without connectivity, we'd return to local monopolies over power transmission. The problem is that the industry is handling connectivity poorly, creating needless vulnerabilities. Control systems can actually be accessed with Bluetooth wireless technology in some cases,[9] like you'd use in a car or by a voice-over-Internet protocol phone. Both these technologies are highly insecure.

In the summer of 2003, a massive blackout shut down a large swath of the eastern and central United States and Canada. The official report on that incident warned that SCADA systems controlling the grid, "many of which were intended to be isolated, now find themselves for a variety of business and operational reasons, either directly or indirectly connected to the global Internet."[10] The trend is worldwide. A recent study of such systems in fourteen countries showed that three fourths of such systems "were connected to the Internet or some other IP network."[11] Repeated studies have warned in watered-down language that this practice is risky: an "unresolved security issue," one of them evasively reports; it "can present" security risks, grudgingly admits another; it "creates potential vulnerabilities," says a third.[12] Said in plain English: Connecting SCADA and other industrial control systems to the Internet may create marginal savings, but it also creates massive vulnerabilities. If you know how to break into the electronic system, you can alter the words I've written, turn off the alarm at the nuclear plant, give someone who isn't supposed to be there access to sensitive facilities, create or change account balances at banks—or take down the power supply. Defenders of this practice say it makes remote monitoring of the power system more efficient, and no doubt it does.[13] Power generators must be able to monitor and audit their systems efficiently in order to manage overhead costs.[14] But the bulk power industry—which keeps the lights on, makes the trains run, and powers American business—has been unwilling to mitigate the risk this efficiency creates.[15]

Some companies deny—or don't even realize—that they've connected their industrial control systems to the Internet; others reportedly do it so they can patch their software efficiently as soon as vulnerabilities are discovered.[16] (A "patch" is a software fix distributed by a manufacturer, like Microsoft, to close a vulnerability.) They say that if they don't patch, their software vendors won't support them. This would be more persuasive if owners and operators of the grid systematically patched their vulnerabilities, but they don't. One recent study found that firms running SCADA systems took 331 days on average to implement patches.[17] A 2004 survey of U.S. electrical operators found "loosely controlled system access and perimeter control, poor patch and configuration management, and poor system security documentation."[18]

In fact, automatically patching an industrial control system can be dangerous; it creates the risk of crashing or slowing the industrial controls unless it's done at the right time with the right sort of expertise.[19] Some experts say that because such systems often combine hardware and software, they can't be updated easily or quickly under any circumstances.[20] The patching rationale for connecting the grid to the Internet is a red herring. The real issue is money, and the grid's owners have no incentive to spend it. A recent survey of owners of U.S. SCADA systems—including electricity, oil and gas, sewage, and telecom companies—reported that about 25 percent of them expected a government bailout in the event of a major attack. About 30 percent expected ratepayers and customers to pay. And about 45 percent thought insurance would cover it.[21] In short, almost none of them thought they'd incur any financial harm from an attack. So why should they worry?

## "The BP Problem in Waiting"

Mike Assante is an intense but down-to-earth man who lives with his wife and three young children in Idaho Falls, Idaho. A veteran of navy intelligence and military information warfare, Mike assembled the team that conceived the AURORA project. He was then working at the Idaho National Laboratory, having already spent four years as a vice president and chief security officer of one of the nation's largest electricity generators, American Electric Power. Blowing up a generator with a keyboard was a shocking idea to the engineers and businessmen in the bulk power business. "I thought if I showed people you could do it, they'd understand the implications and take the threat seriously," Assante said.[22] "At first nobody wanted to do it." It took a lot of persuasion and several rounds of congressional appearances before he got the necessary go-ahead. "Then when we proved it, the reaction was: 'This can't happen in my system.' That was baloney." After that Assante became the vice president and chief security officer of the North American Electric Reliability Corporation, or NERC. Assante was also the executive director of the Electric Sector Information Sharing and Analysis Center and cochair of the Electricity Sector Coordinating Council. If there's one man in America who understands cyberattacks, industrial control systems, *and* the electricity grid, it's Mike Assante.

Here's how the grid regulatory system works: NERC is composed of the owners and operators of the grid. It is charged by Congress to "establish and enforce reliability standards for the bulk-power system," subject to oversight by the Federal Energy Regulatory Commission, or FERC. The Federal Power Act instructs FERC to "give due weight" to NERC's views. But the act also requires NERC to endorse any reliability standard the regional utilities agree on unless NERC can prove the standard is not in the public interest.

This is a cascading system of deference by which a regulatory commission (FERC) gives "due weight" to an industry membership organization (NERC) that must, by law, defer to what the boys in the regional organizations want. As a practical matter, no reliability standard is set without the consent of the regional associations that are being regulated. Because those associations don't want standards that restrict their ability to connect ICSs to the Internet, there are no such restrictions.

FERC understands the limits on its power. In 2007 it nonetheless declined to approve certain reliability standards, stating that while they met statutory requirements, they failed to address recommendations in the report on the 2003 blackout.[23] The commission then ordered improvements—but without stating what they should be, because it had no power to do so.[24] NERC, in turn, has begun warning about the dangers of remote electronic attacks on the grid.[25] But no standards explicitly address this risk.

According to Assante, "This is the BP problem in waiting."

The BP problem is the explosion that blew up the Deepwater Horizon rig, killing eleven men and roiling the Gulf of Mexico into an oily stew. The common factor between the BP disaster and the danger to the grid, in Assante's view, is uncritical deference to an industry with weakly regulated cybersecurity—as opposed to plant safety. "There are people in the industry, right up to the CEO level, who do understand the cyber risk, but they're very much in the minority," he said.

"When you have a weak standard, complying with it gives people a false sense of security," he explained. "I mean, if they meet it, they check the box and forget about it." There are more than eighteen hundred owners and operators in the North American bulk-power system, with some two hundred thousand miles of high-voltage transmission lines, thousands of generation plants, and millions of digital controls.[26] Charged with auditing the industry's critical infrastructure while at NERC, Assante calculated it would take seven years just to figure out which assets were being protected—much too long to get a working picture of security in the industry. So he launched a series of surveys to determine whether bulk-power operators were complying with the reliability standards that the industry itself had adopted. For starters, all he wanted them to do was to *identify* the assets that "if destroyed, degraded, or otherwise rendered unavailable would affect the reliability or operability of the Bulk Electric System," which is how NERC defines a critical asset.[27] His reasoning was simple: If you can't identify the elements of critical infrastructure, you won't know what to protect. Unfortunately, there was no common understanding of what was "critical," and no criteria for making that determination.[28] Assante's insistence on a wide understanding of critical assets made some of the operators "very unhappy," he said, and the survey results—or rather, Assante's publication of the results—made them unhappier still. Assante told them, in a letter to industry members in April 2009, that the "survey results, on their surface, raise concern" about whether industry members could even identify the critical assets, including cyberassets, "that support the reliable operation of the Bulk Electric Power System." Which was a polite way of saying that they could not. In one survey, only 31 percent of respondents said that they had any critical assets at all, and only 23 percent said that they had critical cyberassets. In another, 73 *percent of respondents claimed to have no critical assets.*[29]

"The industry engineers didn't understand the nature of cyber risk," Assante told me later. They were trained to use abundant data to calculate the risk that, say, a piece of equipment would wear out after a certain period of time. You can predict such events statistically, and you can plan for them; the industry's good at that. But the risk of malicious manipulation of the grid by hostile attackers is a different story. "It's a low-frequency, high-impact event involving a thinking, planning adversary. It's not probabilistic," so the engineers don't know how to think about it, he said. Or don't want to.

What would it take to start changing their minds?

## "Code for Chaos"

In June 2010, a security firm in Belarus issued a warning about a computer worm[30] it called "RootkitTmpHider."[31] The virus used USB devices to spread itself and it infected operating systems in ways they hadn't seen before. By mid-July the antivirus firm Symantec had seen enough of this bug, which it called "W32.Temphid," to adjust its detection software to catch it. Three days later Microsoft issued a security advisory regarding a Windows vulnerability that could allow "remote code execution" by this kind of malware. Advisories like this get the attention of cybersecurity analysts. Remote code execution means that someone can tamper with your system from afar, and it looked like this malware was designed to steal secrets, so analysts in the cybersecurity business paid attention. After another three days, Symantec said it was investigating reports that the malware was infecting SCADA systems manufactured by the German industrial giant Siemens, and it called the bug W32.Stuxnet.[32] Three more days went by, and Siemens offered assurances to its customers and free assistance in dealing with the bug. However, there was "no evidence that this was motivated by industrial espionage," a company spokesman said.[33]

By the end of the summer, however, it was clear that Stuxnet was the most sophisticated piece of industrial espionage—or more precisely, sabotage—in history, and that its target was the Iranian nuclear program. Before it was discovered, it had existed for at least a year and had replicated itself through removable drives by exploiting not one, but at least four previously unknown vulnerabilities in Microsoft Windows.

It spread in several ways and copied and executed itself automatically. And it hid its own code, so it was invisible. If programmers tried to view all the code on an infected computer, they'd see everything except Stuxnet. It exploited Siemens's default passwords and reprogrammed the computers. It knew what system the virus was running on, and adjusted accordingly. Peer-to-peer connections enabled it to update itself.

But it didn't steal information.[34] Stuxnet wasn't designed to find things out; it was designed to bring things down. Reports were filtering out of Iran that the malware was attacking computers in its nuclear complex.[35] This was consistent with infection statistics showing that about 60 percent of infections were in Iran. The next highest infection rate was about 18 percent in Indonesia and about 10 percent in India. After that, no nation's infection rate reached even 3.5 percent. (It was less than 1 percent in the United States, Britain, and Russia.[36]) In late September Iran admitted that the worm was infecting computers at its Bushehr nuclear site, but it denied the infection was serious.[37] Then, in early October 2010, Iran announced it had arrested an unknown number of "nuclear spies" in connection with Stuxnet.[38]

By mid-November it was clear that the worm was calibrated to send nuclear centrifuges spinning out of control by causing their rotational speed to fluctuate. It was also introducing fake data into systems, making it appear that the centrifuges were operating normally, confusing their human masters.[39] Without explanation, in late November Iran stopped feeding uranium into the centrifuges at its main plant. Apparently those centrifuges were no longer working.[40]

A remote electronic sabotage program this good required the services of a dozen or more world-class experts. It also required the ability to conduct electronic and probably physical reconnaissance of the Iranian systems. Whoever did this had to conduct tests in a closed environment that mirrored the Iranian systems, complete with the same expensive hardware the Iranians were using.[41] In short, this operation cost millions of dollars to pull off, and possibly a year of planning, and it very likely required the collaboration of human and electronic intelligence services.

Almost certainly this operation was carried out by a government or under government direction, and speculation turned quickly to the Israelis and Americans, especially after the discovery that a small piece of Stuxnet code might contain an obscure reference to the Book of Esther, in which a tyrant threatens the Persian Jewish community, only to be overthrown in a sudden turn of fate.[42] The Israelis are not above such chutzpah, and the operation would have been consistent with Israeli policy. It would also have been consistent with U.S. policy but not with previous U.S. methods, which avoided computer operations likely to damage others besides its intended targets. While the Stuxnet worm disproportionately harmed Iran, about 40 percent of the infected computers were elsewhere. That's a lot of collateral damage.

The French and Russians also could have engineered this operation, and the Russians had opportunity as well as motive. Russian engineers work in Iran, and some of them have access to Iranian nuclear installations.[43] We know the Russians have used thumb drives to propagate malware in U.S. military systems in Afghanistan; this is a signature modus operandi for their intelligence services. The Russians want to maintain friendly ties with the Iranian regime in order to do business there and exclude the West, but they don't want a nuclear-armed Iran on their border. A covert Russian operation could have accomplished all of these goals and is as plausible as an Israeli one, especially because the Israelis were likely to be blamed (or congratulated). The leading theory, however, is that Stuxnet was a joint Israeli-American operation: The Americans knew the Siemens equipment inside out, and the Israelis reportedly duplicated the Iranian centrifuge array to unlock its secrets. The attack was not a total success; it disabled about a fifth of Iran's nuclear centrifuges but left the rest unharmed. It was successful enough, however, to delay Iran's nuclear weapons program by about five years. An armed attack on Iran's nuclear facilities would not have achieved a better result.[44] In any case, nobody's talking.

Stuxnet will not be a one-off affair. The malware is now out of the box for amateurs to analyze and copy—and it will be copied. If systems are electronically isolated from public networks, and if physical access is limited, as in Iran, a successful attack might require the concentrated efforts of one of the world's better intelligence services. But much of the North American electrical grid is not isolated from the Internet. The fact that Stuxnet was aimed at Siemens equipment should give no comfort to the makers and owners of other brands of industrial controls. That specific code was simply the last stage of a multistage attack. That means, said Joe Weiss, "this isn't a Siemens problem and . . . they could have substituted [General Electric], Rockwell or any other" brand of industrial control equipment as the target.[45] Ralph Langner, the German security consultant who was among the first to grasp the significance of the Stuxnet attack, agrees. "The problem is not Stuxnet," he said. "Stuxnet is history. The problem is the next generation of malware that will follow."

That brings us back to the vulnerability of our electric grid.

## Targeting Electric Power

"We know that cyberintruders have probed our electrical grid," President Obama has said, "and that in other countries cyberattacks have plunged entire cities into darkness."[46] Presidents don't say such things without significant, validated intelligence. Obama was apparently relying, at least in part, on intelligence disclosed more than a year earlier by a senior CIA official who, according to the *Wall Street Journal*, "told a meeting of utility company representatives in New Orleans that a cyberattack had taken out power equipment in multiple regions outside the U.S."[47] Later that year, CBS News identified one of the countries involved as Brazil, which reportedly suffered a series of attacks, one of which "affected more than three million people in dozens of cities over a two-day period" and knocked the world's largest iron ore producer off-line, costing that company alone $7 million. The utility's later assertion that the blackouts were caused by routine maintenance failures are difficult to credit.[48]

Senior intelligence officials believe the Russians and Chinese are already inside the U.S. grid, or parts of it, and Iran has shown an interest in following in their steps. "Authorities investigating the intrusions have found software tools left behind that could be used to destroy infrastructure components," one of them said. "If we go to war with them, they will try to turn them on."[49] You can also put al-Qaeda in the group of wannabe intruders, and al-Qaeda would have far less compunction about trying it than a nation-state. Computers seized from al-Qaeda operatives contain details of U.S. SCADA systems,[50] and the industry knows it.[51] According to the report on the 2003 blackout, "The generation and delivery of electricity has been, and continues to be, a target of malicious groups and individuals intent on disrupting this system."[52]

In 2003 a group of extremists affiliated with the Pakistani group Lashkar-e-Taiba conspired to attack the Australian grid. This is the same terrorist group that was behind the mass murders in Mumbai, India, in November 2008. Other terrorists plotted to attack the UK grid in 2004, 2006, and 2009. Physical security has been breached at some U.S. plants. These incidents are well-known to NERC officials. In America, security-related incidents tend to be criminal—copper theft, for example—but extremists have tried to disrupt or sabotage generating plants and transmission.[53] If would-be attackers had an ally inside a power plant, the odds of a successful attack would rise sharply—and there are, unfortunately, malicious and disaffected employees in every large organization who can identify critical systems, open virtual and literal doors, and provide details of security setups.

So far we know of more than 170 cybersecurity incidents in industrial control systems, most of them unintentional.[54] But this figure is undoubtedly low, because nuclear plants are the only power utilities required to report such incidents. As a result, neither the regulators nor the operators have a complete or reliable picture of the type, severity, or frequency of cyberevents that could take down parts of the grid.

The bulk power owners and operators have regrettably been

reluctant to wrap their minds around the possibility that their industry could be the target of an intentional, sophisticated attack—or even suffer an unintentional cyberevent.[55] "There's evidence of advanced, persistent penetrations in control systems," Assante said, but he wouldn't name any company. And then he paused. "It's a sad state of affairs. The analytic tools are so bad," he said, speaking about those in use at some of the companies, "that you couldn't even do the analysis. They couldn't see the communication flow on their own networks. They weren't grabbing that traffic, so they weren't analyzing it. . . . When you asked the engineers those questions it was like speaking Greek. They had no idea why you'd want to do those things." And because they couldn't see the cybertraffic in their own systems, they had no idea who had penetrated them. Then, when he went to the owners and operators with his concerns, Assante said, "they'd insist there was a lack of evidence [that] they were penetrated." Catch-22.

Assante recalled the thefts of a couple of laptops from utility vans during his days working in the industry. The laptops contained the keys to the kingdom—lots of information about how to access SCADA controls and field systems. "Somebody broke into their field engineering vans. They"—he meant the utility—"assumed it was a smash-and-grab operation," he said, a run-of-the-mill burglary aimed at stealing and fencing laptops and tools. Smash-and-grab thieves don't care about the information on your hard drive. They just want the equipment. The utility's management "wouldn't act on the risk that somebody had actually targeted those laptops" for the information on them. "They wouldn't even change their compromised passwords after that. They thought it was too expensive."

The system also discourages disclosure when it should require it. As Joe Weiss puts it, "If two organizations have the same vulnerabilities and only one is willing to share the information, the organization sharing the information will be punished as not being cyber secure, while the organization that does not share will be viewed as cyber secure by default."[56]

Apparently there's at least one firm that's paying attention. In 2008 a power company challenged Ira Winkler, a penetration-testing consultant, to hack its network and the power grid it oversees. Winkler won't disclose the company that hired him, but he got into the network within a day. "We had to shut down within hours," Winkler said, "because it was working too well. We more than proved that they were royally screwed."[57] But still most owners and operators don't want to believe it, even as the evidence of their vulnerability mounts higher and higher. They'd rather dance in the dark, figuratively—and raise the risk that the rest of us will be dancing in the dark, literally.

OFFICIALS AT NERC have now acknowledged that "[a] highly-coordinated and structured cyber, physical, or blended attack on the bulk power system . . . could result in long-term (irreparable) damage to key system components in multiple simultaneous or near-simultaneous strikes."[58] Under persistent prodding from Assante and like-minded colleagues, NERC has warned that if such an attack were "conducted on a large enough scale, it is possible that the bulk power system could not recover in its present form."[59] The Chinese have understood this for some time. Unlike us, they have designed key parts of their electric grid so it can be isolated quickly from the Internet.[60] But that arrangement requires real-time awareness of what's going on in your system. You have to constantly monitor the electronic traffic coming in and going out; otherwise you wouldn't know you were in danger until the lights went out. As Mike Assante's survey showed us, however, the state of network awareness in North America is dismal.

Yet NERC has been unwilling to propose any rule that would discourage, let alone forbid, connecting bulk-power industrial control systems to the Internet. Why? Because NERC is essentially a member-based organization, and in spite of its ostensibly independent board, it is unwilling to cross the wishes of its powerful members. This power structure is reflected in existing NERC standards for critical infrastructure protection. Their approach is based on size: the bigger the plant, the bigger the risk. This makes sense when you're concerned only about equipment failure. But when the risk is cyberpenetration, size is irrelevant. An attacker is just as happy to get into your system through one of those insecure, remotely monitored field devices as through your main server. Once he's in, he's in. From this point of view, Weiss says, a relatively tiny twenty-megawatt facility in rural California "that normally would have no effect on the reliability of the grid can potentially bring down the entire California grid by providing compromised packets" to the system run by the California Independent System Operator.[61]

NERC's regulations are unsatisfactory for other reasons, too. They permit each utility to develop its own risk assessment methods. This directly undercuts our national policy on critical infrastructure, which calls for *standardized* risk assessments. In 1998, President Clinton directed the preparation of the National Infrastructure Assurance Plan, based on sector-level proposals and organizations, like NERC.[62] In 2006, the Bush administration followed up with its National Infrastructure Protection Plan, which was based on standardized assessments.[63] The Obama administration has followed with an Energy Department plan to establish a national energy sector cyberorganization that is supposed to do the same thing.[64] That's the policy. But in the electricity sector it hasn't happened. And so long as Congress allows the owners and operators to remain in control of the standards they apply, it isn't likely to happen. "Priority should be given to designing for survivability," NERC has rightly said.[65] Survivable systems are resilient and can recover quickly from failure, in part because of built-in redundancy. If one part of the system is down, another part takes over. The more redundancy, the greater the security. For ordinary contingencies, the North American system may have enough.[66] But "ordinary contingencies" as previously understood are likely to be a poor guide to the future. As the report on the big blackout of 2003 told us, many operators are skating close to the edge of reliability. As a result, we can expect an increase in large-scale disruptions.

In the years since 2003, the system has actually become less resilient. As NERC has warned, "[R]esource optimization trends have allowed some inherent physical redundancy within the system to be reduced."[67] *Translation:* By continuing to squeeze the last penny of short-term operating efficiency from our electric grid, we have reduced the already insufficient redundancy in the system that would let us recover from a large-scale outage, let alone from a well-coordinated malicious attack.

Another characteristic of a resilient system is that it can replace damaged equipment quickly. On this score we could be in serious trouble. *It would take two years to replace the heavy-duty generators necessary to supply large cities.* Why so long? Because we rely on foreign manufacturers for these heavy goods. Nearly all North American industrial electric generators are made abroad, and nearly all the really big ones come from China and India—mostly China.[68] This trend is accelerating; according to Scott Borg, director and chief economist of the U.S. Cyber Consequences Unit, an independent, nonprofit consultancy. World production is limited and could not be increased quickly.[69]

Nor is the electric grid the only critical infrastructure in danger. Worldwide, owners and operators of all types of critical infrastructure report that their cybernetworks are being attacked repeatedly by sophisticated adversaries. American infrastructure is no exception. In one survey, 60 percent of U.S. companies reported experiencing a large-scale attack.[70] The oil and gas sector reported the highest level of stealthy infiltration, and more than half of the companies in that sector had multiple stealth attacks every month.[71] Malware has interfered with freight and passenger rail signaling systems,[72] and the government's own reports have concluded that our air traffic control system is vulnerable to cyber-attack.[73] As we've seen, American firms have lost critical information through cyberespionage, and if you can penetrate a network to steal information, you can also shut it down.

---

**THERE'S AT LEAST** one other possible motive behind the penetration of any enterprise's electronic networks: extortion. This is the least understood aspect of cybercrime, and perhaps the most important. One in four infrastructure companies had been the victim of extortion through real or threatened cyberattack within the previous two years, according to one study of critical infrastructure operators around the world. Some suggested that the real figure might be higher, since no company wants to admit it has been had. Eighty percent of these companies had experienced a large-scale DDOS attack, and 85 percent had been infiltrated. The victimization rate was even higher in the power industry, and higher still in the oil and gas sector.[74] So far, this kind of extortion has been reported most frequently in India, Saudi Arabia, the Middle East, China, and France, and least frequently in the United States and Britain.[75] Some people insist it couldn't happen here. But what starts a long way off has a way, sooner or later, of ending up on our own doorstep.

*The phone rings in the chairman's office. It's 7:15 P.M. and the lights have just come on around the lake outside his expansive suite. The chairman is alone, plowing through a stack of reports in preparation for a meeting of the compensation committee of the board of directors. His package of salary, bonuses, and stock options is up for renewal, and he'll be making a pitch for a generous increase. His assistant in the outer office doesn't screen this call; it's ringing on one of his private lines—the one number known only to his wife and son. Even his personal lawyer doesn't know this number. He answers it.*

*"You don't know me," the caller says, "but I have information about your last trip to Geneva, when you opened an account at Union Bancaire. Judging from the photographs we have of you coming out of your room at the Le Richmonde with Madame Hottiger, you appear to have had a lovely trip." Madame Hottiger is not his wife.*

"Who are you?" the chairman blurts out. "How did you get this number?"

"Mr. Chairman, we have all your numbers. Please listen carefully. My associates and I . . ."

His assistant pops her head in the door and mouths the words "Is everything okay?" He waves her off and sits down heavily.

". . . have completely penetrated your corporate information networks. Don't take my word for it. Please go to your own Web page and click on the link to 'The Chairman's Message to Shareholders.'" The chairman, who is used to giving instructions rather than taking them, takes this one. "Are you there?" He grunts. His photograph has been replaced with a photo of Adolf Hitler, in full Nazi regalia. "Don't worry. We will take that down in a moment. That is just to get your attention. Now please look out your window. In about ten seconds, watch the lights blink on and off around your beautiful lake." The chairman's heart beats the count, rather too fast; the lights blink. His heart rate rises, and he holds the phone away from his ear, tempted to slam it down.

"Do not hang up. There is more. If you hang up we will be forced to make more forceful demonstrations of our capabilities in your networks, and that would be difficult for you to keep to yourself. No, quite impossible to keep to yourself. You would force us to take harsh measures. You may decide to ignore what I say, but at least you should have all the information you need before you decide.

"Mr. Chairman, if you would please return to your computer, you will see that the system has gone down. Don't worry. We won't keep it down long." The wheels are turning in the chairman's head. Whom can he call?

"In half an hour your IT geniuses will have it back up, and they will no doubt have a silly explanation for what happened. As you see, we own your IT system—all of it."

His general counsel? The FBI? His chief information officer?

"I know you have a backup system," the voice continues. "The servers are in Ohio. But you're not dealing with children. We own your backup too. Every time your IT geniuses back you up, they send our . . . How shall I say? Our commands. They back up our commands along with your *own files to those pointlessly expensive servers in Ohio. We can alter your budget figures, destroy your records, or take you down completely. We own you. We could also make bank transactions on your behalf—but we prefer not to do that. It might trigger conversations between the bank and your staff, and that would draw attention to our relationship rather too quickly for either of us."*

*"What do you want?" the chairman says, perspiring heavily. His CIO won't do him any good; he knows that. He considers other options.*

*"I'm getting to that. But I know what you're thinking. It would be unwise for you to call the police or the FBI. Don't be unintelligent. You can always call them later, but remember: Once you do, you can't call them off—and they won't be able to act fast enough to stop us from crashing your operations."*

*"What do you want?" the chairman repeats, his anger boiling over. The catch in his voice surprises him. He clears his throat.*

*The caller ignores the question. "Besides, if you call them, you won't be able to avoid reporting a material problem with your internal controls. If I'm not mistaken, last quarter you signed a financial statement saying you didn't have any problems like that. Think of the shareholder litigation, Mr. Chairman. And that meeting tomorrow with your compensation committee—we want it to go smoothly, don't we?*

*"Now please get a pen and paper. I'm going to give you wire instructions—for the first payment."*

---

**IT CAN HAPPEN** here. If disruption is possible, so is extortion. Long-lasting disruptions of the power grid, parts of our transportation network, or other critical infrastructure could probably be pulled off only by a nation-state or its surrogates. But the resources required to do it would be modest. Sami Saydjari of the nonprofit Professionals for Cyber Defense thinks it could be done for about $5 million and with three to five years' preparation.[76] The chief requirement would be expertise, which for the time being is limited to a small number of intelligence services. A cooperative insider would change that, however, and there are plenty of those. In October 2010, a programmer for Fannie Mae, the Federal National Mortgage Association, was convicted of trying to destroy data on the organization's five thousand servers. Five days after he was fired investigators discovered a "logic bomb" set to go off about three months later. It was designed to spread through the organization's servers, destroying mortgage and financial data.[77] They stopped that one, but some companies weren't so lucky. When one company fired its system administrator for abusive behavior, his logic bomb did go off. The Secret Service won't identify the company, but it cost them more than $10 million and led to more than eighty layoffs.[78] In 2008, a disgruntled employee of the city of San Francisco's technology department snarled the city's payroll and e-mail systems and many vital services by setting secret passwords and refusing to divulge them for *twelve days*. People didn't get paid; many city services came to a standstill.[79]

Electronically engineered disruption by corporate insiders could have disastrous environmental as well as economic effects. In 2009 a temporary employee of Pacific Energy Resources, angry because he hadn't gotten a permanent job there, sabotaged the leak-detection system on an oil rig off the California coast. Fortunately there was no leak before the sabotage was undone, but the company suffered thousands of dollars in damage.[80] It would be surprising if there were not more such incidents involving offshore drilling equipment. *Jane's Intelligence Review* noted in late 2009 that "with many offshore oil rigs increasingly using unmanned robot platforms, hacking into their control systems could cause major damage to systems and disrupt or potentially halt oil production."[81] Not to mention cause another environmental disaster.

There is no shortage of people who get satisfaction from harming others, often with self-righteous intentions. And if we have learned one lesson about technology, it's that it disperses itself quickly. Capabilities, materials, and expertise that only a few years ago belonged to only a small number of nation-states—the ability to launch a satellite, for instance, or access to high-resolution space photography and high-tech materials such as titanium—are now widely available. This trend is accelerating. And just as the rain falls on the just and unjust alike, technology is available to do evil as well as good. Cyberattack expertise that today is found only in espionage agencies and state security bureaus will percolate quickly into the hands of those whose uses for it we will not be able to control.

Sophisticated attacks using advanced, persistent malware are increasing, and as the Stuxnet episode demonstrated, the risk of large-scale disruption to the grid and other critical infrastructure is on the rise. The cost of ignoring this risk could be disastrously high for the nation and could put many firms out of business. Rational businesses and a rational government buy down risk, but those who run our critical infrastructure are not doing that.

Here is yet another lesson that we've failed to take to heart, unlike our chief rival. The Chinese lead the world in adopting security measures to protect their critical infrastructure.[82] As we'll see in the next chapter, China has also displayed remarkable foresight by imagining a new kind of warfare that takes the fight far away from the traditional battlefield—perhaps to our doorstep.

# 6

===

# BETWEEN WAR AND PEACE

[W]ar will not be waged by armies but by groups whom today we call terrorists, guerillas, bandits and robbers, but who will undoubtedly hit on more formal titles to describe themselves.

—Martin van Creveld, *The Transformation of War*[1]

[T]here is a gray area between peace and war, and the struggle will be largely decided in that area.

—Richard M. Nixon, *The Real Peace*[2]

IN 1988, five years after the U.S. military's walkover invasion of the Caribbean island of Grenada, and a year before the Berlin Wall crumbled, an obscure lecturer on information warfare announced at Beijing's National Defense University that the battlefield of the future would be invisible. That battlefield would consist, he said, of "information space." The phrases "information warfare" and "information space" elicited quizzical expressions among military officers and civilians alike, in China as well as in the United States, in the 1980s. Apart from top-secret practitioners of electronic spying, at which China was decidedly in the minor leagues, only a few cognoscenti had any idea what such phrases meant. Nonetheless, the lecturer insisted that the main factor in determining future victors would not be heavy armaments and massed armies, but information. And the objective in warfare would not be killing or occupying territory, but rather paralyzing the enemy's military and financial computer networks and its telecommunications. How? By taking out the enemy's power system. Control, not blood-shed, would be the goal.

The lecturer's name was Dr. Shen Weiguang, and although he's now regarded as the founding sage of Chinese information warfare theory, his views were then on the fringe in strategic circles in the Middle Kingdom. "Virus-infected microchips can be put in weapon systems," he pointed out. "An arms manufacturer can be asked to write a virus into software, or a biological weapon can be embedded into the computer system of an enemy nation and then activated as needed. . . . Preparation for a military invasion can include hiding self-destructing microchips in systems designed for export." Tactics like these, he said, could have profound strategic implications if carried out carefully and systematically. They could "destroy the enemy's political, economic, and military information infrastructures, and, perhaps, even the information infrastructure for all of society." If China could do that, Shen said, it could achieve the greatest of all strategic military objectives: It could "destroy the enemy's will to launch a war or wage a war."[3]

This was a startling and completely untested application of strategic theory in the new information age, but Shen was firmly within China's ancient tradition of strategic thinking. Subduing the enemy without battle, the salient abandoned because no longer defensible, the manipulation of the enemy's mind-set: these concepts are familiar to readers of Sun Tzu's twenty-five-hundred-year-old *Art of War*. But Shen was now proposing to apply them in a new way. His military audience must have been skeptical. The People's Liberation Army was Mao Tse-tung's army, and Mao had founded it on long marches, popular uprisings, and human wave attacks by masses of peasant soldiers fed on millet. "People's war" was bedrock PLA doctrine. "The richest source of power to wage war lies in the masses of the people," Mao had taught. "[D]estruction of the enemy is the primary object of war . . . because only by destroying the enemy in large numbers can one effectively preserve oneself."[4]

Against this history, the notion of "invisible battlefields" must have seemed bizarre. It was also overstated, as many all-too-visible battlefields have demonstrated in the intervening years. Shen had nevertheless grasped a fundamental truth, but it would take more than a lecture to awaken the PLA to what was happening to modern warfare.

## Wake-Up Call

The wake-up shock arrived in January 1991. The previous August, the Iraqi army under Saddam Hussein had invaded Kuwait, installed a puppet regime, and begun looting the country. International condemnation quickly ensued, and in the following months the United States assembled a remarkable coalition of international military forces on the Saudi side of the Iraqi border. President George H. W. Bush issued an ultimatum to Saddam: Get out of Kuwait by January 15 or be attacked. Saddam was unmoved. On January 17, coalition aircraft began a thirty-eight-day bombing campaign as a prelude to invasion. The coalition then launched a ground war against the Iraqi army and Republican Guard—a fight regarded as more evenly matched than the air campaign. That was an illusion. By the time the Americans called a halt a mere one hundred hours later, the Iraqi army had suffered tens of thousands of casualties, and many had died. It had completely fallen apart. In contrast, the entire coalition suffered only about a thousand casualties, mostly wounded. Although Bush's skill in quickly cobbling together an international coalition was of paramount political importance, the war itself was fundamentally an American affair. Indeed, none of the other coalition armies, even the British, were technologically equipped to fight on the same battlefield with the Americans. And the results were awesome. One much-quoted Chinese source summed it up this way: "The U.S.-led multinational force crushed 42 Iraqi divisions, and the Iraqi forces suffered 30,000 casualties and 80,000 prisoners; 3,847 tanks, 1,450 armored vehicles, and 2,917 artillery pieces were destroyed, while the U.S. forces only lost 184 people, but incurred the enormous cost of $61 billion."[5]

The first Persian Gulf War made the Chinese sit up straight and pay attention. They had seen an Iraqi army of some 650,000 men (backed largely by Chinese tanks) utterly smashed in its own backyard, with unheard-of speed. They were shocked. If the Americans could do that to the Iraqis, what would stop them from destroying the PLA? From the Chinese point of view, the Gulf War "changed the world."[6] There would be no repeat of Chinese victories in 1950, when waves of Red Army troops swept across the Yalu River into Korea and forced Allied troops under General Douglas MacArthur into retreat. For decades to come, a head-to-head fight with the Americans would be suicide.

So, like other militaries around the world, the PLA went to school on what the Americans had done and how they did it. And what they saw was a global electronic system of communications, command, control, and intelligence—C3I—that took their breath away. Here's an amazed Chinese account of how Patriot missile defenses worked during that war: "After a [support] satellite identified a target, an alarm was sent to a ground station in Australia, which was then sent to the central command post in Riyadh through the U.S. Cheyenne Mountain command post, after which the 'Patriot' operators were ordered to take their battle stations, all of which took place in the mere ninety-second alarm stage."[7] Computerized command and control meant almost instantaneous information, and the Chinese war planners began to understand that control of information was, as they put it, "the new strategic high ground"[8] and the linchpin of the modern American way of war. Nor did the Chinese fail to notice the birth of a new age of "overnight" alliances, bringing to an end, some of them thought, to "the age of fixed-form alliances which had begun with the signing of the military alliance between Germany and Austria-Hungary in 1879."[9] Finally, the Chinese saw that war—and therefore national security—was a matter of economics. Who else but the Americans could spend $61 billion on a war halfway around the world with the world's best armor and weapons supported by a network of satellites and far-flung ground stations? The Soviets had tried—and had gone bankrupt trying. By the end of 1991 the Soviet Union had collapsed without a shot being fired, a victim of American economic warfare—or, as we would say, of competition. If you could not compete with the Americans economically, you could not fight with them either—at least, not on a grand scale.

Meanwhile, an influential group of American thinkers was cheerfully reaching the same conclusion. But this group, which consisted principally of neoconservatives, went further. In their view, the fog of war, the inevitable confusion that envelops commanders and soldiers alike in the heat and confusion of battle, had been *permanently* dissipated. With the world's best C3I, perfect, total situational awareness during battle was now achievable. No nation, they concluded, could ever again challenge the United States militarily. This assessment had profound implications for the future structure of American military forces, and it was an important factor in making U.S. forces lighter, more flexible, and more technologically dependent. We could begin to move away from a heavy army, heavy equipment, and heavy but immobile artillery.

Donald Rumsfeld was among the group that saw this possibility, and when he again became defense secretary under President George W. Bush, he pushed this agenda hard. But like any really important idea, when pushed too far it led to serious mistakes. Victory may teach lessons, but it also breeds self-satisfaction. Defeat and fear are better instructors. So as the victorious Americans were preening over what they had done, the Chinese were drawing other conclusions. If the Americans could not be directly confronted militarily, at least for another twenty-five years, who said China's challenge to the United States had to come as a direct military confrontation? There were other ways to weaken the beast. China would rise economically and assert itself diplomatically. It would become an innovator, not a copier (like the Japanese). And if China needed technology faster than it could invent it, China could steal it—electronically. As for the U.S. military, C3I might be its greatest strength, but the Chinese saw that C3I was fragile, so it was also the American military's point of greatest vulnerability. Just as control of information had been the key to the American victory, paralyzing or corrupting information systems would be the key to preventing American victory. If the U.S. military could be made suddenly blind and deaf, it would be a useless instrument. The fog of war had not disappeared permanently. On the contrary, with the right preparation it could be reimposed at will. This would be information warfare. Dr. Shen had been right all along.

### Eight years later, 1999

NATO is conducting bombing operations against Serbian forces that were seizing large parts of Kosovo and systematically killing Albanians and Muslims. James Rubin, the State Department spokesman, is explaining why NATO, which had the power to take down the Internet in Serbia and Kosovo, was keeping it open: "Full and open access to the Internet," he proclaims, "can only help the Serbian people know the ugly truth about the atrocities and crimes against humanity being perpetrated in Kosovo by the Milosevic regime."[10] *Translation:* We can keep Milošević from using the Internet by taking it down, but if we do that, then we won't be able to use it either. And we need it.

The Kosovo conflict is sometimes described as the first war on the Internet, but Kosovo did not involve a battle to take the Internet down or control its use; the United States decided not to do that. Rather, the conflict involved a struggle for hearts and minds in which the Internet was the main tool. Governments and nongovernment organizations competed fiercely on the Internet to put out their own stories and attack one another. Hackers and activists used it to assail the Belgrade regime or NATO—or both—and to deface each other's Web sites. Individuals used it to describe the horrors they had been through—all for an international audience.[11] In this sense Kosovo was merely a new chapter in the ancient tradition of wartime propaganda, but with one very big difference. The mass propaganda machines of the twentieth century had been perfected in the era of radio, whose potential the Nazis had immediately grasped, and which they exploited brilliantly. Mass radio, and later television, were easily controlled by totalitarian regimes. You broadcast from one place that was easy to find, using equipment that was difficult to hide, and your point of view was disseminated to the world. The input was centralized and active, the listeners dispersed and passive. The Internet was different. Users were dispersed but they were not passive; input came from everywhere. The Internet was becoming the chief tool of mass communications, especially when radio and TV stations could be destroyed or silenced. If NATO wanted to keep the Net open, it had no choice but to let its enemies use it too. And they did. Not only were the Serbs using the Net to communicate; they were also using it to harass their enemies. Hackers in Belgrade, for example, sent streams of ping commands to NATO's Web servers in an elementary denial-of-service attack—a tactic first used a year earlier by Tamil insurgents in Sri Lanka. ("We are the Internet Black Tigers and we're doing this to disrupt your communications."[12]) In this kind of war, where was the information advantage? Nor could NATO reply in kind, because so long as NATO wanted to use the Internet too, its forces had no targets to hit. Here was an asymmetric advantage to the weak side.

Meanwhile, a version of war fog was creeping in through the backdoor, unnoticed by NATO air commanders. NATO battle-damage analysts did not figure it out until later, but the Serbs were impressively adept at spoofing juicy bombing targets with decoy tanks and aircraft, which they made using painted canvas and wooden frames. Some of

the decoys even had heat sources to attract heat-seeking missiles from
NATO aircraft.[13] This was a low-tech deception triumph against the
world's most high-tech aircraft. In the classical fog of war you knew
when you were confused. Here, in contrast, deception was masquer-
ading as perfect clarity, aided by NATO's wonderfully self-convincing
real-time aerial video of blown-up matériel. Only a systematic study
of after-action photographs of the supposedly destroyed armor would
later disclose the truth.

The Chinese watched all of this, fascinated.[14] As a leading PLA
source on information warfare put it, "[I]n spite of NATO's near total
information superiority, its battlespace awareness was manipulated
by the Serbian armed forces" repeatedly and effectively, and "Serbian
civilian and military personnel were able to use civilian telephone and
radio links to pass military information."[15] At the same time, the American information masters were finding that *too much* information could
lead to the same result as too little. Admiral James Ellis, the American
commander in Kosovo, called it "information saturation." And as every
meteorologist knows, when the atmosphere becomes saturated, the
result is fog.[16]

The United States and its NATO allies achieved some of their
aims during the Kosovo campaign, but they did not succeed in removing
Milošević from power. The Balkan forests and mountains were not the
Iraqi desert, in which destroying massed armor had been like shooting
fish in a barrel for unmolested allied aircraft. And Serbs were not Iraqis.
Culture and terrain still mattered in war. In spite of overwhelming technical disadvantages, the Serbs continued to communicate effectively on
the Internet during the conflict, and their low-tech deception campaign
had been enormously successful in distracting coalition aircraft from
high-value targets, inducing them instead to waste tons of expensive
ordnance on worthless decoys.

Information dominance remains a bedrock principle in both
U.S. and Chinese war-fighting doctrine, essential to establishing naval
and air superiority.[17] In Kosovo, however, the Chinese saw the issue

through the other end of the telescope. By corrupting NATO's information flow, the Serbs had significantly reduced the importance of air superiority. Here was an example in information space of a venerable concept in Chinese strategic thought: the defeat of the superior by the inferior. But the Chinese were not interested in partial success and canvas decoys. They saw bigger possibilities.

## "The War God's Face Has Become Indistinct"[18]

If the First Gulf War made PLA military planners pay close attention to American battle prowess, the appearance in Beijing in 1999 of a volume called *Unrestricted Warfare* returned the favor. This book gave Pentagon strategists an alarming window into Chinese thinking about the nature of their engagement with the Western world, particularly the United States. The authors were two senior PLA colonels from China's rising military elite, Qiao Liang and Wang Xiangsui, whose work obviously had official sanction.[19] Qiao and Wang argued that China should use all means, armed and unarmed, military and nonmilitary, and lethal and nonlethal, to compel the enemy to accept its interests.[20] That sounds ominous—it was meant to sound ominous—but the thesis is actually pretty ordinary. How else and why else does any nation use its military and nonmilitary levers of power? But the authors' shrewd and brash analysis of the impact of technology on warfare and communications since the first Gulf War, their embrace of electronic operations, and their discussion of virtually all international engagement in the vocabulary of war gave their work a sharp edge among the small cadre of professionals who think about such things.

Three years later the alarm bells grew louder when an obscure publisher in Panama published an English translation of the book with the subtitle *China's Master Plan to Destroy America*, along with a color cover photo of the burning towers of the World Trade Center.[21] Those embellishments distorted a work that was less bellicose but more deeply threatening than images of 9/11 could convey. The authors were also highly intelligent and displayed an impressive familiarity with Western sources—literary and philosophical as well as military. The Prussian Carl von Clausewitz, and Mao after him, had called war "politics by other means." Qiao and Wang seemed to be saying the reverse: Politics—and economics and communications and everything else—was war by other means. And while von Clausewitz had preached the doctrine of the decisive battle, Qiao and Wang said there would be no more decisive battles. Henceforth, they said (paraphrasing Eliot), when empires perished they would crumble like the Soviet Union, "not with a rumble, but a snicker."[22]

The agents of imperial demise would certainly be backed up by military power—the Chinese have never wavered in that view—but the agents would be many and varied: economic, legal, public relations—and electronic sabotage. The success of George Soros's then recent speculative attack on the currencies of several East Asian nations impressed but appalled the Chinese (who have pegged their own currency to the dollar in part to discourage such tactics). Soros and his traders had driven down the value of these currencies, *forcing them into line with their true worth!* But that point was lost on Qiao and Wang, as it was lost on noncapitalists (i.e., most people) around the world, who saw only economic chaos in Asia created by Western capitalists. To the authors of *Unrestricted Warfare*, these attacks were a form of economic terrorism on par with bin Laden's bombings of U.S. embassies in East Africa, Aum Shinrikyo's sarin gas attack in the Tokyo subway, and the depredations of malicious hackers on the Internet. They "represent semi-warfare, quasi-warfare, and sub-warfare, that is, the embryonic form of another kind of warfare." Such warfare knows no boundaries, and against it, borders have no meaning.[23]

This was the kind of warfare that Qiao and Wang predicted and advocated. The American military could be stopped in its tracks because its command and control rode on porous networks that could be penetrated, corrupted, or brought down altogether. Only arrogance could make Americans think that their seamless electronic brilliance had brought an end to the fog of war, for as any grade-school dialectician knows, every capability calls into being its countercapability. Military commanders and strategists (whether Chinese or American) who could think only in terms of heat, blast, and fragmentation would be left in the past—quietly outgunned, one might say, by the nonmilitary war actions happening around them. "[T]hose who only understand an imposing array of troops on the battlefield and who think that war is just killing people," wrote Qiao and Wang, ". . . have been unable to understand this point."[24]

From now on, according to the two Chinese colonels, it would be "difficult for the military sphere to serve as the automatic dominant sphere in every war. War will be conducted in nonwar spheres."[25] Using financial instruments to attack a nation's currency could be seen as a form of battle. A CNN broadcast that showed the naked corpse of an American solider being dragged through the streets of Mogadishu could affect America's determination to fight. In effect, CNN was conducting a nonmilitary action with warlike results. Nonwar actions like these, the colonels said, were what future war would be about. It would transcend all boundaries and limits. It would be, in short, "unrestricted warfare."[26] Theirs was not a Hitlerian vision of total war, however. Bloodshed and lebensraum were not its goals. "'Although ancient states were great,'" the colonels warned, quoting the ancient Chinese strategist Sima Rangju, "'they inevitably perished when they were fond of war.'"[27] Could Americans understand these things? Qiao and Wang thought not. Americans, they said, only understand technology.

**THE POSSIBILITIES FOR** cyberconflict went on prime-time display in April 2007, in the tiny Baltic republic of Estonia. The Estonians had decided to remove a monument to the Russian war dead of World War II from the center of their capital, Tallinn, and move it to a military cemetery. To them the Russians weren't liberators from the Nazis; they were just the next occupiers. Russian nationalists were insulted; Russia had lost tens of millions to combat, massacres, disease, and starvation in the war against the Nazis, and the perceived insult to their war dead produced widespread outrage. The Russian-speaking population in Estonia went on a two-day rampage. At the same time, Estonian governmental and financial institutions were hammered with a distributed denial-of-service attack from thousands of captive computers organized into botnets. Estonian banks were shut down, remittances from abroad didn't arrive, and government departments came to a standstill. In self-defense, the big credit card issuers shut down their networks, which made the situation worse. Not surprisingly, many of these attacks could be traced to Russia, some perhaps to the Kremlin. Estonia closed its electronic borders and began adding redundant capacity to their external connections as fast as they could, but the attacks continued for weeks.[28]

The Russian government took a "who, me?" approach to international accusations of complicity while refusing to cooperate in an investigation that could have proven who was involved. The following year an ethnic Russian Estonian was convicted of participating in the attack and, according to a report commissioned by the U.S. Air Force, "[c]onsiderable evidence suggests that he had help from parts of the Russian mafiya, which helped organize the hijacked computers for him, but there is still no solid evidence that the Russian state was involved."[29] That the Kremlin was complicit in these attacks seemed obvious, but in what ways? Did the government simply turn a blind eye? Were the attacks perpetrated by outraged Russian nationalists or by Russian criminal organizations that deal in botnet scams day in and day out? Did the Russian government at least implicitly encourage the attacks? Were the criminals in some cases working at arm's length for the Russian security services? The answer to all of these questions is probably yes—but to what degree we don't know. Very likely what began as a spontaneous and disorganized affair received state encouragement and cover, but so long as the Kremlin refuses to permit an investigation, nobody can prove it.

Was this "war"? In the law and culture of the West, war and peace are an on-off toggle switch. Peace is what you have when you don't have war, and wars are declared. There is no middle ground.[30] Such dualism is naive—and never more so than in the period since the end of World War II. Since 1945 the U.S. military has fought three conventional wars for a cumulative period of less than four years. In the same period it has engaged in counterinsurgency operations lasting a cumulative twenty-three years.[31] In Estonia the war/not war inquiry was not an idle question. Estonia was by then a member of NATO, and some in Tallinn were calling for the government to invoke Article V of the NATO treaty, which states that an attack on one NATO member is an attack on all of them. NATO members, including the United States, glanced over the brink of this cliff and said no. And there must have been at least three good reasons. First, declaring war means you must go to war. No American president could afford to declare war and then fail to make war. Nor was there a rule that a conflict that began in cyberspace had to remain there. American doctrine states that the United States is not obliged to respond in kind to an attack: cyber for cyber, missile for missile. We reserve the right to respond in whatever manner we think fit. A cyberwar could therefore have turned hot quickly. Second, the attacks had produced no physical damage and no death. Calling such a cyberattack "war" would therefore have lowered the threshold definition dramatically. And third, when you declare war, you must declare it against somebody specific. In this case, if the cyberattacks had produced physical damage and death, the evidence of Russian involvement might have sufficed, but the precedent of declaring war in a case with ambiguous attribution, when the identity of an attacker can be spoofed, could not have been appealing.

In the end, the cyberattack on Estonia did not produce war among states, but it did result in NATO beginning to pay lots of attention to cybervulnerabilities.[32] Nevertheless many Western commentators began to refer to Estonia as the "first cyber war." But that's not how the Chinese saw it. They remembered earlier U.S. cyberoperations against Iraqi networks on the eve of the first Gulf War, and they knew very well that they had themselves turned a blind eye, much as the Russians did, toward semiorganized attacks by their own nationalistic hackers against anti-Chinese targets in Vietnam, Indonesia, and elsewhere, beginning as early as 1997.[33]

The Chinese see conflict on all fronts—but they do not see conflict as inconsistent with cooperation where interests intersect. They refer to conflict as "warfare" or "subwarfare" in the international arena as readily as Americans refer to various domestic programs as "wars" against this, that, or the other undesirable social condition. In contrast, the rigidity of American doctrinal dualism—either we're at war or we're enjoying peace—crudely simplifies our understanding of international relations. To the Chinese, it must seem childish. But within the American national security establishment, the vocabulary of conflict is also warlike in the absence of declared war: We are stocked with self-described cyberwarriors who for the most part are not soldiers in the usual sense but geeks employed by a military or intelligence organization. Alvin and Heidi Toffler foresaw this happening as early as 1993, when they wrote, "If the tools of warfare are no longer tanks and artillery, but rather computer viruses and microrobots, then we can no longer say that nations are the only armed groups or that soldiers are the only ones in possession of the tools of war."[34] This blurring creates genuine confusion about who's a soldier and who's not, and this confusion is both substantive and legal, since a nonsoldier engaged in war is an irregular combatant and not entitled to the protections of the Geneva Conventions.

War talk has changed in other ways too. As Colonels Qiao and Wang see it, "All of the prevailing concepts about the breadth, depth and height of the operational space already appear to be old-fashioned and obsolete."[35] Strategists everywhere have therefore stopped talking about "battle*fields*." They now talk about "battle*space*," which has created confusion about who's in that space and where that space is. As the colonels point out, this confusion is deepened with the dissolution of the boundary between military and civilian technology. In their view, the battlespace is now everywhere.[36]

### "Water does not have a constant shape."[37]

The Chinese are forcing Mao's PLA into the twenty-first century as fast as they can, and have launched the most ambitious naval modernization program since the PRC was founded in 1949.[38] Yet the principle of the "people's war" remains a pillar of military doctrine as well as national mythology, and they have not abandoned it.[39] But instead of embodying this principle in masses of poorly armed peasants, the Chinese now see it living in legions of hackers ready to defend the nation in cyberspace. "In the high-tech local war which we will face in the future," writes a prominent military strategist who enjoys official approval, "the role of the masses" looms large, and the "great power of the people's war" will be unleashed through military and nonmilitary means in all aspects of life.[40] As applied in cyberspace, however, this was a doctrine chasing the reality of hacker life in China. In 1997 there were just seven Chinese hacker Web sites, all of them rudimentary, all of them with content copied from abroad. That began to change when anti-Chinese riots broke out in Indonesia in 1998, and nationalistic hacker groups like the Green Army and the Red Hacker Alliance retaliated against Indonesian networks.[41] All of a sudden, patriotic hacker groups were blooming like a hundred flowers all over China.

In May 1999 the Red Hacker movement got a huge boost of energy when NATO bombed the Chinese embassy in Belgrade during the Kosovo War.[42] Red Hackers were outraged and quickly launched a powerful DDOS attack that shut down the White House Web site for three days.[43] "Never has such an emotional impact on a nation occurred since the advent of the Internet," declared one Chinese blogger three days later. "Even though I was just facing a computer monitor, I could feel the patriotic spirit of my friends on the Internet." Another pleaded, "Hackers, who love and protect the motherland, please teach me how to hack the Yanks. I hope you will accept me as a follower so that I can make my contribution to the motherland." The outpouring of electronic patriotism in the face of national injury was overwhelming. New members of another hacker group, the Chinese Eagle Union, solemnly pledged "to put the interests of the Chinese nation above everything else" and "to do everything in my power to make the Chinese rise up."[44] No Western country has experienced such a spontaneous wave of unofficial support from a self-identified cyber national guard, and a prominent Chinese hacker explained why: "Unlike our Western counterparts, most of who [sic] are individualists or anarchists, Chinese hackers tend to get more involved with politics because most of them are young, passionate and patriotic."[45]

The midair collision two years later over the South China Sea between a U.S. Navy EP-3 reconnaissance plane and a PLA fighter—the latter piloted by a cowboy whose risky antics were well-known to our crews—set off another round of electronic skirmishes. Never mind that our plane was in international airspace or that the collision was caused by the recklessness of the Chinese pilot; the Red Hacker community was enraged. Members of these groups are not controlled by the central government, which from time to time has arrested some of them for criminal behavior. Yet the government whips them into a frenzy when it suits its purposes, with patriotic injunctions to counter "foreign forces subverting China via the Internet," and so on.[46] The PRC recruits its own network techies through hacker Web sites to harness this energy.[47]

Between these amorphous hacker groups and the PLA's network professionals lies a murky middle layer whose shape, not surprisingly, is indistinct, but whose mission—information warfare (IW)—is not. In 1998 the PRC launched what may have been its first experiment with a cybermilitia: a forty-person unit in a state-owned enterprise in Datong City, Shanxi Province, which had a rich talent pool drawn from some twenty universities, institutes, and companies.[48] Militias are neither official government cadres nor freelance hackers. They operate in ambiguous space, connected to one or another government office by a loose string. A twitch of a government finger tightens the string, either to restrain or direct an operation. The PLA has been actively creating IW militias since about 2002, recruiting from universities, research institutes, and commercial IT companies, especially telecom firms. Some accounts call these cadres an "active reserve," comprising eight million network operators under direct state control.[49] We can't count on the accuracy of these estimates, but we do know that such cadres receive government funding, work in government-affiliated institutions or front companies, and are subject to some degree of government control. We also know that China's Academy of Military Science has endorsed the formation of cybermilitias and "directed the PLA to make the creation of such units a priority." In some cases they undergo light military indoctrination.[50]

The Chinese attacks on Google in late 2009 allowed us to glimpse how some of these militia units work.[51] The attacks were based on a previously unknown vulnerability in Microsoft's Internet Explorer that had been mentioned in Chinese language publications. The attacks themselves were pulled off by a combination of security professionals, contractors, and consultants, and at least some of them were routed through servers at two Chinese educational institutions. Routing an attack through an educational institution makes attribution especially difficult, because the user of any particular machine is often impossible to identify, and security practices at universities are notoriously weak. As we saw in chapter 3, one of the institutions was Lanxiang Vocational School. Lanxiang is particularly close to the government. It actually helped create one of China's principal censorship tools, which is known as the Great Firewall of China, and many of Lanxiang's graduates end up as network operators in the PLA. *Of course* both Lanxiang and Jiao Tong denied any involvement—which may simply mean (if it's true) that the academic administration was not involved. Could a group of students or faculty have organized these attacks without the knowledge of the schools' administrations? Perhaps. Was it technically possible for third-country actors to run these attacks through China? Yes, if they also had cyberwarriors fluent in Chinese who had combed Chinese language journals in search of the code involved. In that case, however, the Chinese had the forensic tools to trace the attacks backward from Chinese servers to their source. Yet the PRC kept mum. And why would a third-country actor have used the attacks to spy on internal Chinese dissidents—which is what happened? As we saw earlier, we now have other intelligence that confirms the attacks were authorized by high officials of the Chinese state—but conducted at arm's length from the government.

The Chinese never tire of criticizing Americans' lack of subtlety, even as they praise us for our flexibility, adaptability, and ingenuity. "Most Americans," Shen said dismissively, "see IW as a way of fighting. This is because they approach IW mainly on a technical or purely military level." Chinese thinkers find this tendency "childish."[52] No doubt the Phrygian elders similarly thought Alexander childish when, according to legend, he was unable to untie the Gordian knot. Alexander's method of resolving the conundrum—he cut the knot with his sword—was certainly not subtle, but it proved entirely effective. The American dislike of subtlety and our bias toward technical and military solutions are undeniable; so is our difficulty with dialectics and other modes of nonlinear thought. Airs of intellectual superiority are the first refuge of an old culture resenting the new, however; and military officers who see inevitable conflict between China and the United States are probably more common there than here. Chinese and American military doctrines regarding cyberspace are today quite similar,[53] though our idioms differ. As we've seen, the Chinese often speak of war when referring to any point on the continuum from economic competition to armed conflict. Americans are careful (for legal as well as operational reasons) to distinguish computer network exploitation from computer network attacks. Exploitation is espionage; attacks are attempts to degrade or paralyze an adversary's information systems. The Chinese speak of "informationalized" warfare, whereas Americans speak of "netcentric" warfare.[54] Both mean essentially the same thing. Both seek "information superiority . . . capable of putting disparity in the enemy commander's mind between reality and his perception of reality."[55] Both seek to employ "the core capabilities of influence operations, electronic warfare operations, network warfare operations, in concert with specified integrated control enablers, to influence, disrupt, corrupt or usurp adversarial human and automated decision making while protecting our own."[56]

So why did *Unrestricted Warfare* create a furor among American military thinkers when it appeared in 1999? Because it made plain that the Chinese saw information warfare as a means of disruption, whereas military planners in Washington in the 1990s saw nothing but unchallenged information superiority and unobstructed operations long into the future. Americans saw their superiority as so great that we could enter an era of "not fighting," because no one would challenge us. The Chinese saw instead a new way of fighting. According to Timothy Thomas of the U.S. Foreign Military Studies Office, the West hoped notions of not fighting would lead to clean information warfare rules to play by—"no casualties, just a victory from a stand-off position." *Unrestricted War* upset this thinking. It showed that some in China might actually prefer conflict that wasn't so clean. In information control, Americans had seen efficiency and order, command and control. The Chinese saw that too, but they also saw the value of chaos and asymmetric advantage. As Colonel Qiao put it, "[T]he stronger side is never the first to break the rules and use irregular methods."[57] This sounded like a bald threat to strike first in an electronic war.

In Chinese thought, asymmetric information warfare holds the potential to maneuver the United States—not into open traditional warfare, but rather into inaction. China has made no secret of how it would fight the United States, if it came to a fight. PLA strategy calls for combining network and electronic warfare against an adversary's information systems at the start of any conflict.[58] They would target the communication and control nodes and so lead us to distrust our own systems[59] and undermine our decision making, operations, and morale. Electricity, transportation, and financial networks would be punched out. Blindness and paralysis would follow—at least, that would be the plan.[60] The PLA lays special emphasis on "public opinion war" and "psychological war."[61] Their goals are to "force the enemy side to regard their goal as our goal" and to "force the opponent to give up the will to resist and end the confrontation."[62] All this would be coordinated with hard power,[63] until finally the enemy—that would be us—would be "forced to sign a dishonorable peace."[64]

Let's see how that strategy might play out.

# 7

## JUNE 2017

INCREASINGLY WARM RELATIONS between Taiwan and the mainland turn sour in November 2016, when Beijing restricts certain airfreight traffic from the island in an attempt to protect its homegrown business in computer peripherals. Revelations in the *Taipei Times* of payoffs by PRC agents to several Taipei television news stations and civil servants in the governing Nationalist Party send tremors through the island and within the party. When the revelations are followed by the unmasking of a highly placed PRC spy in the office of the president, a third-party candidate for president of Taiwan—anticorruption but pro-mainland—throws his hat in the ring. His candidacy will produce a fractured vote, as in 2000 when Taiwan elected Chen Shui-bian from the DPP, or Democratic Progressive Party. Chen's four-year term—the only time since 1949 that Taiwan's government was not led by Nationalists—was a period of nonstop strife with the mainland. The elections will occur in late March.

## February 10, 2017

A PLA navy destroyer in the South China Sea harasses commercial geological survey vessels from Vietnam and Brunei. These vessels are operating in their own exclusive economic zones, which conflict with those of China. They're looking for oil. The South China Sea is ringed by the Philippines, Malaysia, Brunei, Vietnam, and China, and by Taiwan to the north, but China ignores their overlapping claims. China claims the entire South China Sea not only as its exclusive economic zone but also as its sovereign national territory. China's foreign minister had told his Singaporean counterpart, while staring him down in a meeting in Hanoi in July 2010, "China is a big country and other countries [around the sea] are small countries, and that's just a fact."[1] In line with that neighborly view of international law, China had for several years been warning international oil companies against surveying off the coast of Vietnam, and on several occasions the PLA navy had chased their vessels away.

The South China Sea is one of the world's most crucial waterways. More than forty-one thousand ships pass through it every year. That's more than twice the ships that pass through Suez, and more than three times the number traversing the Panama Canal. From the southeast, the sea is a bottleneck: More than half the global merchant-fleet tonnage enters it every year through the Strait of Malacca, a skinny neck of water between the Indonesian island of Sumatra and the Malay Peninsula. For the U.S. Navy, the strait is one of the world's most important strategic passages, because it links the Pacific and Indian oceans. Control of the South China Sea would effectively give China control over the strait, and vice versa. Avoiding this passage would add thousands of miles to a voyage from Suez to Hong Kong.

## February 16

Public opinion polls released in Taipei show a dead-even three-way split among likely voters in next month's presidential election.

## February 22

The unarmed USNS *Sumner*, an oceanographic survey ship, is tracking the HAN-class attack submarine 405 as it leaves its base through a huge underground tunnel on Hainan Island, heading southeast. This cat-and-mouse game goes on every day between blue water navies. As the *Sumner* approaches 10° north latitude, however, a PRC Jianghu III–class frigate passes dangerously close in front of its bow and switches on its gunnery control radar. This is like cocking a pistol in someone's face at six feet. The *Sumner* veers sharply away, avoiding a confrontation. A shrill exchange of diplomatic protests follows, with the United States complaining about Chinese interference with international right of passage in the South China Sea, and the Chinese asserting that the United States was engaging in warlike activities within their exclusive economic zone. This is a replay of the dispute over the 2001 midair collision off Hainan Island between a U.S. Navy EP-3 surveillance plane and a Chinese fighter plane. This is not the first time PLA navy warships have bullied unarmed U.S. Navy survey vessels, but turning on the radar is a step up the escalation ladder, and both sides know it. In Taipei and Washington, reaction to the confrontation is immediate and loud.

The conflict between freedom of navigation and exclusive economic zones has been an unresolved sore point among maritime powers and coastal powers since the advent of the UN Convention on the Law of the Sea in 1982. The convention has been ratified or acceded to by 161 nations.[2] The United States signed it in 1994 and generally abides by it, but the U.S. Senate has never ratified it. It has been so widely accepted, however, that it has arguably become customary international law, regardless of ratification. The convention requires that nations "refrain from any threat or use of force against the territorial integrity or political independence of any State."[3] The Chinese regard this provision as a weapon—not warfare exactly; call it "lawfare."[4]

## February 23

The Chinese foreign minister summons the U.S. ambassador in Beijing and tells him in blunt terms that the Chinese government regards with the utmost

gravity the conduct of warlike activities, including espionage, within its exclusive economic zone and sovereign territory, and China reserves the right to take
all necessary measures to prevent their recurrence. In diplomatspeak, this is a
threat to sink U.S. surveillance ships in the South China Sea—but it is not made
public.

An hour later, through public channels that are well covered by the international media, the foreign minister states that, consistent with the convention's
requirement that nations resolve their differences peacefully, China proposes
immediate bilateral consultations to avoid further confrontations between naval
vessels of the United States and the PRC. In response to a planted question, the
minister rejects the suggestion of a regional conference on the issue. The same
day, the Web site of the English-language *China Daily* quotes a "senior government source" suggesting that the United States should exert itself more strenu-
ously to bring renegade Taiwanese politicians into line. After all, such a course
would be in accordance with the American One-China Policy, which has not
changed since the Nixon administration. China's only interest, the source says,
is regional peace and stability.

## March 19

China's naval confrontations and aggressive rhetoric have the opposite
effect on Taiwanese politics than Beijing intended. By a squeaky margin in a split
vote, Taiwan elects a DPP government that is implacably anti-PRC.

## April–May

U.S. attempts to cool off the new Taipei government get nowhere. Beijing
condemns U.S. hypocrisy and meddling in "purely regional" issues and begins
to reinforce mobile missile units on the mainland coast opposite Taiwan, raising
the threat of invasion. On April 11, the PLA announces that its East Sea Fleet will
begin amphibious exercises with the 1st Army Group, Nanjing Military Region.
It simultaneously warns South Korea and the United States against holding
naval exercises in the Yellow Sea, which China also claims. Intense consultations

are held in New York. Over private U.S. and very public PRC objections, Taipei announces a referendum on independence, to be held in mid-September. A red line is about to be crossed.

## June 19

It's Sunday, and the East Coast of the United States is sweating through the worst heat wave since the brutal summer of '10. The lead editorial of the *New York Times* sharply criticizes the Taipei government. The United States had been prepared to go to war over Soviet arms in Cuba, it says; Taiwan is even closer to mainland China than Cuba is to Florida. It recalls that Douglas MacArthur called Taiwan an "unsinkable aircraft carrier" off the Chinese coast, but surely bellicose World War II–era metaphors like that have become irrelevant; no one envisions invading China. And what was America's interest in Taiwan, really? Economic integration between the island and the mainland was already extraordinary. The principal U.S. interest in this regional issue, opines the *Times,* is that it be resolved peacefully. Though the *Times* is left of center, its point of view resonates widely with an American public that still suffers significant unemployment and has no taste for more wars in far-off places.

In another editorial on the same day, as New York experiences its first rolling brownouts in years, the same newspaper notes that calls for voluntary curtailment of energy use by both the White House and the mayor of New York City have been unavailing. The paper calls for aggressive regulation of energy use. It runs a story on the front page about three homeless people who have died from heat prostration in New York. Similar stories run in Atlanta, Washington, and Cleveland, which are all experiencing record heat.

## June 21

Bilateral talks at the UN in New York break down as China, in an attempt to "encourage" diplomatic progress and warn Taiwanese voters, restricts commercial aviation between the island and the mainland. The following day a PLA navy frigate leaves the port at Ningbo, guns sheathed, and stands off Taipei in view of land for twelve hours. It later circumnavigates the island and returns to base. Several amphibious units on the mainland go on active alert.


## June 22

A carrier group from the Seventh Fleet, led by the USNS *Gerald R. Ford,* the United States' first superclass carrier, steams east, ready for war.


## June 23

### Washington—12:20 P.M.

The temperature reaches 105 degrees for the third straight day. The electricity grid in the northeastern United States goes out. The *Times*'s immediate online editorial says, in effect, "We told you so."

### Washington—1:15 P.M.; Beijing—1:15 A.M. the following day

At a secret meeting in "the tank," a secure room in the basement of the White House, the president turns to the four-star commander of U.S. Cyber Command, who is also the NSA director, and demands to know whether our grid is being attacked, and if so, by whom. "Sir," she says, "under standing executive orders, the NSA has nothing to do with protecting civilian networks. That's DHS's responsibility."

Annoyed, the president turns to the secretary of homeland security. "Well, damn it! Are we being attacked or not?"

The secretary, whose chief qualification for the job is that he ran the president's victorious campaign in Ohio, turns to his new undersecretary for cyberdefense, who stammers, "Sir, uh, we're evaluating that now. Very aggressively, sir."

### Washington—1:21 P.M.; Honolulu—7:21 A.M.

A marine colonel enters the tank and hands the president an urgent intelligence report from the U.S. Transportation Command, aka TRANSCOM: Five Marine F/A18-Cs from Guam, bound for Okinawa, have ditched in the Pacific, eight hundred miles from their intended rendezvous point with a tanker that was to have refueled them in midair. "All pilots successfully ejected, CSAR ongoing," the colonel says.

"What the hell is CSAR?"

"Combat search and rescue, sir. It will be some hours before we can get them out, sir."

### Washington—1:24 P.M.

TRANSCOM reports that just before Mayday calls went out, radio traffic from the ditched fighters indicated their rendezvous coordinates were different from those given to the tanker—for reasons the TRANSCOM commander will later be unable to explain to the secretary of defense. This is a Whiskey-Tango-Foxtrot moment—military slang for "What the fuck?"

### Washington—2:09 P.M.; Beijing—2:09 A.M. the following day

CNN, Fox, BBC, and Al Jazeera are running PLA video showing Chinese sailors heroically plucking our exhausted fliers from heavy seas, safe and sound and expressing gratitude to their saviors. The frigate happened to be in the right place at the right time, at some distance from its usual area of operation.

### Washington—3:15 P.M.; Honolulu:—9:15 A.M.

An hour later—following a video hookup between the president, the secretary of defense, and the commander of U.S. Pacific Command, or PACOM, overlooking Pearl Harbor—an additional carrier group detaches from the Fifth Fleet in the Indian Ocean and sails full speed for the Strait of Malacca.

## June 24

### Washington—12:41 A.M.; Honolulu—6:41 P.M. the evening before

A Chinese submarine surfaces undetected within half a mile of the *Gerald R. Ford* in midocean. The sub is powered by a quiet electric drive engine developed in a top-secret U.S. Navy program. Satisfied it has been seen, the Chinese ship submerges and disappears. The message is unmistakable: You can't see us coming—and we could sink you if we wanted to.

Washington—9:45 A.M.; California—6:45 A.M.

The traffic control system in San Diego begins to blink. Back in the tank, the DHS secretary reports that his analysts have concluded that, yessir, we are being attacked. "No kidding," the president mutters. He authorizes CYBERCOM (the U.S. Cyber Command) to retaliate against six specific parts of the Chinese grid.

Washington—10:32 A.M.; Beijing—10:32 P.M.

The Chinese have taken four of the six intended targets offline; they can't be taken down remotely. The other two targets are hit: Xiamen and Chengdu go dark.

Washington—12:00 P.M.; San Diego —9:00 A.M.; Honolulu:—3:00 A.M.

The San Diego grid goes down, followed by the grids in Seattle (another big navy base) and Honolulu. In California's Central Valley, turbines in three electric generators mysteriously blow up. The secretary of energy tells the president that this kind of equipment takes twelve to twenty-four months to replace.

"What?!" the president says. "Don't I have emergency powers to deal with that?"

"We don't make those generators in this country anymore, Mr. President—haven't made them for years."

"Who does make them?"

"India, sir. The Indians make them, and the Chinese."

Meanwhile, for reasons the USPACOM commander in Honolulu can't understand, we begin losing track of several more Chinese submarines. Frantic efforts by the director of White House communications have kept the story of the blown-up generators off the evening news, but it won't stay quiet long.

Washington—3:00 P.M.

The treasury secretary informs the president that the Chinese have begun selling Treasury notes on the open market. In the next hour, all market indexes go into free fall and trading halts on U.S. markets—but not overseas. The dollar is being clobbered. The secretary has spoken with the Chinese finance minister, who regretted very much that domestic economic pressures had caused them to start selling. The consensus of his staff, the minister said, is that they should sell much more—half a trillion worth—but that he, the minister, felt they should hold the line for now at $100 million. He sincerely hopes to begin buying as soon as domestic conditions in China permit.

### Washington—5:45 P.M.; Beijing—5:45 A.M.

The president of China calls the White House. I am happy to say, he tells our president, that your airmen are safe and sound in our military hospital in Xiamen, which has excellent modern electrical generating capability, and we look forward to releasing them in a day or so, when they are fit. I also want to say how much I regret the difficulties you are having with those old electric generators in California. My staff tells me the Indians have a terrible production backlog. So do we, Mr. President, but in light of the great value we place on Sino-American friendship, we would be pleased to replace these generators as a high priority, and on favorable terms. That might be particularly important to you in case others were to go down, perhaps in more critical locations.

"One moment." The president hits the mute button. "The son of a bitch is threatening to take out more generators. Can he do it?" The CYBERCOM commander looks at the DHS secretary. "Sir," the secretary says, clearing his throat. "Sir"—his voice has gone squeaky—"we don't know."

"Don't know! Didn't you assure me last week that your critical infrastructure protection program was a one hundred percent success? Didn't you?" The president is screaming. He turns to his secretary of energy: "The rest of the grid—is it safe?" The energy secretary shrugs and extends his hands as if to say, No idea, sir. At that point the secretary's BlackBerry goes off.

"Goddamn it," the president shouts, "I thought I told you never to bring one of those things in here!"

"Sorry, sir, I . . ."

"Sorry my ass. Get it out of here—now. For all you know, that thing is a direct pipe to Beijing." The DHS secretary turns pale and slips his hand into a pocket to make sure *his* BlackBerry is turned off. A colonel breaks in with a message: The Omaha Public Power District is reporting erratic behavior on its SCADA networks. Omaha is home to U.S. Strategic Command.

"Jesus Christ," the president says, and hits the mute button again.

"Mr. President," our president says, "thank you for your call. I'm sure you'd agree that it is in the interests of both of our countries to reduce the current dangerous level of tension. Our defense secretary is prepared to open talks with your side immediately to achieve that . . ."

"Mr. President," their president says, "I appreciate your attitude, but I think perhaps you do not understand. The progress of your carrier groups toward China's coast is an immediate threat to China's security and integrity, and we will not tolerate it, sir." And he repeats, his voice rising, "We will not tolerate it! If the carrier group from your Fifth Fleet does not alter its course within forty-five minutes"—he's now practically yelling—"we will disrupt the power grid in your northern midwestern states and throughout your Pacific coast. If this naval war party—or any American warship in the future—enters the Strait of Malacca we reserve the right to treat its progress as an act of war. If the *Gerald Ford* or its sister ships proceed east of 122 degrees east longitude, our missiles will sink them." Then, more quietly: "We respect your navy, Mr. President, but please— please do not underestimate our capabilities. They are based, as you undoubtedly know, on excellent technology!

"I do not wish to be impolite, Mr. President; I will not ask you to reply now. I will know your reply in forty-five minutes. I sincerely hope, Mr. President, that our foreign secretary and your secretary of state can meet within thirty-six hours to produce a joint communiqué restating that the bedrock foundation of our relations since 1972 remains intact, and that any effort by the current regime in Taipei to alter that foundation would be vigorously opposed by both of our governments. Thank you, Mr. President, and good-bye."

Click.

Half an hour later the carrier changes course.

Thus it was that in a dispute in 2017 that appeared to be entirely about Taiwan, the United States of America lost the freedom of navigation through the South China Sea. As a result, China's effective defense perimeter was pushed outward one thousand miles south of Indonesia and east of the Philippines, drawing Vietnam, Cambodia, Thailand, Malaysia, Singapore, Indonesia, Brunei, Papua New

Guinea, and the Philippines much more tightly into the ambit of Chinese "persua-sion," and making it clear to the governments in Canberra and Tokyo that they had serious thinking to do about their geopolitical allegiances.

The joint communiqué that followed was the most vigorous statement of international cooperation that China and the United States had issued in many years and was hailed in Western capitals as a triumph of statesmanship.

The referendum proposal in Taiwan? That was defeated.

## Could This Happen?

I'm not predicting this scenario, but it's well within the realm of possibility. And we would be foolhardy not to prepare for it. With the exception of successful attacks on our electricity grid—and we know the grid is vulnerable—virtually every aspect of this fictional scenario *has already happened*. The Chinese contention that their economic zone overrides the right to free navigation in international waters is a matter of record. Confronta-tions between PLA navy warships and unarmed vessels in the South China Sea have already occurred much as described. The capabilities of Chinese warships are in fact catching up fast with our own—because they're based in significant part on stolen U.S. Navy technology. The mismatch between the Department of Homeland Security's cyberresponsibilities and its capa-bilities (they're extremely weak) is well-known. Chinese hackers really have penetrated networks at TRANSCOM, which controls tanker refueling schedules. The incident of the Chinese submarine surfacing undetected amid a U.S. Navy carrier group really did happen. Diesel-electric genera-tors that keep our lights on really do come from India and China; we don't make the big ones any longer. And of course the People's Republic of China is the largest holder of U.S. government debt. It would be foolhardy for U.S. government officials to believe that such events could not be made to occur in a choreographed sequence like the one described above. But so far in the United States we've been able to talk about this danger only as an argumentative replay of the old black-and-white, war/not war dichotomy. Here's what the discussion sounds like so far:

> The United States is fighting a cyberwar today, and we are losing. It's that simple.
>
> —Admiral Mike McConnell,
> former director of national intelligence[5]

> The biggest threat to the open internet is not Chinese government hackers or greedy anti-net-neutrality ISPs, it's Michael McConnell, the former director of national intelligence.
>
> —Ryan Singel, blogger[6]

This kind of exchange easily degenerates into a shouting match that obscures the complexity of the problem, perpetuates confusion about the meaning of war, and confirms the Chinese view that American thinking on the subject is superficial. Words like *cyberwar*, *netwar*, and *information war* mean different things to different people. So let's simplify the issue and assume that these three terms are synonymous (as indeed they usually are), and then let's ask: What *is* a cyberwar, anyway?

At least six different situations have been called cyberwar:

1. Electronic propaganda
The Kosovo War in 1998–99 involved frantic competition for propaganda advantage using the Internet. None of the parties sought to bring the Net down. There were plenty of attacks on infrastructure, but they involved physical bombs, not logic bombs.

2. Massive DDOS attacks
The first Internet war was a series of DDOS attacks by Russians against Estonian banks and government institutions in 2007. This was indeed a cyberattack against a nation-state. We have suffered similar attacks in the United States. On July 4, 2009, for example,

a DDOS attack that *probably* originated in North Korea shut down the White House's Web site—but not its communications—for three days. We do not treat DDOS attacks as acts of war, however, and we are pretty good at fending them off. It is highly unlikely that the United States could be similarly paralyzed by such attacks. The U.S. communications infrastructure is too robust and redundant, and the country is much larger than Estonia.

3.  Strategic cyberwar

A strategic cyberwar would be a solely electronic war against infrastructure—railways, the power grid, or air traffic control, for example—or against forces. This has not happened, and it is very unlikely to happen. Its effects would be too difficult to predict, in part because the state of an adversary's defenses would be uncertain. The diplomatic, electronic, and possibly physical consequences of attempting such an attack would also be too severe to warrant the risk. Just because a conflict begins in cyberspace doesn't mean it must remain there. In addition, a massive strategic attack could probably not be limited to a single target country, so the risk of disrupting international financial markets, telecommunications, and infrastructure would be significant. No nation wants to do that.

4.  Electronic sabotage

Electronic sabotage operations generally occur through what is known as a supply chain operation—that is, compromising sensitive electronics to make them fail, as the CIA brilliantly did during the 1970s.[7] Starting during the détente years of the Nixon administration, the Soviet leadership understood that they were years behind the West in technology. So Soviet intelligence agencies geared up to steal from Western—especially American—sources what they lacked, particularly computers and microchip technology. To this day, no commercially viable computer chip has ever been manufactured in Russia. The Soviets packed trade and agriculture delegations with intelligence officers, and in one case, a Soviet guest visiting Boeing put adhesive on the soles of his shoes to pick up metal samples. Still, nobody wanted to believe warnings from CIA counterintelligence officials that the Soviets were engaged in wholesale economic espionage, because nobody could *prove* these incidents were part of a grand design. Meanwhile, the Soviets, often through front companies, were stealing radar, machine tools, and semiconductors—all items that were embargoed to the Soviet bloc during the cold war. American views changed in July 1981, however, when the French disclosed to President Reagan that they had a Russian defector in place who had revealed the entire Soviet operation, known as Line X. The defector was Colonel Vladimir I. Vetrov, known to the French as Farewell. So in early 1982, the CIA and National Security Council officials proposed to launch a classic counterintelligence operation: Rather than roll up this espionage network, they would use it to advantage. They now had the Soviet shopping list, why not help them fill it—but with "improved" products designed to pass initial Soviet quality control tests but later fail? President Reagan readily approved the plan, and in due course, flawed microprocessors were built into Soviet military equipment, turbines designed to fail found their way into a gas pipeline, and thoughtfully imperfect plans wreaked havoc with chemical plants and a tractor factory.[8] William Safire of the *New York Times* finally broke this story in 2004. According to Safire's source, the Soviets wanted to automate the operation of their new trans-Siberian gas pipeline but lacked the technology to do so. They applied for an export permit, and when we rejected it, the KGB sent a spy into a Canadian company to steal what they needed. Farewell tipped us off to the plan. The CIA then made sure our friends got what they wanted—sort of. The goods the Soviets so cleverly filched were programmed to run the pumps to produce pressure far greater than what the pipeline joints and valves could withstand. As Safire reported, "The result was the most monumental non-nuclear explosion and fire ever seen from space."[9]

Supply chain attacks involve corrupting a product at the place of manufacture or—more often—somewhere along the line between the manufacturer's loading dock and the point of delivery. Supply chain integrity is a major concern of every large company, whether a food supplier, an electronic manufacturer, or a medical device company. The food supplier does not want to sell poison. The electronics firm wants software that does what it's supposed to do—and that does *not* do something else. The medical device company wants to know its titanium screws really are made of titanium and machined to the right tolerance. Counterfeits could kill patients and lead to massive liability. But food, electronics, and medical devices come from all over the world, so policing supply chains is a major headache—including for the military. The Pentagon has found counterfeit computer chips in military jets, for example.[10] The equipment on modern fighter aircraft uses hundreds of computer chips, but many of them come from abroad—which increases the ease of sabotage—because that's where most of the manufacturing capacity has moved. Whether the Pentagon fell for a foreign intelligence service's supply chain operation (probably not) or simply bought chips from a corrupt contractor intent on making more money, counterfeits invariably mean degraded performance. In January 2010, a software flaw in the Pentagon's GPS network disrupted satellite communications. In 2007, six brand-new stealth F-22 Raptor jets were lucky to find their way back to base when their computers went down.[11]

5. Operational cyberwar

Cyberoperations as part of hot war are here to stay. This is operational cyberwar, and it has already occurred at least three times. In 2003, before U.S. and coalition troops moved into Iraq, the

U.S. military already owned Iraq's supposedly closed military communications system, and U.S. commanders used their control to great effect. They not only successfully frightened many Iraqi commanders into surrendering without a fight, they also gave the Iraqis instructions, which were followed, on how to park their armor close together before abandoning it—so we could blow it up more efficiently.[12]

The second and most breathtaking instance of operational cyberwar occurred in 2006, when the Israeli air force fighter-bombers flew undetected along the Turkish-Syrian border and blew up a nuclear weapons facility the North Koreans were building for Syria. The next day the media carried the story of the bombing but not the backstory: Syria's air force didn't even scramble to meet the attack because Syria's tip-top Russian-made radar (which Iran also uses) showed nothing unusual. Syrian military radar operators might as well have been looking at cartoon pictures of the clear night sky—pictures made in Tel Aviv. This was indeed electronic magic of an advanced sort, and worthy of the name cyberwar.[13]

The third instance of operational cyberwar occurred in 2008, when Russia invaded Georgia. Though the Russians contend the Georgians started the cyberfight, the Russians definitely finished it, paralyzing Georgian communications. In the future, cyberoperations will accompany all hot wars. In this chapter, my fictional example illustrates how cyberoperations could also be used in connection with operational hot war threats in ways that actually avoid a hot war—but lead to a dishonorable peace with strategic implications.

6. The criminal-terrorist symbiosis

Cyberoperations are cheap. The physical tools of the trade are not secret, and they're readily available the world over. What separates advanced nation-state capabilities from the lesser capabilities of criminal organizations and terrorists is expertise, not expensive equipment, and expertise is bound to proliferate. When China's Dr. Shen wrote more than twenty years ago, "[E]very computer has the potential to be an effective fighting unit; and every ordinary citizen may write a computer program for waging war,"[14] he had in mind a version of people's war waged on behalf of the Chinese state. But the ability to wreak havoc on networks is not limited to nation-states and their proxies. Al-Qaeda and other terrorist groups are thinking about network disruption, and so are groups of a different ilk:

> We do not believe that only nation-states have the legitimate authority to engage in war and aggression. And we see cyberspace as a means for non-state political actors to enter present and future arenas of conflict, and to do so across international borders.[15]

This is the bravado of the Electronic Disturbance Theater, a hactivist group "working at the intersections of radical politics, recombinant and performance art, and computer software design."[16] This kind of talk would have been unthinkable, literally, only a few years ago. The idea that a collection of artsy, self-righteous geeks would have either the nerve or the imagination to issue a threat of "war and aggression" against nation-states was so preposterous that no one would have thought of it when war was synonymous with the concentrated application of heat, blast, and fragmentation, as it had been since the time of Napoleon. But if this group's bravado was exaggerated, and their skill thus far limited, their threats are no longer entirely preposterous. In 1998, in order "to demonstrate solidarity with the Mexican Zapatistas," its members organized DDOS attacks against Mexican president Zedillo's Web site, and later against President Clinton's White House Web site, and then against the Web sites of the Pentagon and the Frankfurt and Mexican stock exchanges.[17] If those tactics seem ho-hum now, they did not seem so in 1998, and the skill level of nonstate groups is increasing.

In the late 1990s the Chinese authors of *Unrestricted Warfare* predicted exactly these sorts of "sundry monstrous and virtually insane destructive acts" by groups like EDT. They also pointed out the asymmetric advantage that nonstate actors would have, because a nation-state "adheres to certain rules and will only use limited force to obtain a limited goal," whereas terrorists (artistic or otherwise) "never observe any rules and . . . are not afraid to fight an unlimited war using unlimited means."[18] In the intervening years the convergence of criminal and terrorist organizations has given the EDT manifesto a far more sinister ring than it had when it came from a group interested in "recombinant performance art." Crime finances terrorism, and terrorism in turn enhances the market for criminal extortion. For instance, large-scale drug dealing financed the Madrid bombings in 2004, which were set off electronically. Spanish police later seized nearly $2 million in drugs and cash from the plotters. Indeed, almost half the groups on the U.S. government's list of terrorist organizations raise money through drug trafficking.[19] As a general rule, large criminal enterprises are increasingly networked rather than hierarchical, both in their organization and in their means of communication.[20]

In 2000 the U.S. National Intelligence Council predicted that in "the next 15 years, transnational criminal organizations will become increasingly adept at exploiting the global diffusion of sophisticated information, financial, and transportation networks." The council predicted that these organizations would form ad hoc alliances both with one another and with political movements. With income from trafficking in arms, narcotics, women, children, and illegal immigrants, they would corrupt unstable and economically fragile states, insinuate themselves into businesses, and cooperate with insurgents on specific operations.[21] By 2008 the council's predictions were even more ominous: "For those terrorist groups active in 2025, the diffusion of technologies and scientific knowledge will place some of the world's most dangerous capabilities within their reach." These groups will "inherit organizational structures, command and control processes, and training procedures necessary to conduct sophisticated attacks."[22]

In a word, advanced network operations will cease to be the special province of a few advanced states. Nonstate actors, who cannot be deterred with threats of cyber retaliation, have crashed the party.

# But When Is It War?

Is Admiral McConnell right to say that we're already fighting a cyber-war? Or are his critics right that he's just engaging in scare tactics? Make no mistake about it: Our government and our corporate enter-prises are being attacked relentlessly, McConnell is certainly right about that. But calling these attacks war transforms the dispute into an argument about categories and not about the nature of the world. Determining when an attack amounts to war is important, but it won't enlighten us about the nature and urgency of the threat or how to deal with it. It won't even tell us how to respond to specific attacks. These attacks are coming in waves and are growing more sophisticated every week. Yet we use the term *cyberattack* to include everything from net-work nuisances to systematic espionage to disabling electronic sabo-tage. Estonia's networks were systematically attacked from Russia, but when faced with deciding whether that was war, NATO said no. So attack and war are not necessarily the same thing.

The war/not war question has also become more difficult—and less useful—because the line between war preparation and war fighting has become blurred. Consider what happens, for instance, when net-work operators in Country A penetrate the electric grid of Country B. And let's assume that Country A's infiltrators intend only to look around and figure out how the network is configured; they have no intention of disrupting the grid, though they may want to do that later. In the course of that operation, however, Country A doesn't simply sneak into the system; it also makes changes to the network—like creating backdoors to enable it to get back in later. But looking around, or surveying, a com-puter network is not an act of war. It's just spying. Everybody does it.

Now suppose Country A's intention is more sinister. Assume it is intentionally laying the groundwork for sabotage. In U.S. military doctrine, this is called preparing the battlespace, and if our side were doing it, it would be done by the armed forces under the military legal authorities found in Title 10 of the United States Code—not under the intelligence authorities of Title 50. We did this on the eve of the second Iraq war in 2003, when we took over Iraqi networks. We used some of them for propaganda, and we took some of them down.[23] Most other countries don't bother with such cumbersome and sometimes artificial distinctions between military and intelligence authorities, however; they just do the operation. But regardless of legal authorities, *what they would do if they were preparing sabotage is exactly the same as if they were just looking around*: They'd create backdoors to enable them to attack the network later.

How would we know the difference between an intelligence operation (not war) and a preconflict subversion of a U.S. network (possibly an act of war)? The answer is: *We couldn't*—not unless the attacker went further and left destructive logic bombs that were instructed to go off later, *and* unless we discovered the trick. But logic bombs are just a few lines of computer code buried in a software program that might contain a million or more lines of it. And as we learned in earlier chapters, in the current state of technology they're almost always impossible to discover. This is one reason why offensive cyberoperations currently enjoy a great advantage over defensive ones. So the answer remains: In almost every case imaginable the line between an electronic intelligence operation and a presabotage act of electronic war is impossible to see. This is why penetrations of military and infrastructure networks cannot be dismissed as "just espionage."

Nor is it wise to conclude blithely that the Chinese (or the Russians, or any other actual or potential adversary) don't intend to go to war with the United States. Even assuming that assessment is currently correct (it probably is), intentions can change on a dime. Capabilities and defenses cannot. They take a long time to build. A nation that puts its faith in a potential adversary's benign intentions rather than its own strength and capabilities is a nation that is psychologically and practically incapable of defending itself.

# SPIES IN A GLASS HOUSE

In 15 years, there will be no more secrets.

—Don Burke, CIA analyst[1]

**AT 12:30 ON** the morning of Tuesday, January 19, 2010, a slim woman in a wide-brimmed hat disembarks from Air France flight 526, and after presenting a doctored Irish passport to an emigration official of the United Arab Emirates, emerges into the marble-clad halls of Dubai International Airport. Her passport says "Gail Folliard," and that's what we'll call her, because we don't know her real name.[2] On the airport's closed-circuit television we watch her emerge into the warm night of the Persian Gulf coast, hop into a taxi, and drive off. At 1:21 A.M., on another closed-circuit TV system, we watch her at the front desk of the Emirates Towers Hotel as she checks into room 1102. Ten minutes pass. A bald man who took the same Air France flight but a different taxi arrives at the same hotel and checks into room 3308. His Irish passport, also doctored, identifies him as Kevin Daveron. That's somebody's name, but not his. Folliard and Daveron are members of a surveillance team that is converging on Dubai from France, Switzerland,

Germany, and Italy and, in the wee hours of that Tuesday morning, is checking into various Dubai hotels. Some of them will emerge in disguise. We know this because we are watching them. Their hotels all have closed-circuit video systems.[3]

Back at the airport people depart and arrive from all over the world, and cameras capture them all. Who is worthy of interest? We do not know yet. Later we will notice the arrival from Zurich at 2:29 A.M. of a man claiming to be Peter Elvinger. Apparently in his late forties, this man holds a doctored French passport and carries an unusual piece of luggage. Seven minutes later we watch him leave the airport—then quickly return, walk across the lobby, and exchange a word with another man before they depart in different directions. Elvinger leaves in a taxi; the other man enters the parking area. Both are caught on camera.

At 2:46 A.M., Elvinger—or whoever he is—checks into room 518 in a hotel. He remains there until 10:30 that morning, when he leaves to go shopping. At exactly the same time, three other team members arrive at the Dubai Mall, which has closed-circuit video. Ten minutes later, Folliard and Daveron—the woman and bald guy from the Air France flight—arrive at the same mall. All these people are using cell phones, or pretending to use them, but none of them is calling any of the others on this team, not once. Instead they call a number in Austria, no doubt using an encrypted line.

At 11:30, Folliard leaves the mall—alone. At 12:18, her traveling companion, Daveron, and another man also leave, followed some twenty minutes later by the others. Daveron returns to the Emirates Towers, then at 1:37 P.M. he checks out. Eight minutes later he arrives at another hotel, disappears into the men's room, dons glasses and a wig, and then departs for a third hotel, the Fairmont, where he will soon be joined by two colleagues.

At 2:12 P.M. two men in tennis gear bumble through the revolving door and into the lobby of the Al-Bustan Rotana hotel. Only later will anyone note that they spend all of their time walking around the hotel with tennis rackets and no time playing tennis.

Meanwhile, at 2:30, someone is making inquiries at still another hotel: Mr. Abdul Ra'ouf Mohammed—has he checked in yet? The desk clerk checks his records and replies: No, sir. The clerk explains that Mr. Mohammed is expected at the Al-Bustan Rotana. Thank you. A critical detail has been cleared up.

At 3:15 P.M., the man he had inquired about, Abdul Ra'ouf Mohammed, arrives at the Dubai airport on Emirates flight number EK912 from Damascus. The flight is packed. Usually Mr. Mohammed travels with two bodyguards, but this time he is alone. Outside customs, surveillance team members are pacing about, on camera. Five minutes later we watch Abdul Ra'ouf Mohammed pass through immigration. Actually Abdul Ra'ouf Mohammed is an alias—one of five aliases he is known to use. His real name is Mahmoud al-Mabhouh, and he is a cofounder of the Izzedine al-Qassam Brigades, the paramilitary wing of Hamas, and an active weapons buyer for Hamas in Gaza. Such a man has many enemies. The Israelis have imprisoned him several times. He is alleged to have organized the capture and murder of two Israeli soldiers during a Palestinian uprising in the 1980s. Egypt arrested him in 2003 and imprisoned him for a year, and the Jordanians are looking for him. Fatah loathes him. Already, at only age forty-eight, al-Mabhouh has survived several assassination attempts.[4] At the moment, however, on the video screen he looks like just an ordinary arriving passenger, somewhat tired perhaps, pulling a wheeled suitcase behind him as he squeezes around a fellow in a white baseball cap and T-shirt chatting on a cell phone.[5] The man in the baseball cap is not there by accident.

Moments later, at 3:21 P.M., Folliard checks out of her room at the Emirates Towers, only to check into another hotel a few minutes later. She alters her appearance.

At 3:25, the man from Hamas, al-Mabhouh, arrives from the

airport at the Al-Bustan Rotana, checks in, and is given two plastic key cards to room 230. He enters the elevator—followed by the two men in tennis togs who have been loitering around the hotel. They follow him out of the elevator onto the second floor and down the hallway, noting his room number and also that of the room across the hall, number 237. Al-Mabhouh does not appear to notice them. He inserts his key card and enters. His room has no balcony, and the windows are sealed—just as he likes it. He takes a shower and changes clothes.

At 3:51 P.M., from the business center of the Crowne Plaza Hotel, the man calling himself Peter Elvinger books room 237 in the Al-Bustan—the room across from al-Mabhouh. Elvinger also books a flight out of the country. Meanwhile, Folliard and Daveron—the two from Paris—arrive at Fairmont and are joined by several others. At 4:14, Daveron leaves Fairmont for the Al-Bustan, followed two minutes later by Folliard and the others. Meanwhile, a new surveillance team has taken over at the Al-Bustan.

At 4:23 P.M., al-Mabhouh leaves the Al Bustan. He is going to the mall to buy sneakers. He is followed. Ten minutes later Elvinger arrives at the Al-Bustan, which al-Mabhouh has just left. He checks into room 237, but he doesn't go to it. Instead he gives the keys to the bewigged bald guy, Daveron, who has arrived from the Fairmont. Elvinger then departs, soon to be out of the country. Daveron hands the keys to his original traveling companion, Folliard, who goes to the room and is joined by several men. They wait.

Two hours and eleven minutes later, at 6:34 P.M., members of the assassination team arrive at the hotel. Seven minutes after that, a new surveillance team takes over. Al-Mabhouh is still out of the hotel, having dinner, but his hunters are frantically busy. At 8:00 they attempt to enter his room by reprogramming the software in the door lock but are interrupted when a hotel guest enters the corridor. Daveron, posing as a member of the hotel staff, calls them off. The software in the lock retains a record of the attempt.

At 8:24 P.M. we watch al-Mabhouh, the Hamas arms buyer with

so many aliases, walk slowly along the second-floor corridor to his room, glancing at himself in a full-length hallway mirror on his way. He slips in his key card and leans a little against the door, but it does not open. A second try, a third—it opens.

Twenty-two minutes later, at 8:46 P.M., four men emerge from al-Mabhouh's room, put a DO NOT DISTURB sign on the door, and leave. Indeed, al-Mabhouh will not be disturbed again, even by a phone call from his wife half an hour later, which he does not answer. He's dead—shocked five times with an electric device, tranquilized with the drug succinylcholine,[6] and suffocated. When his visitors depart they leave the door locked and chained from the inside. If the Dubai police know how they gained entry to the room, they haven't said. Did they pick the lock on a second try? Was al-Mabhouh overpowered after answering a knock at the door? Was there a bribe? We don't know. The Dubai police have not released all the tapes.

At 8:47 we watch Folliard pay her bill in cash and grab a taxi for the airport. Daveron follows, still wearing a wig. They return to Paris. That night others fly out for Zurich, Johannesburg, Hong Kong, and Frankfurt. By morning they're all gone, long before hotel staff enter the room at 1:30 P.M. and discover the guest who is not waking up.

**A FEW YEARS AGO** the assassins and surveillance teams would have vanished without a trace, but not this time. This was the first political assassination in history where most of the operation—all but the actual killing—was recorded on 648 hours of video,[7] supplemented by electronic passport, travel, and key-card entry records. Within twenty-four hours of finding the body, the efficient Dubai police had assembled and correlated closed-circuit video and other records from public and private sources and figured out what had happened and how it had happened. This supposedly covert intelligence operation unfolded in a fishbowl. Without a doubt, such a synchronized, expensive, labor-intensive, and deadly operation could only be pulled off by one of the world's most sophisticated intelligence agencies. And as far as the Dubai police and international opinion were concerned, the whole affair bore the fingerprints of Israel's foreign intelligence service, the Mossad. Yet how could a sophisticated intelligence service fail to understand that the world had become transparent? How could Mossad—if it was Mossad—permit its agents to be photographed over and over again? By February 16, when the Dubai police went public with the story, they had splashed photographs of eleven foreign suspects all over the Internet, along with the pictures used on the passports and footage of the operation itself. They also wrapped up two local Palestinians and charged them with aiding and abetting the crime. The eleven foreigners all traveled on European passports—six British, three Irish, one French, and one German. Ten of the passports had been issued to persons with dual Israeli citizenship, but there was no suggestion that any of the people whose identities had been used were involved in the operation. On February 25, the Dubai police charged fifteen others with participating in the crime and posted their photographs too. Training an agent costs millions and takes years. Twenty-six of them were now finished forever—or, as they say in the trade, "burned."

Was Mossad behind it? That's the leading theory, but even good theories leave loose ends. How to explain that two of the suspects left Dubai by boat *for Iran*? How to explain that the two arrested Palestinians worked for a real estate company owned by Mohammed Dahlan, a senior security official in Fatah, Hamas's rival?[8] Fatah, as it turns out, regularly shares intelligence with Israel.[9] Was this a joint Fatah-Israeli operation? But if so, how to explain the Dubai police chief's claim that a member *of Hamas* leaked al-Mabhouh's travel itinerary to Mossad?[10] Evidently Mr. al-Mabhouh had more enemies than he knew. In the intelligence business, a good rule of thumb is that nothing is what it seems. People play double games. The Dubai police are indeed very good, but are they *that* good—or were they tipped off? Many powerful players in the Middle East would have been glad to get rid of Hamas's murdering arms dealer *and* embarrass Israel. One of those players could have been working with the Israelis (or Fatah, or Hamas) *and* with the Dubai police. Nobody's telling the whole story.

One thing is certain, however: In an age of mass surveillance and instant electronic storage and retrieval, covert espionage operations will never be the same again. The intelligence business, like everyone else, now operates in a glass house. This isn't a case of heavy-handed government surveillance. It's a case of pervasive light-handed surveillance by just about everybody, producing massive amounts of information that can be correlated with a few keystrokes or mouse clicks. Transparency has come to the intelligence business.[11]

# Managing Identity in the "Participatory Panopticon"[12]

Is transparency in intelligence good or bad? Before you answer, remember that the surveillance technology that exposed the Dubai operation is the same technology that captures you scratching where it itches in public, tracks your movements as you pass through tollgates and in and out of elevators, records when you use a key card to enter and leave your office, recalls that you like your coffee with soy milk and light sugar, sends you targeted advertising from places you've never heard of, and records every keystroke you make at work. Surveillance can be used for good or ill, and judgments about it will vary among thoughtful people. The good/bad question surely has its place; if we are going to make any rules at all about how technology can be used, we will have to deal with it. But while passing judgments leads to moral self-satisfaction, it won't help us understand what's happening around us. Whether on balance we like these developments or not, relentless transparency is a fact of life.

Transparency is not an unadulterated virtue to be preferred without reflection over discretion, modesty, privacy, and tact. We cannot have unlimited amounts of both privacy and transparency. Privacy

implies opacity; it throws a veil over our lives. Transparency demands:
Open up! Privacy says: Here you may not go. This you may not see.
That you may not hear. Transparency laughs: Get over it! The technology that gathers and culls data, compares photographs, and forgets
nothing does not come with built-in discretion. It gathers and culls
indiscriminately, compares faces regardless of motive, and remembers
with efficient indifference to motivation, profit, or nationality. The
technological threat to personal privacy and the technological challenge to the secrecy of intelligence operations are therefore essentially
identical. Or as I put it earlier: Secrecy is to government what privacy
is to persons. They both rise or fall—at present they're falling—on the
same technological changes and on the same cultural proclivities for
modesty on the one hand or exhibitionism on the other.

One of the most basic functions of intelligence work is protecting
the identities of the people who do that work. The most obvious challenge is preventing someone from knowing whether your employee is
who he (or often she) says he is. If your agent is living under an alias,
you've got to make the alias credible to prevent others from seeing
through it. The Russians are—at least until recently—masters at this.
They specialize in a class of agents known as illegals, and used them
heavily from 1917 onward. An illegal was a Soviet intelligence officer
working abroad under an alias and having neither diplomatic cover nor
any apparent connection to Soviet institutions.[13] The Russians, who
still use this practice, embarrassed themselves badly when the FBI
rolled up ten of their illegals in mid-2010.[14] That blown operation may
have been remarkable for its insignificance, but it would be a mistake to think the Russian flair for this kind of penetration is a thing of
the past.

Intelligence and security services reflect the talents, tendencies,
and especially the insecurities of the cultures that create them, and the
Russians have been running illegals for generations. This is unlikely to
change. These operations require extraordinary patience, which is a
commodity in short supply in American culture. In the same way, the

American lack of deep familiarity with foreign languages and cultures and our tendency to seek solutions to problems through technology are reflected in our intelligence agencies. When the United States was at war with Germany in 1917, for example, there were tens of thousands of native German speakers living in New York City, but there was only one German-speaking Allied intelligence agent in New York—and he was British.[15] Nine decades later, in 2006, there were only six Arabic speakers among the one thousand employees of the U.S. embassy *in Baghdad*—and most of them were not fluent.[16] This was disgraceful—but characteristically so. On the other hand, our prowess at technical intelligence is unmatched, though we have serious rivals in areas such as cryptography and certain types of electronic eavesdropping. Of course, Western intelligence agencies also run agents under cover, but more often than not, Western agents operate under their true names. In either case, the question of identity not only involves knowing the person's true name but also whom that person is really working for. The man's name may truly be Adnan Hakim al-Aziz, and he may really be an Egyptian citizen employed by the Cairo (electric) Generation Company—but if Mr. al-Aziz (whose name and circumstances I have invented) is really working for French intelligence they would not want you to know it.

Creating and protecting that kind of deep cover has become more difficult than ever, as the Dubai episode demonstrated. But the technology used by the Dubai police to unravel that caper was actually elementary compared to capabilities now available. Microsoft, for example, has created software that will find, link, tag, and correlate every electronically available image of the same thing. If you have someone's photograph from a passport or a surveillance camera, you can find every other photo of that same person that has ever been posted online. You can also enrich that image with every bit of information that has ever been associated with any of those images—biometric data such as fingerprints, for example. Such data are increasingly embedded in passports, credit cards, driver's licenses, and other documents. You can also pull up their credit history, bad jokes about them from a high school yearbook, photographs, social information from Facebook, and so on. When your agent tells the foreign immigration official he's visiting the country on business for Acme Metallurgy, Inc., but he has posted a Twitter link to a photograph showing him at a football game with pals known to be from army intelligence, he's got a problem. If you're running a counterintelligence investigation, capabilities like this are wonderful. If you're trying to protect cover identities, they're a nightmare.

Pervasive social media also make it difficult to protect cover identities. While in the counterintelligence job in late 2008, I learned that the chief public diplomacy official in one of our Eastern European embassies had decided that everybody in the embassy had to be on Facebook. The local intelligence services must have been salivating with glee. If this directive had been implemented there would necessarily have been a handful of exceptions: Officials working undercover don't do public diplomacy. But a quick comparison of the embassy's telephone directory with Facebook would have shown who they were, and their covers would have been blown. Facebook and similar networking sites are a gold mine for intelligence officers whose business it is to spot and assess embassy workers who may be amenable to bribery (because of debt), blackmail (because of indiscretions), or simply closer cultivation as a source (greatly enhanced if you know your target's interests, friends, and habits). Facebook is also a mother lode for phishermen and hackers.[17] As I write this a Russian hacker is offering 1.5 million Facebook credentials for sale on the black market, and has reportedly already sold almost half of them.[18] Public diplomacy is to the State Department what marketing is to Madison Avenue. It's important, and this country has not been doing it well. But it must be done by people with a clear and cold-eyed view of the world they live in. I had this misguided effort at compulsory self-exposure stopped, but social media are now pervasive and their use cannot be fully controlled.

The chief objective of an intelligence service is to persuade other people to commit treason. You can sugarcoat this any way you want, but that's the bottom line. In order to recruit others into treachery, you begin by learning as much as you can about the habits, likes, dislikes, indiscretions, and vulnerabilities of potential targets. For this work there's no such thing as insignificant information. Is my target's wife a serial adulterer? That's useful if I want to stoke his resentment. Does my target fancy a certain restaurant or health club? Then if I want to meet him, that's where I will dine or exercise. Does she repeatedly visit the same understated but elegant hotel on the Amalfi Coast? What a coincidence! *That's my favorite hotel too. We have so much to talk about.* Ordinarily it takes months, even years to compile this kind of profile on a potential target. With sites like Facebook you can do it in ten minutes. Again, this is a blessing when you're recruiting agents and a nightmare when you're in counterintelligence. The lesson is not that people who work in embassies can't use social networking sites. These sites are part of the world now, and they're not going away. It does mean that diplomats and others who work in embassies need better training about how to handle them.

Score another point for transparency.

Planes began arriving from Afghanistan, all of them
registered to American companies.

—News account

Tracking satellites as they orbit the earth is a favorite pastime of amateur astronomers. On a clear night you don't even need a telescope to watch some satellites passing overhead, and with inexpensive optics you can find most of them in your latitude. All the information you need to do it is available free online: latitude, longitude, azimuth, speed, elevation, and the bird's location right now.[19] If you're an amateur astronomer, gathering this information is fun. If you're loading missiles onto a freighter in the harbor at Chinnampo, North Korea, in violation of a UN resolution, or trying to conceal the preparation for a missile launch from Bakhtarun in western Iran, knowing when the satellite is going to pass overhead is not about having fun. It's vital information that tells you when you can load the cargo or transport the missile undetected. In international relations this is the equivalent of knowing where the radar traps are on the interstate—except it's easier to move radar traps than to change satellite orbits.

Closer to the ground, an unorganized band of aviation enthusiasts known as plane spotters enjoy photographing and recording the take-offs and landings of aircraft from civil and military airfields around the world. Getting a photo of any kind of aircraft in service anywhere is a cinch.[20] And if you can see the registration number on the tail, you can find out not only who owns it, but also who used to own it, and if its registration number has changed, you can learn that too.[21] Some of this information has always been public but hard to find. Now it's compiled in advance and easy to find.

In 2004, stories began to surface about alleged CIA flights carrying prisoners from Afghanistan and Iraq to Guantánamo Bay, Cuba, or "black sites"—secret prisons—in Europe and elsewhere. A tip here, a whisper there, and an amateur photograph of a certain twelve-seat Gulfstream jet: These details were the end of the skein; pulling on it began to unravel the whole ball of yarn. In October 2004, stories appeared in the Irish press of mysterious U.S. military flights in and out of Shannon Airport, though there seemed to be no official record of their takeoffs or landings. "The Gulfstream jet with the call-sign N379P has landed in Shannon on at least 13 occasions in the past four years," reported the Dublin *Sunday Business Post*. "The privately-owned aircraft is on a permanent lease to the US military and is known to have transported al-Qaeda suspects on at least two separate occasions."[22]

Web sites were also popping up with the same kind of information. As one of them explained a month later, "Analysis of [another] plane's flight plans, covering more than two years, shows that it always departs from Washington DC. It has flown to 49 destinations outside America, including the Guantánamo Bay prison camp in Cuba and other US military bases, as well as Egypt, Jordan, Iraq, Morocco,

Afghanistan, Libya and Uzbekistan." Changing the registration number of the aircraft no longer hid anything; it was merely further evidence of something shady.[23] According to an article in Britain's *Sunday Times*, "The movements of [yet another] Gulfstream 5 leased by agents from the United States defence department and the CIA are detailed in confidential logs obtained by *The Sunday Times* which cover more than 300 flights."[24]

As official and self-appointed investigators caught the scent, their hunt for evidence of these flights—and of secret prisons—intensified, and they would not let up for several years. Witnesses began to talk. "Everything was unusual, from beginning to end," said the woman who had managed a Polish airfield. "I was told to accept these flights even when the airport was closed." The flights originated in Afghanistan, and the planes, mostly Gulfstream jets, were registered to American companies. Parked at the far end of the runway, the planes "would be met by government vehicles. The planes would stay no more than an hour or two before taking off. Their onward destinations were also unusual: Morocco, Uzbekistan and Guantánamo Bay, Cuba."[25]

The initial sleuthing was unofficial: plane spotters, human rights advocates, and journalists all got into the act. Then national and international officials hustled to catch up. The once covert operation was now the subject of investigations by the Council of Europe, the European Parliament, and the UN; by the governments of France, Germany, Portugal, Spain, Italy, the UK, Romania, and Kosovo; and by nongovernmental organizations, including Amnesty International and the World Policy Council. As the *Chicago Tribune* noted, although the leader of the Council of Europe's investigation "had no subpoena powers, his team of investigators used public records, satellite imaging, news accounts and interviews with officials to lay out a strong circumstantial case for what he described as a 'spider's web' of clandestine CIA flights and secret detention centers."

Views from Earth of what happens in the Earth's orbit now belong to everybody. Views from orbit of what happens on Earth are moving in the same direction. As I recounted earlier, commercial satellite imagery is widely available at amazingly good resolutions, and Google Earth has made much of the globe an open book to everybody, for free. Score another point for transparency.

## Leaking on a Mass Scale

> WikiLeaks has released more classified intelligence documents than the rest of the world press combined.
>
> —WikiLeaks[26]

About thirty times a day, somebody somewhere sends an electronic copy of a secret document to an amorphous and suddenly well-known organization called WikiLeaks, hoping the organization will post it electronically for the world to see.[27] Depending on your point of view, the senders and recipients of these messages are heroes or villains, whistleblowers exposing injustice or rootless subverters of international public order—or both.[28] WikiLeaks's sources scour and send every sort of document imaginable: classified intelligence reports, secret corporate memos, personal correspondence and embarrassing videos.

Of course, the leaking of official secrets predates and extends well beyond WikiLeaks. It's a huge headache for any counterintelligence official, and I've taken my share of aspirin. Officials in both the executive branch and Congress do it without compunction for political advantage. Civil servants leak secrets from a real or imagined sense that an activity is illegal or from moral outrage, as with Daniel Ellsberg and the *Pentagon Papers,* or with the terrorist surveillance program run by the White House through the NSA. And an innocent slip of the tongue can be as damaging as an intentional disclosure. In 2009, for example, the chairman of the Senate Intelligence Committee, Senator Dianne Feinstein, mentioned at a televised hearing that the United States was launching drone aircraft from bases in Pakistan, a fact the Pakistani government had denied. Feinstein is no fool—she was apparently just exhausted—but the damage was done. The press, meanwhile, is very effective in ferreting out information. As the investigative reporter Seymour Hersh once told me, "Your job is to keep secrets; our job is to find them out."

But Hersh was talking about retail leaking. WikiLeaks is a wholesale operation. If information is liquid, WikiLeaks has turned on the hose. After going live in 2007, WikiLeaks published the classified standard operating procedures from the prison at Guantánamo Bay, the "Climategate" e-mails of scientists at England's University of East Anglia, and private e-mails from Sarah Palin's Yahoo account. WikiLeaks has no office, no paid staff, no fixed address. It keeps no logs—so there are no logs to subpoena—and it uses high-grade encryption to protect its sources and other information.[29] Run by volunteers from more than a dozen countries,[30] the group hit its stride on April 5, 2010—and achieved the notoriety it craved—when it posted video footage of a U.S. military helicopter attack in Iraq that killed eleven people. The dead included two unarmed civilians as well as men carrying assault rifles and rocket-propelled grenade launchers, and it was accompanied by a sound track of the brutal language one might expect of soldiers under stress but that civilians far removed from battle find profoundly disquieting.[31] The seventeen-minute, edited footage of the aerial attack was headlined COLLATERAL MURDER and was met with fierce criticism from the secretary of defense and media commentators, who attacked both its inflammatory title and partisan editing. It was also greeted with voluntary contributions to WikiLeaks from people around the world, and soon it led to a *New Yorker* profile of its founder and guiding light, Julian Assange.[32]

The episode involving the helicopter footage was a mere skirmish compared to the firestorm that erupted a few months later, on July 25, 2010, when WikiLeaks released a document trove that it called, "[T]he Afghan War Diary, an extraordinary compendium of over 91,000 reports covering the war in Afghanistan from 2004 to 2010."[33] To WikiLeaks the release was a triumph of transparency and candor over secrecy and lies, comparable to Daniel Ellsberg's leaking of the *Pentagon Papers* during the Vietnam War. Anticipating criticism of unvetted documents, however, WikiLeaks broke from its past practice of releasing raw documents and instead offered them to three news organizations: the *New York Times*, the *Guardian* in London, and *Der Spiegel* in Hamburg. These organizations published simultaneously, but each made its own decisions about what to release, and each wrote its own analyses.[34] Assange claimed that about fifteen thousand documents were withheld to protect identities,[35] but lives were undoubtedly put in jeopardy by those that got out. Assange's colleagues said that the decision to release them without first deleting the identities of Afghan intelligence sources was his alone.[36]

Contributions to WikiLeaks again shot up, and so did criticism. On the day of the leak, the *Times* (London) stated that "in just two hours of searching the WikiLeaks archive, *The Times* found the names of dozens of Afghans credited with providing detailed intelligence to U.S. forces. Their villages are given for identification and also, in many cases, their fathers' names."[37] Among those named were people who had risked their lives to expose Taliban members, and shortly after the leaks a Taliban spokesman declared that the Taliban had set up a "commission" to determine who was spying for NATO.[38] Critics of WikiLeaks's undifferentiated information "dump" emerged from many quarters. They ranged from Reporters Without Borders, which called the posting of identities "incredibly irresponsible,"[39] to General Michael Hayden, formerly the director of the NSA and the CIA, who pointed out that the released material included reams of technical information about military operations that was of keen interest to foreign military and intelligence services but of no interest to the public.[40] Releasing that kind of information doesn't trouble Assange, however; it pleases him. In 2007 he was incensed when the press failed to notice that he'd leaked reams of pages of secret military information about the U.S. Army in Iraq and Afghanistan. "I am so angry," he said. "This was such a fucking fantastic leak: the Army's force structure of Afghanistan and

Iraq, down to the last chair, and nothing."[41] After the more recent dump on the Afghan war, *Der Spiegel* quoted him as saying that he "loved crushing bastards," which led the *Wall Street Journal* to "wonder if the 'bastards' he has in mind include the dozens of Afghan civilians named in the document dump as U.S. military informants."[42]

Australian by birth and an eccentric nomad by inclination, Assange is not an attractive poster boy for his cause. *The Daily Beast* described him this way: "With his bloodless, sallow face, his lank hair drained of all color, his langorous, very un-Australian limbs, and his aura of blinding pallor that appears to admit of no nuance, Assange looks every inch the amoral, uber-nerd villain, icily detached from the real world of moral choices in which the rest of us saps live."[43] After the Afghan leaks he lived for months in fear of arrest, moving from country to country and from one supporter's apartment to another, staying out of sight when he wasn't giving interviews to *The New Yorker*. The habits and language of war and secrecy infect even those who oppose them: Assange's former quarters in Reykjavik were rented on a subterfuge—his people called it "the Bunker"—and key members of the group are known only by their initials.[44] The Australian government made it clear that if he returned to his home country and were prosecuted in the United States, Canberra would cooperate. Iceland was also turning unfriendly. As an Australian citizen he could stay in Britain, but not indefinitely, and the British government's view of leakers was, if any-thing, even dimmer than that of American officials.

Following the drumbeat of criticism about endangering lives, Assange was also having internal troubles. "We were very, very upset with that," one of his main backers in Iceland said, speaking of dis-closing Afghan identities. When another supporter and coworker chal-lenged his judgment, Assange told him essentially to shut up or get out. "I am the heart and soul of this organization, its founder, philosopher, spokesperson, original coder, financier, and all the rest," he said, and the group would fall apart without him. His critics, he sniffed, "were not consequential people." Resentful of Assange's imperious style and uneasy with his capricious judgment, about a dozen volunteers left the group. And then in August the Swedish government issued, withdrew, and then later reissued a warrant for Assange's arrest on charges of raping two women. The cases involve consensual sex that allegedly turned forceful and nonconsensual. Assange then temporarily went into hiding somewhere in southeast England.[45] In spite of accusations that the charges were trumped up by WikiLeaks's enemies, the publicly disclosed evidence thus far suggests otherwise.[46]

Then in November 2010 the group engineered another massive document dump of secret State Department cables that laid bare conversations among diplomats, monarchs, ministers, cabinet secretaries, and spymasters. The disclosures added little to what the public knew about the policies of their governments but added a great deal, in embarrassing detail, about conversations that would not have occurred at all, or would not have been candid, if their participants had known their words would be leaked. In early December the group released a secret list of worldwide critical infrastructure, including hydroelectric plants; European pharmaceutical facilities that manufacture vaccines for smallpox, flu, and other diseases; and the locations of undersea cables through which pass all the world's electronic communications.[47] Some pundits, who were not themselves in the business of protecting anything, blandly opined that such a list could have been compiled from unclassified sources, but the list was obviously suggestive, especially to would-be terrorists, and it showed terrorists of every caliber what locations probably were (or were not) well protected. Its publication seemed to be motivated by nothing other than malice. The leak of diplomatic cables managed to alarm and offend every nation with which the United States engages, and to most people the leak of critical infrastructure sites was appalling. Under concerted pressure, Assange seemed to be flailing. Already an enemy of the United States, now he had made enemies of governments around the globe. As all of this was unfolding, he was arrested for rape in London on a Swedish warrant and then freed on bail, and as of mid-2011 is fighting extradition. That episode is a sordid distraction from the serious public policy issues that WikiLeaks presents, but it wasn't irrelevant to Assange's predicament. He was now looking less like a principled if fanatical champion of free expression than merely a fanatic who couldn't abide restrictions on his self-aggrandizing personal and social behavior. Meanwhile, PayPal froze the accounts of people who were donating to WikiLeaks. Bank of America, Visa, MasterCard, and some smaller money handlers refused to process financial transactions for the group.[48] A short while later Apple removed the WikiLeaks app from its store.[49]

But Assange was not without vocal support, notably from the loosely affiliated army of politically active cyberanarchists known as Anonymous. Anonymous, or people calling themselves that, quickly launched Operation Avenge Assange "to fight the oppressive future which looms ahead . . ." Their slogan, obviously intended to intimidate their opponents, was "We are Anonymous. We do not forgive. We do not forget. Expect us." Their weapon was the DDOS attack, and after going after PayPal, in December 2010 they succeeded in temporarily taking down the servers of MasterCard, Bank of America, a Swiss bank, and the office of the Swedish prosecutor.[50]

But these vigilante attacks were transitory, and if Anonymous succeeded in intimidating anyone, it wasn't large banks and financial service companies. On the other hand, individuals and smaller companies that could not afford to defend themselves against mass DDOS attacks might think twice before speaking out against the group, whose tactics were, after all, illegal in the United States and Europe but difficult to deflect or prosecute.

Meanwhile, Assange and WikiLeaks were being squeezed like a lemon.

**WIKILEAKS'S STATEMENT** of purpose is high-minded. In its view, "principled leaking" changes history for the better, and "transparency in government activities leads to reduced corruption, better government and stronger democracies." It describes itself as a "multi-jurisdictional public service designed to protect whistleblowers, journalists and activists who have sensitive materials to communicate to the public." Since its founding, it claims that it has "worked across the globe to obtain, publish and defend such materials, and, also, to fight in the legal and political spheres for the broader principles on which our work is based: the integrity of our common historical record and the rights of all peoples to create new history."[51]

"Multi-jurisdictional" means that the group is not only transnational in principle, but also beyond the ability—thus far—of a government to regulate or shut down. Governments, whether democratically elected or not, have no special status in the WikiLeaks worldview. After all, many governments exercise power beyond their own borders, so why shouldn't people outside those borders have a say in how they operate? According to this argument, international organizations are ineffective at policing the activities of other governments, because international organizations are just cliques of the governments. That's where WikiLeaks comes in, because somebody has to decide what information you and I "should" have, and WikiLeaks has nominated itself for this role: "[T]he time has come," it says, "for an anonymous global avenue for disseminating documents the public should see."

WikiLeaks relies on crowd sourcing to test the authenticity of its postings. That is, if you publish something for all to see, then the truth about it should quickly come out, regardless of whether the initial information was false, misleading, or defamatory.[52] Besides, unlike companies that are interested in shareholders' profits, and governments that are interested in power, WikiLeaks's motives are ostensibly pure. It represents "the people" and—here's hubris—functions as "the first intelligence agency of the people."

> Better principled and less parochial than any governmental intelligence agency, it is able to be more accurate and relevant. It has

no commercial or national interests at heart; its only interest is the revelation of the truth. Unlike the covert activities of state intelligence agencies, WikiLeaks relies upon the power of overt fact to enable and empower citizens to bring feared and corrupt governments and corporations to justice.[53]

WikiLeaks's profession of objectivity may be doubted in light of its deeply anarchic, antimilitary, anticapitalist,[54] and anti-American biases, but its ideological leanings are not germane here. An analogous group could arise that devoted itself to leaking documents but that supported a nationalist military agenda. Far more significant is whether WikiLeaks is, as Assange claims, "an uncensorable system for untraceable mass document leaking and analysis,"[55] beyond the reach of public authorities everywhere, democratic or otherwise.

Jack Goldsmith and Tim Wu point out in their fluid, hardheaded account of the birth and shattering of "illusions of a borderless world," that every part of the Internet is owned by someone: servers, routers, wires, transmission towers, switches—everything that makes the Internet work, everything that creates the lived illusion of cyber "space" is a physical thing subject to some government's jurisdiction.[56] Whether it's a question of regulating domain names, enforcing subpoenas for information, or policing crime, nation-states have hardly been powerless when it comes to the Internet. Now WikiLeaks poses a direct challenge to governmental control. Is WikiLeaks really "uncensorable"? Is it beyond the reach of any public authority anywhere? Or, as many people are asking, why don't we just shut it down?

IN FEBRUARY 2008, a Swiss bank called Bank Julius Baer sued WikiLeaks, "an entity of unknown form," in federal court in San Francisco, alleging that WikiLeaks had wrongfully published leaked documents falsely indicating that the bank had laundered money in the Cayman Islands to assist tax evasion by U.S. and other customers. The bank asserted a litany of claims, including defamation. About two weeks later Judge Jeffrey White prohibited WikiLeaks from posting, publishing, disseminating, or giving access to any of the challenged material through any Web site. He further ordered WikiLeaks to block publication of the offending material. The cease-and-desist order extended to "all those in active concert or participation" with WikiLeaks and to everybody else who had notice of the order. That included "DNS host service providers, ISPs, domain registrars, Web site developers, Web site operators, Web site host service providers, and administrative and technical domain contacts, and anyone else responsible or with access to modify the Web site, and that they are to cease and desist." In a separate order the court directed WikiLeaks's domain name registrar, Dynadot, to "lock the wikileaks.org domain name" and disable WikiLeaks's account so that it "remains turned off."[57]

This was about as sweeping an injunction as you can get, and it was met with howls of protest from civil rights and media groups.[58] But before the month was out, the injunction was dissolved by the same court that had issued it. Once WikiLeaks had posted the documents, the cat was out of the bag. The court also realized that its power to suppress publication was seriously in doubt on First Amendment grounds. In any case, by attempting to shut down WikiLeaks entirely, as opposed to ordering the organization to purge certain files, the orders were doubtless far too broad to stand up on appeal. It was also unclear whether the court had power over the foreign parties it sought to reach. But the real problem with the injunction was that the court finally figured out—with amused assistance from the media[59]—that it had no power to redress the alleged harm to the bank *regardless* of the jurisdictional and constitutional issues.

WikiLeaks's principal hosting service is a Swedish firm called PRQ. Sweden is highly libertarian when it comes to freedom of expression, even by Western standards. "If it is legal in Sweden," PRQ says, "we will host it, and will keep it up regardless of any pressure to take it down." Founded in 2004, PRQ has a well-deserved reputation for keeping its mouth shut: A *New York Times* blogger called it "perhaps the world's least lawyer-friendly hosting company and thus a perfect home for WikiLeaks."[60] "With our discreet customer relations policy," says PRQ's Web site, "we don't even have to know who you are, and if we do, we will keep that knowledge strictly confidential. We are firm believers in freedom of speech, commerce, and the right to privacy and anonymity."[61] The company takes pride in laughing off threats from lawyers and public authorities. Nevertheless, WikiLeaks doesn't put all its eggs in PRQ's basket.[62] The group maintains servers all over the world, many of them with mirror images of all of its content. In late 2010 there were about two hundred such sites.[63]

As the judge in San Francisco discovered, you can take one of WikiLeaks's sites down only to find that the same content continues to appear through other servers. This is like playing electronic Whac-A-Mole on a global scale, and the court put an end to the game before its lack of power could be displayed any further. The bank, meanwhile, reaped far more bad publicity as a result of its lawsuit than if it had done nothing. The injunction against the domain registrar, Dyandot, stood, thus freezing a group of domain names, but as an observer put it, "That's akin to removing a person's name from the phone book but not disconnecting his phone."[64] None of the documents that led to the suit has ever been removed from WikiLeaks sites.[65]

**AS THE BANK** Julius Baer case suggests, it is unlikely that WikiLeaks could be "taken down"—at least, not for doing what it has done so far. Even leaving aside the technological features that protect it, WikiLeaks's situation has been prefigured by groups like Amnesty International, Reuters, and the International Red Cross, all of which are transnational organizations that displease various governments from time to time. None of those organizations has ever been shut down. And Western governments would be unlikely to take down WikiLeaks as a matter of principle. Here again, history shows us why: When the *New York Times* published the *Pentagon Papers*, there were principled disagreements about whether that particular publication should be permitted, but no sensible person advocated shutting down the *Times* itself.

But shutting down WikiLeaks isn't technically impossible, and it would be legally and politically possible under certain circumstances. Let's imagine a hypothetical case involving an ordinary crime, like murder, with no political overtones. Suppose an organization like Wiki-Leaks, with reckless disregard for truth, published plainly defamatory information that not only created shame, loss of reputation, and bankruptcy, but also led to some third party stalking and killing the victim of its behavior. To pursue this crime, public officials could first try to break the organization's encryption. That might be difficult, but it could almost certainly be done. Breaking the encryption, after a court-approved warrant to enter one or more servers electronically, would illuminate a great many operational details—bank accounts, names of donors and sources, e-mail and IP addresses, and so forth. Even without such an order, much of this information is publicly available. That would establish a basis to assert jurisdiction over specific people affiliated with the organization—not merely Assange—and would be followed by subpoenas for records and witnesses that would likely be honored across international boundaries. Judicial efforts to bring murderers to justice—unlike efforts to stop the leaking of official secrets—command broad international support across the political spectrum. Bank accounts could be frozen and payments disrupted. Indeed, this has already happened to WikiLeaks without subpoenas or judicial process; for example, Bank of America and PayPal voluntarily stopped processing the organization's donations and other transactions. Establishing the liability of an amorphous group would be a challenge, but responsibility for the activities of unincorporated associations, not to mention the participants in criminal conspiracies, is hardly a new problem. Courts in all Western countries deal with it every day. Witnesses could refuse to talk, but they would go to jail. In other words, given an adequate basis under the law of one or more countries, WikiLeaks's secrecy could be broken and punishment or liability imposed. At this writing, U.S. prosecutors are trying just such a strategy as they investigate whether Assange conspired with the alleged source of the recent leaks, U.S. Army private first class Bradley Manning. If he did, Assange could be charged with conspiracy to commit espionage or computer fraud, and could be extradited to the United States.[66]

Regardless of what happens to Assange in Swedish or American courts, the leaked information will remain public. Assange's claim that the group exists beyond any form of governmental control or sanction may be overblown, but WikiLeaks has thus far managed to publish vast troves of secrets once deeply held by governments, individuals, and organizations—from the U.S. Army to Swiss banks to the Church of Scientology to Kenya's kleptocratic former president Daniel arap Moi. Few people would say that *none* of this information should have been leaked. WikiLeaks may even fall apart, but where it has gone, others will surely follow. Whatever you think of his motives or personality, Assange has highlighted for his followers—and for all of us—the potential for transparency that characterizes so many aspects of our electronically tethered lives. Assange also understood that "the source is no longer dependent on finding a journalist who may or may not do something good with his document."[67] The recent episodes in which WikiLeaks funneled information through three large newspapers suggest a new, more symbiotic relationship with the media, but even in these cases WikiLeaks is leading and the media are following.

Score another point for transparency.

Focusing on how to suppress an organization like WikiLeaks misses the point. Even if WikiLeaks were destroyed, imitators are emerging to take its place. And once information gets into the hands of such an organization, it is for all practical purposes irretrievable. Therefore the important issue is not what comes out of one of these groups, but what goes in: How did WikiLeaks obtain all that information in the first place? That query raises questions we'll address in the next chapter, about how we manage information.

The world of information is changing at light speed. Covert operations run by the top-notch intelligence agencies are uncovered with cameras in hotels and shopping malls. Low-budget terrorists run operations using free imagery from Google Earth. An army of amateur sleuths exposes secret rendition flights from out-of-the-way military airports on several continents. Top-secret State Department cables, once meant for the eyes of a few, are leaked en masse through a phalanx of servers around the world.[68]

In this environment, how can anybody run an intelligence agency?

# 9

---

# THINKING ABOUT INTELLIGENCE

**THE FUNDAMENTAL PURPOSE** of intelligence services is to prevent surprise, especially strategic or grand-scale surprise. "No More Pearl Harbors" was the cry after 1941. And two years after the Second World War ended we created the CIA and the Defense Department. The NSA followed in 1952. "No More 9/11s" was the cry after the Twin Towers fell. And again we adjusted our budgets and made organizational changes. Compared with preventing surprise, everything else is secondary. But preventing surprise is difficult. It requires an understanding of an adversary's intentions as well as its capabilities. Capabilities invariably have physical manifestations. You can count numbers of tanks and missile silos. You can monitor missile tests to observe accuracy and reliability. But intentions are more elusive—and may be detectable only when it's too late to do anything about them. Is a country modernizing its navy to protect its own coast, or does it have expeditionary intentions? Against whom? These questions are difficult to answer.

Preventing surprise also requires that we not be taken unawares by the emerging technologies that erode boundaries, accelerate change, and confound our ability to control them. As we have seen over and over again, these technologies are creating previously unimaginable transparency—voluntary and involuntary, good, bad, and indifferent— in all walks of life: personal, commercial, governmental, and military. These developments profoundly affect intelligence organizations' capabilities and manner of operating. In order to understand how these developments affect them, however, we must first make clear what intelligence is.

**THE CORE FUNCTION** of intelligence is stealing secrets.

Most descriptions of intelligence work break it into two lines of business. Stealing secrets is called "collection"—though, as we will see, intelligence services also collect plenty of information that isn't secret. Collecting is done through human spies, whose principal business is persuading foreigners to commit treason; through electronic penetrations of foreign information networks; or through sophisticated imagery and sensors designed not only to photograph but also to sense radiation, chemicals, and other invisible emanations from installations that a foreign government or transnational terrorist group wants to keep secret—like a clandestine nuclear facility, or a factory for making nerve gas. The same technology lets us monitor the radiation resulting from a nuclear accident in a friendly country. Even people who are uncomfortable with the entire intelligence enterprise want us to know about such things. Other departments of government also collect information, but not secretly. The Department of Agriculture collects information about world grain markets, for example. The State Department collects information about foreign governments, but while diplomatic cables may be classified, diplomats' collection methods are open and aboveboard. In contrast, the core competence of intelligence agencies is stealing information that cannot be gathered openly.

The second principal line of work for the intelligence business is analysis, which is collating classified and unclassified information and making sense of it. These two activities—collection and analysis—are supported by scientific research and other secondary functions, but the collection/analysis dichotomy is basic and is reflected in the organization of our foreign intelligence agencies. In the CIA, for example, the Directorate of Intelligence (analysis) and the National Clandestine Service (spies) are supported by the Directorate of Science and Technology and Directorate of Support. The NSA's organization is somewhat different because that agency also has a defensive function to protect classified networks,[1] but within the NSA's offensive operation, the collection/analysis dichotomy also holds true. Still, bifurcating intelligence this way can't give us a full sense of the business, because it omits a great deal. For example, counterintelligence, which in my view is a core part of the intelligence enterprise, isn't essentially about stealing secrets. It's about defeating the efforts of foreign intelligence services to penetrate the U.S. government and American companies, either by disrupting their efforts or misleading them.[2] The FBI's recent roll up of ten Russian illegals was a counterintelligence operation. So was the CIA's reported booby-trapping of the computer chips that the Soviets secretly diverted to use in the trans-Siberian pipeline, which then blew up. In counterintelligence's defensive mission, which is protecting secrets, transparency is a nightmare, because it makes secrets hard to keep. In its offensive mission, which is disrupting foreign services, transparency is an advantage.

The collection/analysis dichotomy also omits covert operations, which intelligence agencies in all countries have carried out for centuries. Strictly speaking, a covert operation—that is, an operation that may occur in the public eye but whose true author is disguised[3]— is not about gathering or analyzing information. It aims instead to do something openly that nobody wants to admit having done. The Dubai assassination was a covert human operation that achieved its objective but left lots of clues about who did it. Designing and spreading the

Stuxnet worm that corrupted Iran's nuclear command-and-control system was a covert electronic operation. We don't know yet—and we may never know—how successful it was or who did it. Governments assign this kind of covert operation to their intelligence services because the operations require extraordinary access to secret information, whether it's the travel plans of Mahmoud al-Mabhouh or the design and specifications of an adversary's networks and plant equipment. These operations also require the ability to conduct secret business across continents. In the United States, most of the criticism directed at the CIA has been triggered by its covert operations and not by its intelligence-gathering activities.

During wartime, intelligence services find themselves drawn into yet another kind of covert operation. At the start of the current war in Afghanistan, for instance, a small number of highly skilled CIA officers performed extraordinary feats in dislodging the Taliban from power, and since then, CIA officers have run many paramilitary operations in that theater of war. Although these operations require stealth and intelligence support, they are not fundamentally an intelligence function. We assign them to the CIA chiefly because no other organization in the U.S. government is nearly as agile. The military can and does run covert operations too, but compared to the CIA, the military is far more bureaucratic.

The collection/analysis dichotomy also leaves out the intelligence community's huge and growing responsibility for spreading information swiftly throughout the federal government, to state and local governments, and sometimes to private industry. The agencies still think of this as ancillary, if not opposed, to their core lines of business, but it is actually now at the heart of their work. It requires the ability to sort and collate vast troves of data, assess their importance, and send them where they need to go—but not to everybody at the same classification level or in the same level of detail. This work eats up hundreds of millions of dollars annually in equipment and time, and as the WikiLeaks document dumps have demonstrated, unless it's done right it creates pervasive vulnerabilities, by making classified information available to the wrong people. Frankly, this kind of wholesale dissemination effort is anathema to the ethos of intelligence professionals—and not because of bureaucratic jealousy. It's anathema to them because any information that's distributed en masse, whether or not it is classified, simply isn't secret anymore. To understand this, suppose that our man in wherever is the only person who knows certain secret information about a foreign government's intentions. Suppose further that the risk of losing this secret through treachery, negligence, leaking, or any other reason is x. As soon as our man tells his colleague or boss, the risk doubles to 2x. But when our man puts that information into a network to which ten thousand people have access—many of whom are less well trained to keep secrets than he is, or who have never met the source of the information and don't lose sleep (as he does) about his source's fate if he's uncovered—then the risk of losing the secret increases by a factor of more than ten thousand. At that point, the information may still be sensitive, but we're kidding ourselves if we call it secret. Secrets have a half-life; they degrade over time. The more people who know them, the faster they degrade.

Finally, the collection/analysis dichotomy obscures the morphing of analysis into two distinct lines of work. I'll call the first line analysis proper. It consists of the sifting and winnowing of lots of information and figuring out what it means. The second line is classified journalism, or turning conclusions into finished products for the president and other high officials. Journalism is not a pejorative label. The ability to take a complex subject and express it in clear, concise prose is a rare and valuable skill, but it's a different skill from doing analysis proper. Operationally, the two skills have always been closely related, but they are different, and the pressures on them are different, too.

With this background, let's return to the question at the end of the last chapter: How can you run an intelligence agency in a world where secrets, if you can keep them at all, don't stay secret for long?

A casino

Las Vegas, Nevada

10:12 P.M.

The heavyset man in the safari vest had been at the blackjack tables three nights running and his winning streak was impressive. Certainly the sharp-eyed watchers in the video surveillance booth upstairs were impressed. They were also suspicious. The man moved from table to table, every night playing with several dealers. He was a professional, they could see that, and won more often than he lost. That kind of skill costs the casino money and will earn you their attention. So up in the booth one of the security staff began to log this gambler's playing time, rerunning videos from the previous nights and calculating his winnings at each table. This showed her what she had missed in real time: The man gravitated to one dealer more than the others, and he won more consistently with that dealer—for three nights running. Who was he?

According to his California driver's license, which he had presented to get credit for his gambling, he was Edward McNeil Partland, and he lived in a rented apartment in Torrance but picked up his mail at a PO box—nothing too unusual about that. He had an account with the Los Angeles Department of Water and Power and one with T-Mobile for cell-phone service. He didn't use Twitter, but he did have a Facebook account. Partland listed his occupation as security consultant, freelance. He looked legit. But if he was a pro, why did none of the Las Vegas casinos have any record of his previous gambling? He also had a tattoo on his right forearm of the 101st Airborne Division, with its screaming-eagle logo. The security crew upstairs began to dig deeper, checking commercial databases that ordinary people don't buy access to.

Yes, Mr. Partland had an address in Torrance, but he had been at that address for only three months. Yes, he had an account with L.A. Water and Power—also for about three months. Before that, nothing. He had a California driver's license, but why did a nationwide check disclose a driving record that went back less than a year, when he supposedly moved to California? A check of a multistate vehicle insurance database turned up nothing older than twelve months. How could an army veteran who appeared to be about forty-five years old not have a long history of auto insurance? So casino security dug deeper. Why, they wondered, did Mr. Partland have a tattoo of the 101st Airborne on his arm but no record of military service? And why couldn't they find any trace of him in any of the 101st Division's veterans' groups? They looked at his Facebook account, but there was little on it—and no "friends" from the army. Nothing in Mr. Partland's story could be proved false, but the whole story was just too thin, and the security team could smell it. Real people leave lots of trails. Their identities are thick. Meanwhile, "Mr. Partland's" luck held out. He was a hundred thousand dollars ahead of the house. And then, after the fourth night, he stopped coming.

The security staff turned their attention to their dealer. Let's call her Angela Raney. (She's my invention, just like Partland.) Casinos don't hire dealers without investigating them up one side and down the other, and Ms. Raney was no exception. She lived right in Las Vegas, sharing a bungalow with a long-time boyfriend named Ben Taylor. The casino knew about Taylor; if you work for them, they know a lot about you. So it didn't take long to pull his record of military service and discover that he had served during the first Iraq War in the 101st Airborne. A little more digging found that before moving to Vegas, he had lived in Torrance and had used a PO box address—the same PO box used by Partland. Suddenly, using only mouse clicks, a scheme to rip off the casino was coming apart: "Ed Partland's" cover was blown. A crooked dealer, the dealer's lover, and the lover's army buddy were about to get acquainted with the district attorney.

THIS PIECE OF FICTION has nothing and everything to do with intelligence tradecraft: nothing to do with it because it involves a crime scheme to defraud a casino rather than spies and state secrets; yet everything to do with it, because Partland's cover problem is fundamentally the same as the problem of creating deep and effective cover for covert government operatives. Creating effective cover was never simple, but it has now become much more difficult and expensive. Whether or not the cover involves an alias, the tools for prying it open are cheap and readily available. In either case the agent must have a detailed history, and that history must stand up to an intense level of electronic scrutiny available to any novice private eye, who will have access to a rich trove of information going back to the agent's school days.

Several conclusions follow. Serious cover will be used more sparingly than in the past, and fewer risks will be taken with it. This point bears emphasis: Clandestine services will become more risk averse. Training a good agent takes years. If sloppy cover exposes that agent, she is burned forever, and a big investment goes down the drain. The penetrability of cover will affect clandestine services around the world, and the more wired the country, the sooner the effect will be felt. This is not to say that technology is doing away with spies. Spies have been around since before Joshua sent his agents into Canaan, and they are not going out of style. Nor is transparency going to bleed treachery and deceit out of the range of human character traits. Indeed, it is more likely to put a premium on those traits. But the training of agents and the strategies for deploying them are already changing, and the risk that these agents will be stripped of their cover is going up. The Dubai affair will reverberate through the world's intelligence services for a long time.[4]

TO ENTER THE watch floor, you walk up a slightly elevated ramp—the wires that connect all that computer equipment have to go somewhere; they're under the floor—then through a door with a cipher lock. All employees have top-secret clearances, but they can't come in here without a reason. You pass through a comfortable but Spartan outer office, then stop to let your eyes adjust. The lights are low. And it feels chilly, especially in summer: In this environment people adapt to the needs of the computers, not the other way around, and computers must be cooled. The ops center is a kind of miniature amphitheatre, with several levels of elevated seating, like a university classroom. Analysts beaver away on each level, some in military uniform, some not, each with his or her workstation and screens, each working a different issue. Behind them, in glassed-in cubicles, sit the watch supervisors. The front wall is plastered from waist height to ceiling with a bank of big video screens. Information is flowing in from all over the globe, sometimes just strings of numbers that only a specially trained analyst can understand, but there are also video feeds and interactive maps that bring together data from across the entire intelligence community and the military—exactly the sort of high-tech information sharing you had hoped was afoot among government intelligence agencies. It's amazing—even though you have no idea what most of it means. A couple of screens are familiar, however: one's tuned to CNN, another to Fox News.

Now the man in the booth is standing up and pointing. Suddenly the image on one of the screens disappears and another collection of pixels pops up. It's a cartoonish but near real time map with symbols of military units—blue and red, us and them—together with live radio chatter (which you can't hear because you're not wearing headphones). It looks cool, but it isn't. It's a schematic image of a firefight in Ghazni, a town in eastern Afghanistan where a NATO patrol is being ambushed from three sides, and blood is flowing. You're watching an extraordinary display of technological prowess that would have been impossible to pull off even a few years ago. But soon the supervisor sits down; there's nothing he can do. Air support is being called in, but not from here. Military command and control in the war theater takes care of that.

Ten minutes later Wolf Blitzer on CNN breaks off his chatter and cuts to a live video feed from Ghazni. A CNN reporter and cameraman are embedded with the NATO unit, and they're taking fire, but the camera's rolling, and they're pushing out live video and commentary against the barking rattle of machine-gun fire. This, too, is a display of technological prowess that would have been impossible a few years ago. CNN's video actually contains less information than the government's integrated tactical sources, but it's an astoundingly good source nevertheless—which is why some watch-floor screens are tuned to commercial networks. In fact, you don't have to be on a multimillion-dollar, top-secret watch floor to see this video. You could be home drinking beer and watching it on TV.

**FOR INTELLIGENCE PURPOSES,** knowing about that firefight ten minutes before it hit CNN made no practical difference. No one in his right mind would say that our intelligence agencies, let alone the military, should rely on cable news or any other commercial source for tactical intelligence—at least, not now. But in the future questions like these will grow more pressing, particularly when it comes to political and social intelligence as opposed to tactical military intelligence, when minutes matter and commanders must be able to count on the capability to produce the intelligence every time. Whether a government should invest in a particular capability will depend on two factors: Will it be there when we need it? And can we do anything useful with the information if we're getting it only minutes before it hits the commercial source? Depending on the answers to these questions, the government may disinvest in some of the resources on that watch floor.

I have smart friends in the business who insist that this kind of disinvestment will never happen, that the agencies will never rely on commercial sources this way. But I fear that my friends aren't thinking far enough ahead—or looking far enough backward. We already rely to a significant extent on commercial satellite imagery (which is extremely good) to supplement the government's own satellite imagery (which is better). Thirty years ago few people in the Defense Department or the intelligence business would have believed that possible. The convergence of the technologies available to the most powerful governments with the technologies available in your living room will not stop. And it will certainly drive public investment decisions.

Convergence is driving intelligence in another dimension, too. When an intelligence agency can get information that nobody else can get, it gains an advantage. Economists call this "information asymmetry." Everyone else calls it keeping the other guy in the dark. Either way, it's an advantage you want, whether you're the president of the United States, a currency trader, or a washing-machine salesman. Markets achieve optimum results when everybody has the same information, but an individual in a market thrives on having better information than everyone else. When traders get such information, they keep it secret. When governments get it, they classify it. When others can get it as readily as the government, classifying it is pointless, even silly.[5]

Yet most of what is worth knowing in the world is not classified, and technological convergence will make this axiom truer than ever. Everybody knows a lot, and secrets have a very short shelf life. In 1815, a difference in bond prices between the Paris and London markets might persist for days, even weeks. Today traders arbitrage differences between markets around the world in tiny fractions of a second. In 1842, news of the disastrous British retreat from Kabul during the first Afghan war took weeks to reach London. Today we have electronically connected journalists embedded with combat units in Afghanistan. The advantage that intelligence services once held in gaining access to information has shrunk.

The secrets our intelligence agencies steal, and the sources and methods that enable that theft, are valuable—but they usually have less to do with high policy than most people think. Unlike certain diplomatic cables, most of the information we secretly collect does not relate directly to the strategic intentions of adverse foreign governments, such as a planned surprise attack. When we collect information about adversaries' intentions, it's often tactical—a likely position in a negotiation, for example, or the fact that a secret missile test is about to occur, or that the test fizzled. These are real secrets. They are important to know, and our agencies are extremely good at ferreting them out. But these are not strategic intelligence victories.

Strategic failures, on the other hand, don't generally result from a lack of capability but from a lack of imagination. Before December 7, 1941, for example, the U.S. Navy was certain that the waters of Pearl Harbor were too shallow for torpedoes. They couldn't conceive of scientists in another country—an Asian country, no less—solving this very problem, which indeed the Japanese had done. Of course there were other reasons for that disaster. Complex events always have many causes, but failure of imagination caused the greatest intelligence lapse possible—the failure to prevent surprise. North Korea's invasion of the south in June 1950 was another strategic surprise. U.S. intelligence was caught flat-footed—and so was the national security staff in the White House. In 1950, the CIA was less than three years old and the NSA didn't exist. Still, the problem wasn't a lack of an ability to spot massed troop movements. Intelligence agencies attend to the priorities their political masters downtown give them, and gathering intelligence on North Korea simply wasn't a priority. The entire national security establishment was focused on the possibility of war with the Soviet Union in Europe, not Asia. Inability to think beyond one's deeply held assumptions is not a peculiarly American problem, however. Before the Yom Kippur War of 1973, Israeli intelligence had plenty of information about the massing of Egyptian troops on the west side of the Suez Canal. They just couldn't imagine that the Egyptians would dare cross it. And so they suffered grievous casualties in the Sinai and on the Golan Heights before they could turn the military situation completely around.

Lack of imagination was a factor in the 9/11 disaster, too. Nobody took seriously the idea that al-Qaeda operatives would try to fly fully loaded airliners into buildings in the United States—in spite of intelligence suggesting al-Qaeda's interest in that tactic, and in spite of the fact that the FBI knew Zacarias Moussaoui was interested in flying large airliners but didn't care about taking off or landing. Lack of imagination can't be fixed by supplying more information.

Intelligence agencies have little if any competitive advantage over private companies in analytical talent and imagination, and their advantage in global reach is diminishing. As Columbia University's Richard Betts has pointed out, "No one can match analysts from the CIA, DIA, or NSA for estimating what Al Qaeda might do in the next month. But what is their advantage over Middle East experts in think tanks or universities for estimating worldwide trends in radical Islamist movements over the next decade?"[6] The leaders of the American intelligence community and Defense Department know this. That's why they spend many millions of dollars every year consulting with experts in universities and the private sector. This official scouring of unofficial sources of expertise is yet another example of the progressive breakdown of the once-clear boundary between the roles of the public and private sectors.

This isn't simply a matter of privatization. When the postal service hires a farmer's wife to deliver mail in rural areas, or the army hires a contractor to wash dishes instead of using privates on KP, those are limited forms of privatization. When the postal service contracts intercity mail carriage to a trucking company, or the State Department decides to use an armed security service rather than the marines for embassy security, those are deeper forms of privatization. However, all of them involve greater or lesser degrees of control over the activities of the contractors, who are working for the government. But when an intelligence agency elects to supplement its satellite coverage with commercial overhead imagery, and it alters its investment plans accordingly, something more profound is occurring. This isn't privatization in the usual sense. Rather, the government becomes just another large buyer of goods or services that it used to provide internally. It relies on the private sector (whose camera may be on a satellite launched by a French or Chinese rocket) to perform a function once thought integral to one of its agencies and exclusively within the power of the government. Low-budget terrorists already rely on Google Earth for intelligence. In a word, this is an example of unbundling intelligence into component parts, some of which can be done as well—or well enough, or better—by the private sector.

To understand the future of the private sector's role in intelligence, we don't need a crystal ball. We can just as well look backward as forward, because we are experiencing a return to a historical norm. In 1815, for example, news of the French disaster at Waterloo first reached London not in the saddlebags of the duke of Wellington's courier, but in those of the courier paid by Nathan Rothschild.[7] The British government had no advantage in international communications over a wealthy banker. Both could hire couriers, establish a beaconing system using bonfires on hilltops, and hire fast boats to cross the English Channel. The electric telegraph did nothing to change that essential public/private equality. Private parties had access to the telegraph, and any man with pliers, a knife, and the ability to climb a pole could cut the line to disrupt someone else's ability to communicate. Not until the twentieth century, when cryptography and cryptanalysis required large sums of money and the secret collaboration of topflight mathematicians, did a few governments acquire qualitative advantages over everyone else in secret communications. The Second World War and most of the cold war cemented rich governments' near monopoly on intelligence, because only such governments could operate through war zones and on the other side of the Iron Curtain. With the advent of high-altitude surveillance aircraft, followed by surveillance satellites, this monopoly began to seem both natural and inevitable. It might even have seemed "inherently governmental."[8] Only the United States and the Soviet Union could compete systematically on this level. Even in the human spy trade, technology played a role in making the spy game seem like a government-only business. Spy cameras hidden in tie clips, low-voltage recording devices hidden in cigarette lighters, exploding cigars—these were the stuff of state security services (and Hollywood). You can now buy most of this stuff on the Internet, and the tiny camera in your cell phone is as good as any spy camera ever hidden in a tie clip. Our intelligence services remain far ahead of the commercial sector in clandestine technical capabilities, but as the world has accelerated, this advantage is shrinking.

In the nineteenth century security services were largely a private-sector affair. The most famous detective agency in the United States, if not the first, was the Pinkerton National Detective Agency, organized in Chicago in 1850 by a Scottish immigrant, Allan Pinkerton. Pinkerton's business in the early days consisted chiefly of providing security to railroads and their cargo. His contract to protect the Illinois Central was drafted in 1855 by the railroad's counsel, Abraham Lincoln. After Lincoln's election in 1860, security for the president-elect was not provided by either the military or the Secret Service, which did not yet exist.[9] It was provided by Pinkerton and his men. In May 1861, Major General George McClellan asked Pinkerton to create a Secret Service for his army operations in Ohio—essentially a private version of what became the U.S. Army Intelligence and Security Command. Pinkerton also ran counterintelligence operations in Washington, D.C., during the Civil War.[10] The Justice Department was not created until 1870. A year later Congress appropriated fifty thousand dollars to the department for "the detection and prosecution of those guilty of violating federal law." The department found the sum insufficient, however, and engaged the Pinkerton Agency to handle the job.[11] Government lawyers today would regard all these functions to be inherently governmental.

Already by the late 1960s the sums spent by private firms for protection had reached half the amount of public expenditures at all levels for police, counsel, and criminal courts, and at least one social scientist saw the "apparent muddling of the public and private police function."[12] Although some private police may do some investigative work, they mostly perform security functions, which should not be surprising, since the police function has historically had more to do with keeping order than solving crimes after they occur.[13] Universities, hospitals, banks, owners of large apartment buildings, and nightclubs all employ private police or off-duty municipal police who act in a private capacity. So do some wealthy residential enclaves. Starting in 1970 when the District of Columbia Court of Appeals held a landlord liable to a tenant who was criminally assaulted in the common area of his residence,[14] court decisions have provided an incentive for this kind of private policing. By 1970, a study of private police concluded there was "no clear-cut basis for distinguishing public and private police as to service performed."[15]

In today's world protecting the president certainly seems about as inherently governmental as you can get, but President Lincoln didn't think so. He and his advisers trusted Allan Pinkerton to gather intelligence and provide physical security; they didn't have a good alternative. Today, however, federal law (at least on its face) requires agencies to decide whether a particular activity *must* be performed by government employees based on whether that activity is *in its nature* inherently governmental. Indeed, under current federal law there is no middle ground: The categories commercial and inherently governmental are mutually exclusive, and every agency is required to parse all its activities into one of these two bins. This rigid, mutually exclusive duality is practically and logically untenable,[16] but it remains the touchstone of federal law in this area. The civil servants who write regulations like this are intelligent and experienced, but they are less interested in logic than in crafting rules they can administer to control the sprawling world of government contracts. They do the best they can with the legal tools they inherited from a world in which boundaries seemed stable. This tool is rapidly approaching the end of its useful life, however. Not many decades ago most Americans would have thought that delivering the mail was an inherently governmental function, and the history of public mail service supported that view. Then came Federal Express, UPS, and DHL (which began as a private company and was later acquired by the German post office). Military logistics and support also used to seem inherently governmental, but nowadays private contractors deliver ammunition, prepare food, and provide heavily armed security service. Whether any of these developments is good or bad is important but beside the point. Good and bad don't correspond with governmental or commercial. As the world around us changes our assessment of what the government can do best, and of what the government alone should be permitted to do, changes too.

Apart from the deliberate, forceful taking of life, liberty, or property from its own citizens, or binding the government by contract, it is difficult to see what actions are inherently governmental. This isn't to say that the government should outsource everything it is permitted to outsource, but simply that the centralization of power in industrial societies that reached its peak in the mid-twentieth century is ending, and the intelligence business will not remain unaffected.

**IN A VIDEO** commercial IBM's Jeff Jonas is standing by an intersection with cars whizzing by, and he asks, "If all you had was a snapshot of the traffic five minutes ago, how would you know when to cross the road?" You wouldn't. In the future everybody will know a lot, and as Jonas rightly says, successful organizations will be those that can make use of what they know as soon as they know it.[17] Speed, not secrecy, will be the coin of the realm.

This is why the collection/analysis dichotomy in the intelligence community has begun to collapse, though the collapse is lamentably not yet reflected in the way our agencies are organized. Under the old model, operatives were kept rigidly apart from analysts. They were (and still are) organized in separate directorates with distinct cultures and usually collaborated poorly. Both were heavily white, male, and Ivy League, but the operatives were the supersecret guys who did the cool stuff and got to break rules. The analysts formed a mandarinate of well-educated specialists in history, politics, economics, and international relations. They decided *what things meant*, and for the most part they would tell you *what things meant* only when they were good and ready to tell you, if in their opinion you needed to know. They delivered their wisdom in the form of a finished product. These products represented

"Intelligence" (spelled with a capital "I"), which was based chiefly on secret sources, and which they distinguished from less well-informed thinking—or thinking not based on stolen secrets.

Sketching the traits of this community can easily and unfairly degenerate into caricature, however, so I emphasize that intelligence analysts as a whole were and are a highly capable cadre of civil servants who do credit to their agencies. But the isolation and privilege of a top-secret world lead to the sins of pride and self-satisfaction, which lead to error. Besides, working on a model that required a finished product meant their output was too slow. The relentless acceleration of nearly all aspects of life following the end of the cold war has undermined this model, and it has been strained nearly to the breaking point by a decade of terrorism and war in South Central Asia. We no longer face the rigid, slow-footed, technologically clumsy adversary of the cold war. Our adversaries are numerous, and they are deft, swift, and techno-logically skillful. Whether the threat was to the London Underground, a NATO facility in Germany, or a company of soldiers on patrol in Helmand Province, the demand for intelligence was becoming heavily tactical and ever more urgent. The agencies' customers needed infor-mation in real time—not after the mandarins had chewed the intellec-tual cud and uncapped their fountain pens. These customers were also becoming increasingly military. This is hardly a surprise during wartime, but because the pace of war has increased along with everything else, it means that intelligence has been pulled into tactical targeting decisions to a degree previously unheard of. In World War II, in order to be cer-tain of taking out one target, 1,500 B-17s had to drop 9,000 250-pound bombs, which were accurate only within a radius of about 3,300 feet. In the Vietnam War, thirty F-4 fighter-bombers had to drop 176 bombs to destroy one target. During the first Persian Gulf War, in 1991, a single F-117 could reliably destroy two targets with two 500-pound bombs—if the weather was clear. During the current Iraq War, a single B-2 can reli-ably destroy sixteen targets with 16 bombs, in any weather.[18]

This startling qualitative improvement has required more than merely a huge leap forward in weapons technology. It also required a breathtaking leap forward in intelligence capability, *and* the integration of intelligence with weaponry. The army may have a tactical missile that it can guide into an apartment window from twenty miles away to take out a terrorist commander, but the officer who fires it had better know exactly which window to send it through. Precision is useless without intelligence, and the intelligence must be available to the soldier or pilot with his finger on the trigger. Getting this right is not done with carefully polished intelligence products of the sort that were the norm during the cold war. Now it is done by putting fresh tactical intelligence, sometimes with little evaluation, into the hands of battlefield commanders. This requires actually embedding intelligence officers in combat units, and it demands that collection, analysis, and operations be highly integrated.

We have become very good at this integration at the tactical level—that is, on the ground in battle. But regrettably this fluid integration of skills and information is not reflected in the organization of our agencies or even in the prevailing model of how the intelligence business is supposed to work. The orthodox account of intelligence workflow goes like this:

1.  Elected officials determine intelligence priorities (e.g., to understand the nuclear weapons program of a certain country).
2.  Intelligence officials, through an interagency process, translate these priorities into requirements (e.g., determine how long it will take that country to develop a nuclear weapon).
3.  Collectors gather information to fulfill requirements.
4.  Analysts figure out what it all means.
5.  Congress decides how to invest in future capabilities based on executive branch recommendations—in an unrelated process.

In practice, collectors do not gather information to fulfill requirements, which are far too general to provide operational guidance. In the language of the trade, they collect against *targets*, which are specific people, facilities, or systems that may yield information from which the answers to broad requirements can be inferred. Leaving analysts out of the process of selecting targets—which is what the orthodox workflow model does—is unwise, because analysts can enrich the conversation by explaining what information they would need in order to address the requirements. Analysts know the analytic gaps better than anybody else. On the other hand, collectors understand potential access points better than anybody else. Operating in collaboration, these two groups make better decisions about target selection than either can make in isolation. Together they can also advise on both near- and long-term investment decisions: If only we had the means to find out such and such, we could target this requirement more effectively. In the next budget cycle, let's propose to invest in that capability. Creating organizational arrangements in which the analysts and collectors systematically collaborate would improve each of them.

The intelligence community has begun to attack several specific problems in just this way, but these efforts are the exception to the governing organizational model, not the rule. We must change the model. Organizing the business around problems rather than around functions (like collection) or capabilities (like satellites) would improve it greatly. Our budgets should be driven accordingly, but they are not. Instead, we budget around capabilities. Major change will not occur without congressional approval, however, because Congress controls the budget, and capabilities have constituents, particularly the corporate variety that manufacture and support hugely expensive systems. Corporate constituents make campaign contributions; problems don't. Just as there is a military-industrial complex that President Eisenhower warned about, so there is an industrial-intelligence complex with deep interests in the status quo. Both these alliances have a third axis, and that axis is rooted in the Congress of the United States.

At its extreme the pressure to make intelligence immediately available at the tactical level can push analysts completely out of the picture. This is dangerous but not surprising. Insofar as analysis involves the packaging of information for customers, it's a specialized form of journalism, and all forms of journalistic media are being hollowed out by a flood of information that does not flow through the traditional organs of large newspapers, wire services, or television networks. This is a form of disintermediation, or taking the middleman out of the transaction between the consumer and the source of goods, services, or information. And it is happening in intelligence analysis for the same reasons that it has happened everywhere else.

If you want information, you don't have to buy a newspaper; you can get it online. If you want shoes or tires or computers or clothes, you can buy them all online. As for books and music, networks have not only disintermediated the stores that sell them, they're disintermediating the books and CDs themselves. Physical books and CDs are just devices for delivering prepackaged, portable information. Now you can pick and choose the bits and bytes you want, in portions of text, stories, songs, and videos, ignore what you don't want, and download them directly. The ability to move information this way has enormous advantages for intelligence, just as it has in other transactions, but it also carries disadvantages. Much of the information that now circulates so freely is garbage. Intermediaries—that is, editors, publishers, retail stores, and intelligence analysts—performed a filtering function that we must now do ourselves or pay someone to do. They told us what was reliable, desirable, and important.

In intelligence work, the analog to garbage in cyberspace is incorrect or misleading intelligence. More than once I've seen military officers in the field and political ax grinders in Washington draw half-baked conclusions from unassessed intelligence—an isolated intelligence report, for example, that led inexorably to a certain conclusion, but only if you didn't know that the source was unreliable, or that the report was contradicted by three other reports, or that the language didn't mean what it seemed to mean when read in isolation. That's why we prefer analysts to vet raw information before we disseminate it. Analysts are experts, and experts really do know things. Experience matters. But managing the tension between the need for immediate information and the value of vetted, analyzed information is difficult. This is another reason why the boundaries between collection, analysis, and customers are loosening. Not long ago these boundaries were sacrosanct, but they represent industrial-age organization, and they are too rigid to work anymore.

Intelligence analysis has also come to resemble journalism in its feedback loop—the effect of the observer on the thing observed. And here it's essential to distinguish between what I have called analysis proper, or the evaluation of evidence and drawing of conclusions, and the packaging of those conclusions for policy makers, which is a form of journalism. The media not only reflect what goes on in the world, they also affect world affairs by changing perceptions, and by giving publicity to people and events that would otherwise die in obscurity. Election polls affect voter behavior, for example. Reports of bizarre behavior generate copycat bizarre behavior. Reports of terrorist actions generate copycat terrorist actions. The visually spectacular effects of some events generate reactions that are often out of proportion to their real effects, to the point where the distinction between perception and reality vanishes.

Similarly, leaked reports that the intelligence establishment has reached a conclusion will affect diplomacy and the public positions of the president and cabinet. Only a few years ago it was almost unheard of for the conclusions reached in National Intelligence Estimates (our most definitive form of finished product) to be reported in the press or in an open congressional hearing. Now conclusions are leaked with appalling regularity by policy makers and their civil service underlings who disagree with them and seek political advantage by politicizing the analysis. This occurred notoriously in the case of the 2007 estimate stating that the Iranians had at least temporarily stopped developing a nuclear warhead, but that was hardly the first such occurrence.[19]

Leaking has become so common that it has affected the language, manner of presentation, and sequencing of conclusions in some estimates. For a time it also led to pressure to preempt leakers by making at least a summary of the conclusions public. So much for the ability of intelligence agencies to render top-secret analysis! This is transparency run amok. It is also feedback with a vengeance, and the feedback operates in both directions. Of course the analysis may affect the behavior of the policy makers who sought it in the first place, but that is intentional. In the other direction, however, the anticipated reaction of the media, legislators, public, and foreign governments to whom it is likely to be leaked affects the analysis. This is an unintentional and perverse effect of transparency, and we must learn to live with it.

All administrations have been willing to leak information for political advantage. The recent Bush administration was no exception, and the Obama administration has carried indiscretion to new heights— for no apparent advantage at all—even as it has prosecuted leakers with commendable vigor. In his 2010 book *Obama's Wars*, Bob Woodward describes a meeting in Chicago on December 9, 2008, between president-elect Obama, then-CIA director Michael Hayden, and then-DNI Mike McConnell. Hayden and McConnell were briefing the president-elect on the series of worldwide clandestine counterterrorist operations that required the president's personal approval. These are among the most closely held secrets in government. Yet Woodward refers to specific operations in specific countries and to the "tens of millions" the CIA was paying to Jordan's General Intelligence Department and other foreign services.[20] Where did Woodward get this information? No one I know thinks it came from Hayden, McConnell, or the president. Every shrewd person I know thinks it came from one or more of the advisers close to Obama with whom he would normally have shared it. But whoever leaked the information got nothing for it.

The leaks came from people who were simply indifferent—or hostile—to the government's ability or right to keep any information secret.

This kind of indifference has long affected the press and the public. Here, for example, is a sentence of a kind we read so often that we no longer notice its puzzling, even oxymoronic use of the word secret:

> Earlier this summer, the United States resumed secret drone flights performing military surveillance in the tribal areas to provide Pakistani commanders with a wide array of videos and other information on militants, according to American officials.[21]

There is no meaningful sense in which these operations are secret. They may be classified, they may be unacknowledged, but they aren't secret, as this reference to them in the *New York Times* proves. As this indifference to secrecy spreads, it is bound to affect relations between the intelligence and political communities in both the executive and legislative branches. There is again less trust, and where there is less trust there will be less candor. Gresham's law when applied to information will do its work: Bad information will drive out the good. The dross will be shared, and the gold nuggets taken out of circulation and held privately. This would be dangerous in any government, and in a democracy, poisonous. But it is happening.

Candor in official documents is difficult enough in the best of circumstances. In the most recent (2009) edition of the unclassified *Quadrennial Intelligence Community Review*, which is prepared by experts from a variety of intelligence agencies, the authors' task was to forecast America's position in the world in the year 2025. This is a difficult undertaking, to be sure, but psychological ambivalence and political sensitivity muddled the overarching conclusion, as illustrated by this sentence: "Although U.S. influence will decline, America and its ideals will retain global preeminence." Since preeminence is largely measured by influence, it is difficult to know what, if anything, this sentence means, and in any case it is contradicted several pages later,

where we read of "the declining military, economic, and technological preeminence of the U.S."[22] Possibly these inconsistencies resulted
entirely from a breakdown in the usually rigorous editing process, but I
don't think so. This kind of language results from public officials' reluc-
tance to speak plainly about the relative decline of American influence
for fear of being accused of not believing in the unlimited greatness of
the United States. For results that are both imaginative and candid,
projects like the *Quadrennial Review* should be handled by the open-
source arm of the intelligence community and contracted out to three
or four trusted private firms *in several different countries.*[23]

As early as 1992, the chairmen of the House and Senate intelligence committees began pushing for more use of open-source information, to no effect.[24] Four years later the Aspin-Brown Commission
proposed that the collection and analysis of open-source information
be a "top priority." Again, the idea went nowhere. Secret organizations
have a built-in bias in favor of classified over unclassified information.
Any bias is suspect, but in the tsunami of data created by the information revolution, this particular bias is a serious handicap.

Only in the aftermath of the attack on the Twin Towers did the
idea of an emphasis on open-source information gain traction. In July
2004 the 9/11 Commission recommended the creation of an open-
source intelligence agency.[25] And in March 2005 the WMD Commission recommended creating open-source cadres within both the CIA
and the Office of the DNI.[26] Later that year, spurred by these reports,
the new DNI, John Negroponte, and the CIA director at the time, Porter Goss, announced the creation of an Open Source Center, to be
housed at the CIA.[27] But the wizards of Langley immediately put their
stamp on the new center by ensuring that nobody could work in it who
didn't have a top-secret clearance, thus closing the lid on really imaginative change. As a result, the best work on open-source information
now takes place in private companies that contract with agencies to collect and analyze open-source information. This is actually an excellent
arrangement, but the fact that it took years to achieve it is an accurate

indication of the acute resistance to change at big agencies like the
CIA, the NSA, and the FBI.

Operating in a classified environment is a serious constraint—
more serious than most people in that environment realize. It is a drag
on how they communicate, whom they communicate with, and how
they do business, and it disconnects them from the realities of the
commercial world. Yet people who have never operated outside that
environment cannot imagine doing business any other way. Young
recruits entering the business are frequently turned off by our agencies' stodgy business practices, conflict aversion, and mind-numbing
PowerPoint presentations. Dispelling this atmosphere would dramatically improve the intelligence business.[28]

At the same time, clandestine and covert operations are best undertaken by people who have trained for years in the dark-side atmosphere,
and who will never fully trust people who do not share that background.
This ethos is a matter of survival. Efforts to open up that operational
environment are misguided and doomed to fail. So as we examine the
present and future state of our intelligence agencies, we see an increasingly irreconcilable disparity between open-source and covert. The former cannot operate effectively in a top-secret mind-set, and the latter
can't work without it. Secrecy and openness simply cannot get along in
the same organization, and this is why the bundle of activities that con-
stitute the intelligence business will inevitably begin to come apart over
the next decade. This unbundling is overdue. If we are going to protect
what must be kept secret, we must separate it from what is not secret.

A salutary effect of the separation would be to stop funding secret
organizations that produce mere journalism. During the French presidential election of 2007, while I was the national counterintelligence
executive, I did an experiment. Several times a week I read official
reports of the contest between Nicolas Sarkozy, the center-right candidate who eventually won, and Ségolène Royale, the Socialist Party
candidate. I also read accounts of the campaign in the *New York Times*,
the *Washington Post*, and the Paris daily *Le Monde*. There was no

information in the official reports that could not be found in the *Times* and the *Post*, and none of these American sources was as detailed or interesting as what I could read in *Le Monde*. It was obvious that the official "intelligence" was written from unclassified sources, yet the official reports were classified "confidential." Why? *Because that's what we think. The sources may be unclassified*, I was told, *but our conclusions are classified.* In some cases this reasoning makes sense, but in this case the only "conclusions" were a rehash of publicly available polling data.

Another excuse for producing classified intelligence of this ilk is that policy makers want it. Like people in the intelligence business, policy makers in the White House and on Capitol Hill privilege the classified over the unclassified, believing that the top-secret stuff must be the real juice. Besides, access to classified information is a sign of power. Playing to this mystique is craven. When intelligence officials have nothing secret to report, it's their job to say so. The State Department can do the rest. Rehashing unclassified information about foreign affairs is a long mile from the core business of intelligence, which is stealing secrets.

**IN A WORLD** where secrets, if you can keep them at all, don't stay secret for long, the best way to run an intelligence agency is to focus tightly on the parts of the business that are really secret and separate them from the rest. You spend more money on open-source collection and analysis, and let them happen in controlled but unclassified space. You beef up counterintelligence. And you pay much more attention to the electronic handling and dissemination of information—which is the subject of the next chapter.

Transparency exposes the government's secrets in the same way that it exposes corporate secrets and invades personal privacy—and for the same reasons of ready electronic access. Electronic information is liquid, and liquid leaks. Apart from the technology, our culture also disposes us toward transparency and inures us to the exposure of

information that not long ago would have been carefully and successfully hidden. Advertisements for adult diapers or remedies for sexual
dysfunction, and an eager willingness to parade one's marital failures
on television, are enabled by a profound cultural change. Whether
you call this change an increase in candor or a decrease in shame—or
both—is irrelevant. The change cannot seriously be doubted, and it
makes us disinclined to keep secrets, or even to take secrecy seriously
as a useful value in human affairs. The analog at the national level is
a presidential adviser willing to retail information about covert operations to the media, and the everyday occurrence of headlines about
"secret" military operations in Iraq or Pakistan. To the extent we are in
a postprivacy world, we are also in a postsecrecy world.

The terms *postprivacy* and *postsecrecy* are useful if they help us
understand a social sea change and the parallel between privacy and
secrecy, but they are exaggerations. What we can say without exaggeration is that organizational secrecy and personal privacy are both under
relentless assault. Secrets are harder and harder to keep, and matters
that are successfully kept secret are likely to remain so for shorter periods of time, assuming they're of any interest to anybody. This is true
whether the secrets are personal (like your medical records) or organizational (like CIA rendition flights) or both (like the allegedly fudged
expense records involving a personal relationship that reportedly cost
the chairman of Hewlett-Packard his job). If you're unknown and say
nothing controversial, our beehive culture will leave you in peace. If
you do or say something controversial, or simply become well-known,
you risk being swarmed. People will think twice before saying what
they think. This is a nasty prospect created by cybervigilantes.

It would be absurd, however, to think that there will be no more
secrets.[29] As long as people feel any vestige of shame or can suffer from
guilt, they will want to keep secrets. As long as secrets convey power
over others, people will keep secrets. Blackmail is merely the extreme
case of such power. The mere fact that someone knows that you
know his secrets conditions his behavior. "Write nothing down, throw

nothing away"[30] would be the motto of any organization small enough, and secret enough, to get away with it. In business affairs people will keep secrets as long as information conveys commercial advantage. As long as governments want to engage in activities they wish to disavow, as long as governments do not trust one another and fear for their own security, they will go to great lengths to keep secrets and discover what the others are up to—and to try to hide how they go about it.

I have former colleagues who spend most of their working lives dealing chiefly in the most sensitive information imaginable, with lives hanging in the balance. For them the discussion of openness is bewildering. But their world is opening up nevertheless. If we are serious about keeping secret the work such people do, our intelligence agencies should jettison everything that is not demonstrably done better on the dark side. Their kind of work does not thrive in an open environment. More than half a century ago an adviser to President Kennedy, McGeorge Bundy, observed a tendency to protect all information as if it were top secret. "The moment we start guarding our toothbrushes and our diamond rings with equal zeal," he said, "we usually lose fewer toothbrushes but more diamond rings."[31] Today we still classify far too much information, but that persistent tendency has obscured a far more pervasive development: We have gone to the opposite extreme, and as the WikiLeaks fiasco demonstrates, we now treat diamond rings like toothbrushes.

Transparency and network anarchy have disoriented us. Now it's time to regain our balance and manage this predicament.

# 10

## MANAGING THE MESS

EVERY PRESIDENT IN the last two decades has known that our networks are vulnerable to exploitation. The first President Bush told us in 1990, "Telecommunications and information processing systems are highly susceptible to interception, unauthorized electronic access, and related forms of technical exploitation."[1] Nineteen years later the Obama White House was delivering essentially the same message. "Without major advances in the security of these systems or significant change in how they are constructed or operated," its *Cyberspace Policy Review* warned, "it is doubtful that the United States can protect itself from the growing threat of cybercrime and state-sponsored intrusions and operations."[2] But this was no longer news.

In between, President Clinton warned in 1998 of the insecurities created by cyberbased systems and directed that "no later than five years from today the United States shall have achieved and shall maintain the ability to protect the nation's critical infrastructures from intentional acts that would significantly diminish" our security.[3] Five years later would have been 2003.

In 2003, as if in a repeat performance of a bad play, the second President Bush stated that his cybersecurity objectives were to prevent cyberattacks against our critical infrastructure, reduce our vulnerability to such attacks, and "[m]inimize damage and recovery time from cyber attacks that do occur."[4] Bush's objectives were essentially a restatement of Clinton's but with a new and welcome emphasis on resilience and recovery. However, none of these objectives has been met.

Such pronouncements have emerged like clockwork from the White House echo chamber, along with study groups, working groups, and "public-private partnerships" that produce recommendations that gather dust on some shelf. In August 2009, a presidential advisory committee issued a report on persistent insecurities in the public network and noted that previous assessments had reached similar conclusions in 1993, 1995, 1999, 2002, 2005, and 2007! This chronicle of executive inaction will be of interest chiefly to historians and to members of Congress who, in the aftermath of a disaster that we can only hope will be relatively minor, will be *shocked* to learn that the nation was electronically unprepared to deal with cyberespionage or -attacks. Yet the situation is growing worse.[5] In 2010 the commander of USCYBER-COM, the NSA's General Keith Alexander, acknowledged for the first time that even our classified networks have been penetrated.[6]

Most people in government are neither stupid nor lazy, and the civilian and military personnel responsible for our networks are painfully conscious of our vulnerabilities and work hard to minimize them. Some current efforts in Washington to deal with cyberinsecurity are promising—but so was Sisyphus's fourth or fifth trip up the hill. The higher cybersecurity recommendations rise in the bureaucracy, the greater the chance they'll be watered down to achieve consensus, or sidelined. This is why we get continual declarations of urgency but little real progress. Translating repeated diagnoses of insecurity into effective treatment requires the political will to marshal the financial and organizational resources necessary to do something about it. The recent Bush administration came by that will too late in the game.

After his inauguration, President Obama dithered for nine months over the package of excellent recommendations from a nonpolitical team of civil servants,[7] but the administration's lack of interest was palpable. Unfortunately, Obama's cybersecurity proposal of May 2011, coming after a two-year delay, will not move the security needle far. The proposal is not without merit. In place of a patchwork of state laws dealing with notifications following data breaches, for example, it would create a single nationwide standard, and it would strengthen criminal penalties on cybercrime. But these changes deal with the consequences of insecurity; they will not make us more secure. The proposal would strengthen the Department of Homeland Security's cybersecurity authorities, but not by much. It breaks no new ground and would do little to raise security standards.[8] Obama's budget reflects a higher priority for cybersecurity than ever before, though proposals for the increase originated under his predecessor. And the president deserves credit for creating a new joint military organization called U.S. Cyber Command housed with the NSA at Fort Meade, Maryland, and led by the NSA director. But except in the Pentagon, progress on cybersecurity remains poor.

CYBERCOM integrates the defense of most of the Defense Department's networks and other national security networks, like those in the intelligence agencies. When directed, it also conducts military cyberspace operations. Many issues remain to be worked out regarding CYBERCOM's operations, but it is a robust command[9] with meaningful authorities over Defense Department and national security networks, and it is supported by the nation's most advanced capabilities.[10] CYBERCOM also brings under one roof the historically separate offensive authorities of the Defense Department and the defensive and intelligence-gathering authorities of the NSA. This is important for two reasons. First, as we have seen, it is impossible in most cases to tell the difference between a foreign penetration designed merely to gather intelligence and one to preposition a cyberattack weapon. Calling a meeting of lawyers to determine who can deal with that kind of situation and what tools they can use doesn't work when facing threats at network speed.

Second, we need offensive tools for strategic defense. When an aircraft carrier group goes to sea, for example, the admiral in charge of the group flies an air patrol with a radius of perhaps a thousand miles. Fighter aircraft have offensive capabilities, but in this case their mission is to defend ships, and the admiral needs to know what's coming before it arrives. Holding fire till you see the whites of their eyes may have worked at the Battle of Bunker Hill, but not anymore. If you wait for the incoming danger to reach you, you won't be able to defend against it. CYBERCOM solves this problem by letting the general in charge of defending national security networks use offensive tools outside his networks in order to know what's coming.[11] To be blunt, espionage is an essential aspect of defense. To know what's coming, we must be living inside our adversaries' networks before they launch attacks against us.[12]

The side of government that doesn't deal with national security matters (and that's most of it) presents a different and sadder picture. If an adversary launched a slow-motion, coordinated attack to corrupt the operations of the Treasury Department and of our key companies and infrastructure, how many hours or days would it take us to figure it out? We don't even have a mechanism in place to know what would be happening, let alone to do something about it. The departments of the executive branch—State, Treasury, Justice, Homeland Security, and so on—are isolated silos that in most circumstances are incapable of coordinated action. To understand why most government departments work so poorly together while the military coordinates its activities so well, it helps to look back at a time when the army and navy didn't work well together at all.

CONGRESS CREATED THE War Department in 1789 and the Navy Department nine years later, in 1798, and the two remained rigorously and jealously independent until after World War II. The secretary of war was the civilian head of the army, the navy had its own secretary, and each reigned supreme in his earthen or watery realm.[13] As a result, joint operations in wartime were hazardous affairs that produced as much friction as cooperation. Relations between the army and navy were so bad in Cuba during the Spanish-American War that "the army commander refused to turn captured Spanish ships over to the navy or allow a navy representative to sign the surrender document."[14] In theory the president could command them both, but by the twentieth century the task of presiding over the government had become too complex for the president to concern himself with the details of government operations, civilian or military. Unfortunately, this did not become clear until after the Pearl Harbor disaster.[15] During the war and for years afterward, the two services used different management systems, ensuring that logistical coordination was all but impossible.[16] "The whole organization belongs to the days of George Washington," reported Britian's senior liaison officer in Washington, Sir John Dill. His colleague, Air Marshal Sir John Slessor, was even more scathing: "The violence of interservice rivalry in the United States has to be seen to be believed and was an appreciable handicap to their war effort."[17]

In 1947 Congress split the War Department into the Department of the Army and the Department of the Air Force. (Land-based aircraft had previously been part of the army.) In 1949, Congress forced those two departments and the Navy Department into the newly created Department of Defense—but it did not abolish the separate military departments. DoD is still the only department of the U.S. government that contains departments within it, albeit at the subcabinet level, and the secretary of defense must still occasionally struggle to assert his control over the subordinate civilian military chiefs.[18] The National Security Act of 1947 created the Joint Chiefs of Staff, but neither that act nor the reforms of 1949 altered the separate command structures at the service level or the clubby and ineffective organization of the Joint Chiefs. We had a commander of the U.S. Army in Europe, for example, and we had a commander of the Atlantic Fleet, so the fleet and the army were commanded separately even when operating in the same theater. This dysfunctional organization contributed significantly to the vulnerabilities that led to the bombing of the marine barracks in Beirut in 1983, killing 299 American and French servicemen, and to the utter failure of the mission to rescue the hostages in Iran in 1980.[19]

In 1986 Congress shook this creaky system of military fiefdoms to its foundations when it passed the Goldwater-Nichols Act.[20] Goldwater-Nichols demoted the separate military departments into organizations that merely recruit, train, and equip soldiers, sailors, and airmen. It stripped the army, navy, and air force of all operational command authority and for the first time vested effective command authority in joint commands, each headed by a four-star officer from one of the services and today called a combatant commander, or COCOM. The COCOM's staff comes from all the services, and all units from all services within his theater fall under his command. At this writing (mid-2011), for instance, the commander of Pacific command in Honolulu is a navy admiral, but his deputy is an air force general and his senior enlisted officer is an army sergeant major. This pattern, or something like it, is repeated in all U.S. combatant commands, though the mix of forces of course varies depending on the mission. Pacific command is heavily naval for obvious reasons. Central command, which runs the wars in Iraq and Afghanistan, comprises members of the army, navy, air force, and marines working side by side from headquarters to the boots on the ground.

Joint organization has paid extraordinary operational dividends, but it was a struggle to make it work. Overcoming intense service-level loyalties took time. To accomplish that, the law made it effectively impossible to achieve high rank in any of the services without spending a "joint duty" tour in one of the other services. As Admiral Mike McConnell told me when he was the director of National Intelligence, "When I was a young naval officer, if I had said I was interested in a tour with one of the other services, my career would have been finished. After Goldwater-Nichols, I couldn't get ahead without it." Nine years after the act was implemented, one of its leading military opponents hailed it as "a major contribution to the nation's security."[21] This understates the case. This act is one of the most important organizational reforms in the history of the United States government—as important as our technological edge in making our military the most powerful in the world. All our military services are proud of it—and all of them resisted it fiercely at the time.

*Why isn't the rest of the government organized this way?*

**THIS QUESTION SHOULD** be at the forefront of public discussion about our civilian government, but it's rarely even asked. To be sure, there are great differences between the civilian departments and military services that command their members' dress and behavior and can send them to war. But it's simply wrong to assume that the organization of the military can teach us nothing about the organization of our civilian departments. From an organizational point of view, the military side of our government is light years ahead of the civilian side in its ability to attack problems jointly. This picture runs totally against the common perception of the defense establishment as bloated and inefficient, which it *is* when it comes to acquisition, purchasing, and various other support functions. Everyone has heard the stories of hundred-dollar toilet seats, overpriced hammers, and weapons systems that exist only because they benefit the constituents of powerful members of Congress. Operations, however, are a different matter. The American military's ability to plan and execute stupendously complex, efficient operations anywhere on the planet is astounding. This could not occur without the seamless integration of the services in the field. We see this not only overseas but also here at home. Hurricane Katrina and the destruction of New Orleans in 2005 were a humiliation for civilian government at all levels. The problem went far deeper than the incompetence of the then director of the Federal

Emergency Management Agency and various local officials. President George Bush's fumbling and hesitant mishandling of the disaster could not explain it either. Civilian government simply lacked the means to coordinate the necessary actions across the various departments of government: food relief, flood relief, law enforcement, housing, public order, compensation of victims, and so on.[22] At times it seemed that only the National Guard stood between chaos and some semblence of order. The inability to coordinate across departments hamstrings civilian government every day, not just in emergencies. We have fifteen federal agencies that oversee food safety, eighty-two programs to improve teacher quality spread over ten federal agencies, and eighty different economic development programs. These efforts waste billions and are without unified direction.[23]

All strategic problems, including cybersecurity, require cross-departmental integration. But it does not exist, and the interagency "coordination" process is clumsy and inefficient—just like military operations before 1986. Even as we begin to spend hundreds of millions of dollars on cybersecurity, we are pouring the money into the usual isolated departmental fiefdoms. Cross-departmental governance is extremely difficult—and not just in the United States. Doing it well requires an office with authority over the departments and the power to muscle entrenched and often parochial bureaucracies, and we don't have it. I am not suggesting the militarization of civilian departments. I am proposing the creation of a civilian mechanism of directive authority and responsibility above the departmental level, within the executive office of the president. The media, always addicted to the cliché, told us we were getting a cyber "czar" in 2009,[24] but the newly created cyber "coordinator" has no directive power and has yet to prove his value in coordinating, let alone governing, the many departments and agencies with an interest in electronic networks.

This lumbering charade of "coordination" rather than directed integration has been the theme of American federal interdepartmental

relations since World War II.[25] After the war, in 1947, Congress created the National Security Council, but the NSC's role is restricted
to advising the president on national security *policy*.[26] Policies are not
operations. Policies are set in the clouds, operations occur on the
ground, and the NSC has no power to drive policy from the clouds to
the ground. After 9/11, President Bush created a Homeland Security
Council along the NSC model. Its role was merely to "coordinate the
executive branch's efforts" in dealing with terrorism."[27] *Translation*: It
has the power to arrange meetings—but the real power over budgets,
programs, and personnel remains with the departmental secretaries.
Their power is written into law; even the president can't override it.
As a result, America's federal government is run by an awkward compromise among powerful fiefdoms—much like military operations in
World War II.[28] This is not a viable model for governing a powerful
nation in the twenty-first century.

This ineffective arrangement suits Congress, however, because
the power of individual executive departments mirrors the power of
congressional committee chairmen who control their budgets and oversee their programs and personnel. Fragmentation of executive functions
reflects fragmentation on Capitol Hill. The 9/11 Commission saw this
clearly. Of the scores of recommendations made by the 9/11 Commission, *all were adopted except those regarding Congress's appallingly
fragmented committee system*. As the commission noted, "The leaders
of the Department of Homeland Security now appear before eighty-
eight committees and subcommittees of Congress." And they all hold
hearings that squander vast amounts of valuable executive time. This
system is not only irrational, it's abusive of the people who are trying
to make the government work. "So long as oversight is governed by the
current congressional rules and resolutions," the commission said, "we
believe the American people will not get the security they want and
need." Ruefully, the commission added that Congress was unlikely to
reform itself without sustained public pressure,[29] and the last decade

has borne out that pessimistic conclusion. Even the 9/11 disaster was insufficient to produce change among our legislative princelings.

**CONGRESS ISN'T THE** only cause of operational dysfunction in cybersecurity, however, even in defense. For example, the most effective tool we have for testing the security of an information system is "red teaming." We assemble a red team of professional cyberburglars who are really good guys, and set them to work against one of our own systems. Not surprisingly, the gold standard for white-hat breaking and entering is set by the NSA's Information Assurance Directorate, whose red teams are virtually impossible to keep out.[30] But the ways they get in can teach you volumes about how to tighten your security. Unfortunately, however, the NSA's red teams require the consent of the system's owner before they may lawfully test a network, even within the Defense Department. This is like walking into a middle-school cafeteria and asking who wants to take a pop quiz. Not many hands go up. As a result, the Defense Department cannot apply red teaming where, based on risk assessment, it's most needed. Instead they use it haphazardly, with permission.[31] DoD doesn't need Congress in order to fix this.

On the nondefense side of cybersecurity, the story is worse. The Department of Homeland Security is a confederation of twenty-two agencies that were hurriedly nailed, glued, and stitched together in the wake of 9/11. It includes the Secret Service, the Coast Guard, customs, emergency management, cybersecurity, and a host of other functions from organizations with their own traditions, cultures, and incompatible electronic systems. Melding and governing this confederation has been a work in progress, to say the least. It took four decades (some would say five) to make DoD the effective boss of the military services after World War II, and it will take years before the DHS becomes an integrated department. The DHS has the legal authority and role to protect federal information systems other than "national security systems," which include those of the intelligence agencies. But the DHS lacks the talent, know-how, tools, and systems to do the job. The department has therefore struck a reluctant bargain with the NSA to use NSA tools and, in some cases, borrows personnel to improve federal cybersecurity in nondefense departments. Americans want more security, but they don't want our intelligence agencies in charge across the board. Consequently, the job is being done, more or less, with the NSA's help under the umbrella of the DHS's limited legal authorities. There is no alternative. Duplicating the NSA's capabilities would be astronomically expensive, and it could not be done even if money were no object, because there wouldn't be enough world-class expertise to staff two such agencies.[32] Nor should the DHS apologize for an arrangement that, on a limited basis, represents the kind of cross-departmental operations we should be aiming for. Meanwhile, neither the DHS nor the cyberczar has directive power to deal with agencies whose electronic security is poor, and Congress has been unwilling to create a permanent White House office of cybersecurity.[33] Progress on cybersecurity on the civilian side of government has therefore been painfully slow and unsatisfactory.

Meanwhile, we have awakened to the fact that our national security depends heavily on privately owned critical infrastructure and our economic might—assets that lie outside the defense-military-intelligence realm. Outside that realm the government isn't protecting us at all. If nonmilitary targets were attacked from abroad by land, sea, or air, the government would respond. But apparently this is not true when it comes to cyberattacks. This is a little noticed but momentous change in the oldest, most basic function of government, which is protecting the nation. Is this all bad? Maybe not. How could the government be responsible for protecting all our information systems unless we turned over control of all communications to the government? Perish the thought. Besides, the world is flexible and moves fast. Government is rigid and moves slowly.[34]

In short, the executive branch of the federal government is fragmented and Congress is dysfunctional. But why hasn't the private sector delivered better security?

## The Failure of Private Incentives

Change in the private sector is driven principally by two factors: market demand and liability. Unfortunately, liability has played virtually no role in achieving greater Internet security. This may be surprising until you ask: Liability for what, and who should bear it? When you buy software, it comes shrink-wrapped in transparent plastic, with a warning that if you break the wrapping, you accept the manufacturer's licensing terms (which usually limit its liability to the price you paid for the program). When you install the software, the installation program also typically requires you to click a button that says you agree to those terms. No click, no install. So right out of the box, you agree to terms that severely limit the manufacturer's liability for defects. And because software is licensed rather than sold, the implied warranty that might otherwise be available under the Uniform Commercial Code does not apply. Suing the software manufacturer for allegedly lousy security is therefore a game not worth the candle. Besides, how do you put a monetary value on the damages, say, from finding your computer is an enslaved member of a botnet run out of Russia or Ukraine? And how do you prove the problem was caused by the software rather than your own sloppy online behavior?

Asking Congress to create standards for software defects would be asking for trouble: *All* software is defective, because it's so astoundingly complicated that even the best of it hides surprises. Deciding what level of imperfection is acceptable is not a task you want your congressman to perform. Any such legislation would probably drive some creative developers out of the market. It would also slow down software development—which might not be all bad if it led to higher security. But the public has little or no understanding of the vulnerabilities inherent in poorly developed applications. On the contrary, people clamor for rapidly developed apps with lots of bells and whistles, so an equipment vendor that wants to control this proliferation of vulnerabilities in the name of security is in a tough spot.

Banks, merchants, and other holders of personal information do face liability for data breaches, and some have paid substantial sums for data losses under state and federal statutes granting liquidated damages for breaches. In one of the best-known cases, Heartland Payment Systems may end up paying about $100 million as a result of a major breach, not to mention millions more in legal fees. But the defendants in those cases are buyers, not makers and designers, of the hardware and software whose deficiencies create so many cyberinsecurities. Liability presumably makes these companies somewhat more vigilant in their business practices, but it doesn't make hardware and software more secure. This has scary implications. Many major banks and other companies, for example, already know they have been persistently penetrated by highly skilled, stealthy, and anonymous adversaries, very likely including foreign intelligence services and their surrogates. These firms spend millions fending off attacks and cleaning their systems, yet no forensic expert can honestly tell them that all advanced, persistent intrusions have been defeated. (If you have an expert who says he can, fire him immediately.)

Insurers play an important role in an effective liability regime, raising standards because they tie premiums to good practices. Good drivers, for example, pay less for auto insurance. Engineers who follow practices approved by their insurers pay less for professional liability insurance. Without a liability dynamic, however, insurers play virtually no role in raising cybersecurity.

If liability hasn't made cyberspace more secure, what about market demand? The simple answer is that software consumers buy on price, and they haven't been willing to pay for more secure software. In some cases the aftermath of identity theft is an ordeal, but in most instances of credit card fraud, U.S. banks absorb 100 percent of the loss, so their customers have little incentive to spend more for security. Most companies also buy on price, especially in the current economic downturn.

Unfortunately, we don't know whether consumers or corporate customers would pay more for security if they knew the relative insecurities of the products on the market. As J. Alex Halderman of the University of Michigan has noted, "[M]ost customers don't have enough information to accurately gauge software quality, so secure software and insecure software tend to sell for about the same price."[35] This could be fixed, but doing so would require agreed-upon engineering standards for judging products and either the systematic disclosure of insecurities or a widely accepted testing and evaluation service that enjoys the public's confidence. *Consumer Reports* plays this role for automobiles and other products, and it wields enormous power. The same day that *CR* issued a "don't buy" warning on the 2010 Lexus GX 460, Toyota took the vehicle off the market. A software-security rating service along the lines of *CR*, written in plain English (for consumers rather than computer engineers), would be a public service.

In short, the picture is bleak. But it's far from hopeless.

## What the Government Should Do

Here are seven areas in which federal initiatives would significantly improve cybersecurity by driving change in the private sector without legislating government standards that would inevitably prove clumsy and ineffective. They could be accomplished relatively quickly. They would not create new bureaucracies. They would not require reorganizing the executive branch. And they would enhance both privacy and security.

1. Trade regulation and contracting

   - **Use the government's enormous purchasing power to require higher security standards of its vendors.**

     The Federal Acquisition Regulation and its Defense equivalent are the bibles of U.S. government procurement of goods and services. The National Institute of Standards and Technology is the most influential standards-setting body in the United States. Together they could drive higher security into the entire market by ensuring federal demand for better products. These standards would deal with such topics as verifiable software and firmware, means of authentication, fault tolerance, and a uniform vocabulary and taxonomy across the government in purchasing and evaluation. Sound arcane? Maybe so, but we won't have federal standards for products if we can't even agree on how to evaluate them.

     In support of this effort, the Office of Management and Budget (OMB) should collaborate with the Office of the National Counterintelligence Executive to create a model for acquisition risk analysis that should be applied uniformly throughout the government. And the OMB, which wields the budget hammer, should enforce it.[36] Different agencies have different tolerations for risk. What may be acceptable in the Department of Housing and Urban Development may not be acceptable at the NSA, for example, but all our agencies should be measuring risk the same way. At present, that's not the case.

   - **Forbid federal agencies from doing business with any Internet service provider that is a hospitable host for botnets, and publicize the list of such companies.**

     The Department of Homeland Security and the FBI know who these ISPs are. Publishing a list of ISPs with which the government refuses to deal would also give other federal entities, state and local agencies, and private businesses a rational basis on which to take the same step. So

long as businesses make individual rather than group decisions about bad ISPs, they would have no antitrust liability.

• **Direct the Department of Justice and the Federal
Trade Commission to definitively remove the antitrust concern when U.S.-based firms collaborate on
researching, developing, or implementing security functions.**

Companies often cite the fear of antitrust law to explain
their lack of cooperation on cybersecurity. The fear is overblown, but the government can remove it entirely. The Justice Department and FTC have the ability, without changing
any laws, to approve one or more supervised forums in which
government and businesses could exchange threat information in near real time without endangering competition. This
step should be undertaken in collaboration with the European Union's antitrust authorities in order to reduce the risk
of conflicting international standards.

2. Role of the service providers

• **Require Internet service providers to notify customers whose machines have been infected by a botnet.**

The big ISPs, like AT&T, Verizon, and Comcast, could
quickly and easily cause a dramatic drop in Internet crime,
but for a combination of legal and commercial reasons they
don't. These firms monitor their networks 24/7, and they hire
top people to watch and interpret patterns in the network
traffic. They're not eavesdropping on particular conversations; they're observing larger trends in order to route traffic surges efficiently and protect their own networks from
attack—because they are constantly being attacked. So if
thousands of computers suddenly start sending messages to
a server in Belarus, the ISPs right away see an anomaly in
the traffic pattern. And they don't have to watch it very long
to know they're facilitating—or perhaps even hosting—a

botnet. Whether they can trace the botnet back to its source depends on the cooperation of foreign ISPs, which may not be forthcoming, but they can see which computers are enslaved.

"ISPs are in a unique position to be able to attempt to detect and observe botnets operating in their networks." That's the conclusion of a paper submitted by several Comcast officials to the independent Internet Engineering Task Force.[37] There are thousands of ISPs in the world, but fifty of them account for more than half of all spam worldwide.[38] Yet it's unlikely that you or anyone you know has been warned by their ISP that they're part of a botnet. Even a behemoth like Microsoft had to get a court order in 2010 to force the ISP VeriSign to take down 227 .com domains that the botnet Waledac was using to spit out 1.5 *billion* spam messages a day.[39]

If you ask an ISP official off the record why they don't take down botnets as a matter of course, the reason you're likely to get is "privacy." This is confusing if you're not a privacy lawyer, because ordinary people with common sense don't think the electronic privacy laws were meant to protect criminal behavior on the Internet. But under federal law it is a crime for anyone to intercept any wire, oral, or electronic communication.[40] This applies to you, me, Comcast, AT&T, and federal officials unless they have an order from a judge. Most privacy lawyers have thought this means that an ISP can't set a filter for botnet traffic on your computer—again, I mean watching traffic flow, not reading your e-mail— without violating the law. Since the law carries minimum damages in the amount of one thousand dollars per violation, a class action would undoubtedly be filed, and settling it would be very expensive. Fortunately, however, the act contains what's called the "service provider exception." That means that a provider of Internet services, like an ISP, can monitor traffic *if* it needs to do so in order to protect its own network—*but not to protect your network.* When this law was written in 1986, its authors conceived of the Internet as a big bicycle wheel, or a series of connected wheels, and imagined each spoke as a network. Companies were told, in effect, that it's okay to monitor and protect their own spokes—or if you were an ISP, your own hub. But if you're a hub, protecting a spoke is none of your business, so don't do it. In other words, every actor on the Internet, whether the actor was Grandpa or AT&T, was thought to occupy his own little territory that was separate from everyone else's little territory.

This is no longer a realistic conception of how the Internet works, if it ever was. You may think of yourself as just a spoke in a wheel, but you communicate through a hub. Your communications are part of the hub's traffic; they occur over the hub's networks. What's more, if your machine is corrupted, you threaten to corrupt those of everyone else who communicates with you through that hub *and beyond*— because the hubs and spokes are all connected. The reverse is also true: Corrupted users who communicate with you will contaminate you, whether they intend to do so or not. An attack on one part of a network is therefore an attack on the network itself—period. If you're going to defend the network, you've got to be able to defend it at every point. We do this in other aspects of civic life, but so far we don't do it on the Internet. For example, you can't legally drive a car with no brakes or headlights on a public roadway. If you do, you're a menace not only to your own safety, but also to the safety of everyone else. But that's not how privacy law currently works regarding electronic communications.

As presently understood, the service provider exception merely lets an ISP protect its own proprietary system. But

who has the responsibility to protect the whole ball of wax?
Nobody. Thus we have a legal regime that in the name of
privacy and freedom lets fraud thrive. This is perverse. As
currently understood (I believe it could be interpreted more
expansively), the law does not create more privacy and freedom (which would be good). It just creates more insecurity.
At least two ISPs have begun an interesting experiment of
notifying their subscribers when they are infected and putting them into a "walled garden."[41] The walled garden stops
short of a quarantine or blockade, but others will know you're
in it and can decline to deal with you. The incentive to get
cleaned up is therefore strong, and the ISPs are in a prime
position to capture the remediation business.

So far, however, walled gardens have not caught on.
The reason is that ISPs compete on market share. Market
share drives the price of their stock, which in turn drives
their behavior. To drive market share, the ISPs compete on
breadth of coverage—we've all seen the back-and-forth ads
with blue and red maps—but they don't compete so much
on quality, and not at all on security. The plain truth is, they'd
rather have you corrupted *but on their network* than clean
but on somebody else's network. And they fear that if they
told you you're in a botnet, you'd unfairly blame them and
switch to one of their competitors.

Reducing botnets would not solve all the problems of
our Internet security, but it would be the single biggest step
toward cleaning our networks, and one of the easiest. To
accomplish it, we should permit—not require—ISPs to
block traffic from infected customers according to a subscriber's wishes. But we should *require* them to flag all such
traffic, so others could refuse to accept it. Rules like this
should apply in a neutral way to all technologies and companies and to all components of the media, whether e-mail,

Web sites, or proprietary channels such as social networking sites. ISPs could then compete on how well they do this, and customers could decide whether they want the service at all.

These services could be bundled into basic fees or priced separately, like the telephone service that lets you refuse calls from those who block their numbers. If others are put on notice and still want to accept dangerous traffic, let them. You're free to visit bad neighborhoods at 3:00 A.M. for any encounter you choose—but if you come back from an electronically bad neighborhood with an electronically transmitted disease, you should be tagged, so others can avoid you if they choose. Permitting the government to define the network behaviors that trigger this requirement would be a bad idea, however. Governmental regulation cannot keep up with the technology,[42] and letting the government decide whose communications are dangerous would be a bad precedent. Rather, government's role should be limited to stating the general requirement and tasking a private consortium of ISPs to create flexible rules to implement it.

The primary enforcement model here is not the police or highway department; it's public health. Early twentieth-century public health authorities had to deal with highly infectious diseases, such as tuberculosis (alas, they still do). At the extreme they resorted to quarantine measures, but promoting better hygiene was their focus. Cyber systems are becoming like human systems that constantly encounter microbes and viruses but learn to fight them off. One appealing aspect of this approach is that the government doesn't have to do most of it. The ISPs are communication gateways and uniquely well suited to act as health monitors. Another advantage of the steps I propose is that the market would quickly correlate infections with particular software makers and network platforms. This, in turn, could drive competitive improvements in the way software is engineered. Flawless software engineering is an impossible goal. Rather, like an organic system, software should be designed to contain the consequences of failures and to permit recovery with minimal disruption.[43]

The public has no idea how to achieve security, and even if it were willing to be inconvenienced to get it (it isn't), few people or businesses know how. Most people are not computer scientists, just as they are not auto mechanics. They just want seamless convenience—but without creating unreasonable risk to their personal credit or corporate secrets. That's where the anarchic Internet has failed. This is why virtual private networks are becoming the norm in the business world, and why the Internet has begun to fragment into a world of proprietary profit-making channels like social networking sites or Apple's iPhone (which rigorously controls the applications you can run on it).[44] We are watching a classic pattern in which a capitalist culture nurtures innovation, lets it flourish, and finally figures out how to make it pay. There is no point celebrating the first phase while lamenting the last. They go hand in hand.[45]

3. Energy standards

- **Direct the Federal Energy Regulatory Commission (FERC) to require the North American Electric Reliability Commission (NERC) to establish standards that limit the ability of utilities to connect their industrial control systems directly or indirectly to a public network.**

  We saw earlier that our scheme for establishing reliability standards for this critical industry is off the rails. The Energy Department's inspector general has reached the same conclusion, noting in appropriately bland language that current standards do "not include essential security requirements."[46] FERC's ability to create standards has been hamstrung by the legislation that created it, and NERC is heavily influenced by the grid's owners and operators. Amending the statute would be desirable, but it won't happen soon. Meanwhile, FERC should direct NERC to begin establishing standards in this area, where none now exist. If we're serious about protecting our critical infrastructure, we must begin to restrain the connection of the electricity grid to public networks.

4. Tax code

- **The Internal Revenue Code is a powerful driver of corporate behavior. Use it.**

  The Internal Revenue Code is full of incentives and punishments to encourage or discourage behavior according to Congress's collective preferences. If we want to encourage capital investment, for example, we accelerate the rate at which capital depreciates, creating larger paper losses to write off against current income. If we want to discourage fancy business lunches, we limit the percentage of the expense that can be written off. If we want to help working families with modest incomes, we create a child-care allowance. And so on. We'll know when Congress has become serious about securing the nation's networks when it begins using tax incentives to encourage investment in cybersecurity.

5. Research

  Congress should increase support for public and private research in the following areas:

  - **Attribution techniques and identity standards**

    Reliable, swift attribution of hostile foreign or unlawful behavior on our networks is as essential in cyberspace as it is on the sidewalk. It's easy to commit espionage and other cybercrimes because nobody knows who you are unless they devote inordinate resources to finding out, and sometimes it can't be done at all. As we saw in chapter three, this is known as the attribution problem, and it has three levels. First, what machine launched the attack or the malware? Second, who was at the keyboard? Third, whom were they working for? For intelligence and criminal investigation purposes, all three levels are critical, but we're often stuck on the first level. In the consumer context, authentication techniques should vary according to the value of the transaction. Browsing a catalog could be done anonymously, but buying the furniture should require verification of the buyer's credentials. In a business context, authentication techniques should vary according to the sensitivity of the information you want to access. In a criminal context, the government should be able to trace and attribute behavior under legally defined circumstances, which ordinarily should include judicial oversight. In the decades before the recent advent of phone number spoofing, no one thought it was an invasion of privacy when a phone number could be conclusively associated with a particular phone. You could block your caller ID—and others could block anonymous calls. In most circumstances, however, your call could be traced. To return to that level of accountability in cyberspace, we need a robust public-private research effort into better attribution techniques.[47]

- **Verifiable software and firmware, and the benefits of moving more security functions into hardware**

    The greatest technological challenge to cybersecurity is the near impossibility of reliably evaluating the security of electronic systems, hardware, and code. We've known since the mid-1980s that finding subversive code in the much simpler systems of that era was overwhelmingly difficult. Today's systems are far more complex. We cannot assure security by examining a computer chip with millions of logic gates or a software program with a million or more lines of code.[48]

This inability has become a strategic problem for Western countries, because we have mostly offshored our chip manufacturing and software writing to companies in Asia. These companies, with the guiding hand of foreign intelligence and security services, can then plant hooks or backdoors in systems that we depend on but cannot evaluate.[49] This problem cannot be fixed with a mercantilist commitment to buying only your own nation's goods. "Made in USA" doesn't tell you much when a product that's assembled here contains components from several different countries. Or when a U.S. company makes an identical product in three different countries. Or when a product that's actually made in Texas contains software written in Russia. Or when the software was written in this country—by Chinese programmers.[50] The industrial supply chain is global, and reversing that trend would be an economic disaster. But globalization brings security vulnerabilities. Public support for research in this area would increase our ability to evaluate critical components and encourage products to be designed with evaluation in mind.

- **Feasibility of an alternative Internet architecture**

When I was a little kid, I met a big kid who knew how to make long-distance phone calls for free on a pay phone. He'd make pinging sounds into the phone, and these sounded to the operator like he was dropping quarters into the slot, so she'd put the call through. He could do this because the phone company had built the system so that data (his voice) and instructions (his payments, which authorized a connection) resided in the same memory. AT&T had a huge investment in that technology, but eventually AT&T abandoned it for an electronic switching system that was far more secure.

The Internet today works like pay phones did when I was a kid. Joe Markowitz, a former director of the CIA's

Community Open Source Program Office, thinks it's time to move away from that model. "We should get rid of IP"—that's the current Internet protocol—"and go to a stratified network where we take the control channel out of the subscriber space," Markowitz says.[51] Advocating a hugely expensive change in Internet architecture now would be premature. But it is not premature to fund research into alternatives that would address this fundamental weakness of the Internet.

6. Securities regulation

- **Electric utilities that issue bonds should be required to disclose in the risk factors section of their prospectuses whether the command-and-control features of their SCADA networks are connected to the Internet or other publicly accessible networks.**

    As we saw in chapter five, companies that expose their SCADA systems to the Internet have assumed the risk of severe disruption. That risk should be disclosed to the holders of their securities and to bond rating agencies. Issuers might rebel, but many of them that follow this risky practice *know* it creates an "unresolved security issue."[52] SCADA networks were built for isolated, limited access systems. Allowing them to be controlled via public networks is rash.

- **Toughen public audit standards for cybersecurity.**

    Publicly traded companies with insecure networks jeopardize shareholders' investments. To be sure, the degree of risk may vary sharply among companies. A company that processes financial transactions, or whose value depends on its trade secrets, will have a substantially higher risk than a company that does not. But business interruption is a material risk for every public company, so bond rating agencies should evaluate that risk, and the Securities and Exchange Commission should audit for it.

7. International relations

- **The United States should engage like-minded democratic governments in a multilateral effort to make Internet communications open and secure.**

    Electronic outlawry is an international phenomenon. No government acting alone can reduce it to tolerable levels. Concerted multinational pressure should be brought to bear on states that do not punish international cybercrime. To some degree even China and Russia can be enlisted in this effort, but accomplishing this goal will require a willingness to bring severe pressure, including financial pressure, on uncooperative governments.

    Beyond crime prevention, however, the prospect for a broad strategic consensus among the major powers is limited. China, Russia, Iran, and other authoritarian countries would like nothing better than a return to the days when governments could control what their populations could read, know, and publish. These governments will regrettably succeed to some degree within their own countries.[53] During the Egyptian revolution of 2011 we saw an authoritarian government that owned the Internet "pipes" shut down that country's electronic communications in a vain effort to keep its citizens isolated from events in Cairo.[54] In Russia, the Soviet Union may have fallen, but the Leninist tactic of stealing and twisting the vocabulary of freedom to oppressive ends has not. The Russian rhetorical foray against "information aggression" is a prime example of the revival of this tactic. Aggression to the Russian government is anyone's attempt to say anything it doesn't want its population to hear. The effort by Russia, China, Zimbabwe, and other authoritarian governments to drive this view into international organizations and international law has become intense, and it must be vigorously opposed by a united coalition of democratic nations with a common

program. This effort will require more than concerted opposition to an agenda devised in Moscow or Beijing, however. It
will require a clear vision of what we want as well as what we
don't want—and that implies a hardheaded program for Internet communications that includes security as well as liberty.

## What the Private Sector Should Do

But why wait for the government to do something?

The immediate vulnerabilities in most systems are not technological
or legal, and the government does not create them. They stem from the
failure to implement available technology and to manage people and
systems intelligently. A report released in early 2011 showed that 73 percent of companies surveyed had been hacked, but 88 percent of them
spent more money on coffee than on securing their Web applications.[55]
In most public and private organizations I'm familiar with, the biggest
contributors to information insecurity are managerial indifference and
erratic human behavior. Your employees, your partner, and your spouse
and kids don't practice good cybersecurity. You probably don't either. A
recent survey of IT professionals in Europe showed that half of them
failed to follow basic security practices for mobile devices.[56] Posting
cybersecurity rules and expecting your employees or partners to obey
them is a waste of breath and paper. When systems are designed to
leave security in the hands of users, you can forget about security. We
shouldn't expect our colleagues—let along Grandma and Grandpa—to
understand and implement security options on their computers, and
few people of any age or level of sophistication are willing to tolerate
security measures that are even slightly inconvenient. Besides, even
well-trained people make mistakes that can compromise entire systems.
These facts will not change. Systems must therefore be implemented
and managed to take them into account.[57]

Here are seven steps that every organization should take to

enhance its electronic security. This is not a how-to manual or an information security plan, which would be highly detailed and tailored to a specific organization. But these steps indicate some of the basic components of such a plan.

**1. Clean up your act.** A confidential survey commissioned in 2009 showed high levels of botnet code on the systems of a large number of household-name U.S. companies. I'm not at liberty to identify the companies—but it's likely that others will duplicate the survey and make the names public, because the survey was based on data gathered from open sources. It showed that a botnet attack—whether for criminal, political, or military purposes—could be launched from the systems of major U.S. corporations against other U.S. targets. If that occurred, the liability consequences could be devastating. As I noted earlier, cybermilitary operations could be launched against the United States from within the United States. This survey demonstrates that such operations could be launched from the systems of major U.S. companies. When another survey like this is eventually published, the shock wave is likely to be felt on Wall Street. Smart companies will clean up their acts before that happens. The alternative is to behave like the electric utility that had no means to monitor the communications traffic on its networks—but was confident it was secure because it had discovered no intrusions.

**2. Control what's on your system.** If you manage a commercial enterprise, you have the ability to know who is running unauthorized hardware or software on your system. The guy running peer-to-peer software may be undressing your company electronically without your knowing it. The other guy who connects his family laptop to your system may be infecting you with malware that could shut you down. You can monitor this and stop it from happening. You can also learn a lesson from the military and require employees to use only the encrypted memory sticks you issue them, and then clean and reissue them periodically.[58]

**3. Control who's on your system.** This is a matter of both physical and electronic access. Some systems are more sensitive than others and need to be locked up in special rooms accessible to very few. Others can be more open. But physical access to every system should be controlled. Some people have responsibilities that require them to have electronic access to information that others don't need to see. This sort of role-based access control used to be unusual except in sensitive government agencies; that's no longer the case. As the WikiLeaks fiasco demonstrated, there was no reason to give an army private in Iraq access to sensitive diplomatic traffic involving meetings with Zimbabwe's opposition leader or Iceland's economy. Giving your mailroom clerk access to your proprietary engineering drawings is the same sort of mistake. She doesn't need it, and she can destroy you with it.

Deciding who gets access is actually the easy part of access control, however. Companies must also remove access when people change jobs or leave the company. Many employees feel entitled to take sensitive information with them when they leave, and repeated surveys show that many plan to do so. They steal whatever's most sensitive: the customer database, M&A plans, financials, R&D plans.[59] Managing this vulnerability requires close integration between human resources, information security, and physical security.

**4. Protect what's valuable.** You can't protect everything, and you certainly can't protect everything equally well. This is a matter of understanding the difference between diamonds and toothbrushes, as McGeorge Bundy put it.[60] Identify the business plans and intellectual property whose loss would cause serious harm to your company. Personally identifiable and sensitive health care information must also be protected carefully. None of this information belongs on your e-mail server. Design your server architecture and access controls accordingly. And make sure the information is encrypted to a high standard.

Most data breaches are caused by carelessness and bad management—like allowing sensitive information to be carried around on portable devices without encryption. In August 2008, a laptop containing the unencrypted personal information of about thirty-three thousand travelers registered by the U.S. Transportation Security Administration's Fast-Pass program—this is the program that lets trusted, preregistered travelers zip onto airplanes without the usual security hassles—was stolen from the San Francisco airport. A month later Tennessee State University reported as missing a thumb drive with the financial records of nine thousand students. That kind of information does not belong on a flash drive, and it should have been encrypted. If you're a manager, the question is not whether your employees will lose laptops or flash drives. The question is how many will get lost—and what will be on them.[61] Yet most companies have no policies governing mobile media. Even fewer enforce the policies they have.

**5. Patch rigorously.** Patches are software fixes for newly discovered software vulnerabilities; software vendors issue them regularly. Yet studies have shown that many penetrations of commercial systems take place through unpatched vulnerabilities. In 71 percent of those cases a patch had actually been available but not used *for more than a year*.[62] Firms that behave this way are like drivers who leave the keys in their car overnight on a city street with the windows open. They shouldn't be surprised when it's gone in the morning. The patch regimen you should follow depends on the intricacies of your system. Some firms should automate patching. Others, where patching cannot be centrally controlled, should automatically shut out users who fail to install them. Some firms that do have central servers cannot patch automatically, because they must first test the effect of patches on interrelated systems. In any case, a systematic and rigorous approach to patching is elementary. If you can't manage it yourself, providers of cloud services can do it for you.

**6. Train everybody.** If you don't train and retrain your personnel, don't be surprised when they do things that horrify you. The organizers of the DEFCON conference in 2010 ran a contest to see who could get the most information from a Fortune 500 company. Lots of charm and a few lies produced appalling results. One contestant, for example, called an employee out of the blue and said he was a KPMG auditor working under a deadline and needed help, fast. He got the employee talking, and before long he had loads of confidential information.[63] This is a social engineering technique, like sending an e-mail that pretends to come from a friend of the recipient. These scams exploit the weakest link in the system—us. In this world, a company that fails to train its employees in social engineering techniques and other aspects of computer security is running unnecessary risks.

**7. Audit for operational effect.** Audits are not merely tortures you suffer at the hands of the government. They are tools of managerial control. If you can't audit your electronic networks, you have no idea what's occurring on them. If you don't want certain activities to happen on your networks, design them to make those activities impossible. If you want to permit a particular activity only under certain circumstances, design the system so that the activity cannot occur unless it is authorized. Then make sure the authorization can be audited and the audit trail can't be tampered with.[64] Unfortunately, many companies that should be doing this don't.

**8. Manage overseas travel behavior.** In most countries, you shouldn't expect any privacy in Internet cafés, hotels, offices, or public places. Hotel business centers and phone networks are regularly monitored in many countries. In some countries hotel rooms are often searched. Transmitting sensitive government, personal, or proprietary information from abroad—or even taking it abroad—is therefore risky. The risk is not limited to the information you take with you, however. Security services and criminals can also insert malicious software into your device through any connection they control—like in the hotel. They can also do it wirelessly if your device is enabled for wireless. When you connect to your home server, the malware can migrate to your business, agency, or home system, can inventory your system, and can send information back to the security service or freelance culprit. You cannot eliminate this risk, but you can minimize it by following the guidelines published by the Office of the National Counterintelligence Executive.[65]

Steps like these must be driven deep into the bones of an organization to become effective, and that requires leadership and follow-through. Whatever money companies spend on expert advice in setting up and managing their systems will be cheap compared to the cost of losing their intellectual property, or the leaking of sensitive information, or rebuilding their systems from scratch after they discover advanced, persistent malware that their best experts can't clean up.

**I BEGAN THIS BOOK** with an image of Philip Johnson's iconic Glass House, whose transparency eventually became intolerable even for its designer. And then I proceeded to show how all of us—including our companies, our government and military, and even our intelligence agencies—are now living in a collective glass house. Unlike the transparency of Philip Johnson's sleeping arrangements, information transparency now threatens much more than our diminished modesty. The level of Internet crime is staggering. Our companies and government are under relentless cyberassault twenty-four hours a day, and they are bleeding—we are bleeding—military secrets, commercial secrets, and technology that drive our standard of living and create our power as a nation. The astounding advances in the electronic processing and storage of information that have given us so much wealth and pleasure have also left us nearly defenseless against endemic crime and systematic espionage by foreign intelligence services, criminal gangs, and unscrupulous competitors. Much of the crime originates in Eastern Europe and Nigeria. The most persistent espionage—particularly economic espionage—originates in China. Yet as bad as this hemorrhage of vital information continues to be, the impending danger is even greater. As we saw when we examined our electricity grid and other critical infrastructure, electronic systems do not merely create and store information; they keep the lights on and make things work. If you can penetrate electronic networks to steal information, you can also corrupt them or shut them down. And unlike Philip Johnson, we don't have an electronic version of his Brick House we can move into. Put simply, we have become America the Vulnerable.

The United States cannot defend the electronic networks that control our energy supply, keep aircraft from colliding in midair, clear financial transactions, or make it possible for the president to communicate with his cabinet secretaries. We cannot permit this situation to continue and remain in control of our destiny. For the time being, no nation is likely to risk all-out conflict by attacking our infrastructure, but as I indicated in "June 2017," our power can be undermined by incursions that do not lead to open war. In any case, it would be profoundly foolish, and weak, to consign our security to the goodwill of other nations, whose intentions may change. It may be unwise for China, Russia, or the United States to upset the fragile limitations on cyberoperations that each now observes, but other powers will achieve parallel capabilities and may prove less restrained. Meanwhile, the vast gap between the capabilities of advanced nation-states and of transnational terrorist organizations and criminal gangs will continue to narrow, and these groups are unlikely to be restrained by the fears of retaliation or risk of economic collapse that create a measure of stability among interdependent nations. In the meantime, the assaults on our systems continue around the clock, and cyberespionage against American and other Western companies has reached an unparallelled level.

This mess can be managed, and the vulnerabilities reduced, but only with an energized commitment from a government willing to bring concerted power to bear on its own departments and from a private sector willing to harden its systems. It will also require Americans to recognize that the common good depends on the common network, which must be defended and strengthened. The steps I've proposed are a modest but essential beginning.

# ACKNOWLEDGMENTS

Many friends and colleagues supported me in the writing of this book, though I claim all the warts as my own. Professor Harvey Rishikof of the National War College read and commented on the entire manuscript and enriched it greatly. Other friends and colleagues read portions of the book in various stages of completion or have made valuable contributions to my understanding in the course of our working relationship. With most of them I have spent countless hours in discussion: Michael Assante, Stewart Baker, Scott Borg, Spike Bowman, Jonathan Cerrito, Robert Deitz, Thomas Geoghegan, Eric Haseltine, Melissa Hathaway, Jeff Jonas, Thomas Kellerman, Susan Landau, Martin Libicki, Thomas Malatesta, Brian McAndrew, Richard Schaeffer, Joseph Weiss, Rick Wilson, and Prescott Winter. Stephen Spoonamore, a cyberforensics expert and founder of ABS Materials, Inc., also read the entire manuscript and made many useful suggestions, but more than that, he has for several years been one of my tutors in the black and white arts of cybersecurity and defense.

Comments on my various papers and remarks at the Minerva Project on "Explorations in Cyber International Relations" also found their way into the manuscript in one form or another. This a joint program in cyber research between the Massachusetts Institute of Technology and Harvard University, under the direction of professors Nazli

Choucri and Stuart Madnick of MIT, senior research scientist David Clark of MIT, and professors Venkatesh Narayanamurti and Joseph Nye of Harvard. This program does something lamentably unusual: It brings together computer scientists, engineers, policy specialists, and lawyers to deal with a common set of issues. Each of these groups, by itself, tends to get cyberpolicy wrong. The scientists and engineers usually miss the political sensitivities and don't know the law, and the policy types and lawyers rarely understand the underlying technology they propose to regulate or the speed at which it changes. When put into the same room, the enriched perspectives and combined brainpower of these groups can produce really constructive results.

I have benefitted immeasurably from interaction over many years with two distinguished groups. The first is the Standing Committee on Law and National Security of the American Bar Association, whose current chair is Professor Rishikof. The second is a group of scholars and current and former civil servants and military officers who meet together regularly under the benign hand of Jennifer Sims, director of intelligence studies at Georgetown University's Walsh School of Foreign Service.

My superb research assistant, Stephanie Grosvenor, repeatedly astonished me with her swift, energetic, and imaginative pursuit of the telling detail I needed to make an obscure point clear. I take pleasure in knowing that her career has begun to blossom.

I am grateful to General Michael V. Hayden, USAF (Ret.), for giving me the extraordinary opportunity to work for him at the National Security Agency, and to General Keith B. Alexander, USA, for permitting me to continue that service as the agency's inspector general. Without that opportunity this book could not have been written. I am also grateful to General Alexander for bringing me back to the NSA several years later as his senior counsel to advise on public-private cooperation on cybersecurity.

Following my initial tour at the NSA, Ambassador John Negroponte, the nation's first director of National Intelligence, gave me the opportunity to serve as his "NCIX," or National Counterintelligence Executive. I am indebted to him and to his successor, Vice Admiral Mike McConnell, USN (Ret.), for retaining me in that capacity. The impact of my years in their service is evident throughout this book.

For my education in cyberlaw, policy, and operations, however, I am above all indebted to scores of former colleagues at the NSA and the Office of the Director of National Intelligence (including the Office of the NCIX), many of whom I cannot name. From them I learned such things as the elements of traffic analysis, the knotty technical and legal mysteries of electronic surveillance, and the astonishing practical applications of mathematical and scientific principles I could barely grasp. I am proud to have been their colleague and to consider many of them my friends.

In Victoria Pope I am blessed with a wise and lovely wife and an accomplished editor. She watered my spirit, encouraged this project from start to finish, and had no compunction about telling me what didn't work. Our daughters, Clara Brenner and Abby Stanglin, proved to be shrewd as well as supportive critics. Victoria also had the sense to leave the real work to my editor at The Penguin Press, Eamon Dolan, who taught me new lessons in close reading and the uses of a sharp razor. Each pass of the manuscript back and forth between us brought greater precision and clarity, and I thank him for it. I am also fortunate in having the best of all possible agents, Andrew Wylie, and Scott Moyers, formerly of the Andrew Wylie Agency and now publisher of The Penguin Press.

I owe thanks also to my law firm, Cooley LLP, for their generosity in affording me the encouragement and time to complete this work while reimmersing myself in a law practice now devoted in part to grappling with the problems described in this book.

Finally, in keeping with the expansive fashion in these matters, I should mention that while our sybaritic cocker spaniel Travis died midway through the project, he never wavered in his enthusiasm for whatever I was doing, so long as he was well fed. Oliver, our blind, demented, and recently defunct twenty-year-old Russian cat, had an uncanny way of caterwauling whenever I most required peace and quiet, and although I have discounted malicious suggestions that he is a sleeper agent of an unnamed foreign agency, surely this book would have appeared six months earlier without his participation.

# NOTES

## INTRODUCTION

1. The figure of $5 billion comes from the reported cost of developing quiet drive technology for the navy's DD-21 destroyers. Harold Kennedy suggests an R&D figure of $3 billion to $5 billion, but my analysis of the budget suggests the higher figure. "Navy Propulsion System Approaches Critical Stage," *National Defense*, March 2001, at www.nationaldefensemagazine.org/archive/2001/March/Pages/Navy_Propulsion4279.aspx, accessed February 12, 2011.
2. "Red Storm Rising," *Government Computer News*, August 17, 2006, at http://gcn.com/Articles/2006/08/17Red-storm-rising.aspx?p=1, accessed August 22, 2009.
3. Brian Grow and Mark Hosenball, "Special Report: In Cyberspy vs. Cyberspy, China Has the Edge," Reuters, April 14, 2011, at www.reuters.com/article/2011/04/14/ctech-us-china-usa-cyberespionage-idCATRE73D24220110414, accessed April 30, 2011.
4. Wikipedia, "Moore's Law," at http://en.wikipedia.org/wiki/Moore's_law, accessed December 7, 2010.
5. "Global Mobile Statistics 2011," MobiThinking, March 2011, at http://mobithinking.com/stats-corner/global-mobile-statistics-2011-all-quality-mobile-marketing-research-mobile-web-stats-su, accessed April 30, 2011.
6. Executive Office of the President, "National Security Strategy," May 2010, at www.whitehouse.gov/sites/default/files/rss_viewer/national_security_strategy.pdf, accessed December 7, 2010.

## CHAPTER 1: ELECTRONICALLY UNDRESSED

1. Justin Smith, "Fastest Growing Demographic on Facebook: Women over 55," Inside Facebook, at www.insidefacebook.com/2009/02/02/fastest-growing-demographic-on-facebook-women-over-55/, accessed December 8, 2010.
2. This is a statement of Moore's Law, named for Intel cofounder Gordon E. Moore. He initially postulated that the number of transistors that could cost-effectively be placed on an integrated circuit would double every year. Gordon E. Moore, "Cramming More Components onto Integrated Circuits," *Electronics*, Vol. 38, No, 8, April 19, 1965, pp. 114–117. Later he revised his estimate to a doubling every two years. G. E. Moore, "Progress in Digital Integrated Electronics" (1975) at ftp://download.intel.com/museum/Moores_Law/Articles-Press_Releases/Gordon_Moore_1975_Speech.pdf, accessed March 30,

2011. According to Moore, a colleague, not Moore, rephrased Moore's Law to say that performance (rather than the number of transistors) would double every eighteen months. "Excerpts from a Conversation with Gordon Moore: Moore's Law" (Intel Corp., 2005), at ftp://download.intel.com/museum/Moores_Law/Video-Transcripts/Excerpts_A _Conversation_with_Gordon_Moore.pdf, accessed December 31, 2009.

3. Erik Brynjolfsson and Adam Saunders, *Wired for Innovation: How Information Technology Is Reshaping the Economy* (Cambridge, MA: MIT Press, 2010), p. 12, citing Intel Corp., "Moore's Law in Perspective" (2005).

4. Joseph D. Szydlowski, "Federal Officers Use Video Game Console to Catch Child Pornographers," December 8, 2010, at http://axcessnews.com/index.php/articles/show/id/19037, accessed December 8, 2010. If 10 numbers, 52 upper- and lowercase letters, and 8 "special characters" are usable, an 8-digit password would have possibilities of 70 to the eighth power, or 576,480,100,000,000. That's more than 576 trillion. According to one official, PlayStation 3 can run through about 4 million possibilities per second. Ibid. The computing power in an earlier version of this toy, PlayStation 2, is adequate to guide a cruise missile to its target. John Robb, *Brave New War: The Next Stage of Terrorism and the End of Globalization* (Hoboken: John Wiley & Sons, Inc., 2007), p. 9, citing "Military Fears over PlayStation 2," BBC News, April 17, 2007.

5. Scientific and Advanced-Technology Act, 42 U.S.C. §1862(g), Pub. L. 102–476 and Pub. L. 102–588, amended section identically, adding subsec. (g).

6. Unpublished figures provided to the author by the National Security Agency (NSA), Threat Operations Center (2009). Between 2006 and 2009 mobile data traffic increased *fifty* times. Morgan Stanley, "Economy + Internet Trends," presented at the Web 2.0 Summit, San Francisco, October 20, 2009, citing unspecified AT&T data.

7. By 2012, U.S. online retail sales may grow to $335 billion. Forrester Research, at www .forrester.com/Research/Document/Excerpt/0,7211,41592,00.html?cm_mmc =Google-_-Recent%20Research-_-ecommerce%20growth-_-5593380&utm_source =google&utm_medium=cpc&utm_term=5593380&gclid=CP7Xtue0u5UCFSXNIgod wyq_QA, accessed September 1, 2008; Juan Carlos Perez, "Forrester Bullish on US E-commerce Market," March 1, 2011; "U.S. Online Retail Sales, Which Rose 12.6 Percent to US$176.2 Billion in 2010, Are Expected to Grow at a Compound Annual Rate of 10 Percent Through 2015, After Dampening in 2008 and 2009 Due to the Economic Downturn," *PC World* at www.pcworld.com/businesscenter/article/221055/forrester _bullish_on_us_ecommerce_market.html, accessed March 1, 2011; US Online Retail Forecast, 2010 to 2015, at www.forrester.com/rb/Research/us_online_retail_forecast,_ 2010_to_2015/q/id/58596/t/2. For numbers of current Internet users, see Miniwatts Marketing Group, "Internet World Stats," updated March 26, 2011, at www.internet worldstats.com/stats.htm, accessed March 30, 2011.

8. Morgan Stanley, "Economy + Internet Trends," October 20, 2009, as measured by market capitalization.

9. Unpublished figures provided to the author by the National Security Agency (NSA), Threat Operations Center (2009), citing W. D. Sincoskie, formerly of Telecordia Technologies.

10. Nick Saint, "The 'Walk Past a Starbucks, Get a Coupon Sent to Your Phone' Cliché Is About to Become a Reality," *Business Insider*, June 28, 2010, at www.businessinsider.com/ its-finally-here-a-mobile-app-that-texts-you-when-you-walk-near-a-discount-2010-6, accessed March 1, 2011.

11. Reed Elsevier PLC, at www.reed-elsevier.com/investorcentre/presentationsandwebcasts/ Documents/Reed%20Elsevier%202008%20Interim%20Results%20Presentation %20with%20appendices.pdf, accessed September 1, 2008.

12. ChoicePoint also supports law enforcement, public safety, health care, and other government programs. See ChoicePoint, at www.choicepoint.com, accessed September 1, 2008.

13. "MasterCard Incorporated Reports Fourth-Quarter and Full-Year 2010 Financial Results, February 3, 2011," at http://newsroom.mastercard.com/press-releases/mastercardincorporated-reports-fourth-quarter-and-full-year-2010-financial-results/, accessed March 1, 2011.

14. "Learning to Live with Big Brother," *The Economist*, September 27, 2007.

15. For a summary of the data environment in the United States, see Jeff Jonas, "The Landscape of Available Data," Appendix H to "Creating a Trusted Network for Homeland Security," Second Report of the Markle Foundation Task Force (2003), at www.markle.org/sites/default/files/nstf_report2_full_report.pdf, accessed March 30, 2011.

16. Unless you've been the subject of a criminal investigation, served in the military, or held a security clearance the police and FBI probably know nothing about you, but Walmart knows a lot. Walmart, by the way, is on both ends of the surveillance telescope. Wall Street analysts scrutinize satellite photography of Walmart's parking lots. The imagery is a good proxy for sales data (which Walmart keeps confidential), which in turn helps Wall Street predict the company's financial results. Raj Patel, "5 Things You Didn't Know About Supermarkets," *Foreign Policy*, November 2010, p. 104, also at www.foreignpolicy.com/articles/2010/10/11/supermarkets?page=0,2, accessed December 8, 2010.

17. Emily Steel and Julia Angwin, "On the Web's Cutting Edge, Anonymity in Name Only," *Wall Street Journal*, August 4, 2010, at http://online.wsj.com/article/SB10001424052748703294904575385532109190198.html?KEYWORDS=On+the+Web%27s+Cutting+Edge, accessed August 4, 2010.

18. Jeff Jonas, "Your Movements Speak for Themselves: Space-Time Travel Data Is Analytic Super-Food!" August 16, 2009, at http://jeffjonas.typepad.com/jeff_jonas/2009/08/your-movements-speak-for-themselves-spacetime-travel-data-is-analytic-superfood.html, accessed June 16, 2010.

19. Jeff Jonas, e-mail to the author, February 11, 2011.

20. Ibid.

21. Robert Lee Hotz, "The Really Smart Phone," *Wall Street Journal*, April 23, 2011, at http://online.wsj.com/article/SB10001424052748704547604576263261679848814.html, accessed May 15, 2011.

22. The law on this point is in flux. See *In the Matter of the Application of the United States of America for an Order Directing a Provider of Electronic Communication Service to Disclose Records to the Government*, 3rd Cir., No. 08-4227, decided September 7, 2010, at www.ca3.uscourts.gov/opinarch/084227p.pdf, accessed March 6, 2011; *U.S. v. Maynard*, D.C. Cir., No. 08-3030, decided August 6, 2010, at www.cadc.uscourts.gov/internet/opinions.nsf/FF15EAE832958C138525780700715044/$file/08-3030-1259298.pdf, accessed March 15, 2011.

23. My thinking on this point has been enjoyably influenced by many conversations with Jeff Jonas.

24. A census was taken in New France (Quebec) in 1666, which at the time had a population of only 3,215. "Statistics Canada," at www.statcan.gc.ca/kits-trousses/jt2-eng.htm, accessed December 9, 2010.

25. In this respect, Art. I, Sec. 2 of the U.S. Constitution as originally adopted is a record of shame as well as rationality in its provision for counting slaves: "Representatives and direct Taxes shall be apportioned among the several States which may be included within this Union, according to their respective Numbers, which shall be determined by adding to the whole Number of free Persons, including those bound to Service for a Term of Years, and excluding Indians not taxed, three fifths of all other Persons. The actual Enumeration shall be made within three Years after the first Meeting of the Congress of the United States, and within every subsequent Term of ten Years, in such Manner as they shall by Law direct."

26. John Leyden, "Fingerprinting of UK School Kids Causes Outcry," *The Register*, July 22, 2002, at www.theregister.co.uk/2002/07/22/fingerprinting_of_uk_school_kids/, accessed

March 30, 2011. For a good history of fingerprinting, see Wikipedia, "Fingerprint," at http://en.wikipedia.org/wiki/Fingerprint#Fingerprinting_of_children, accessed December 9, 2010.

27. Fingerprinting, "Fingerprinting Products," at www.fingerprinting.com/fingerprinting-products .php, accessed December 9, 2010.

28. Niall Ferguson, *The Ascent of Money: A Financial History of the World* (New York: Penguin Press, 2008), chapter 1.

29. Amol Sharma, "India Launches Project to ID 1.2 Billion People," *Wall Street Journal*, September 29, 2010, at http://online.wsj.com/article/SB10001424052748704652104575493490951809322.html, accessed September 29, 2010.

30. U.S. federal standards for information handling are set by the Office of Management and Budget, which defines PII as information that "can be used to distinguish or trace an individual's identity, such as their name, social security number, biometric records, etc. alone, or when combined with other personal or identifying information which is linked or linkable to a specific individual, such as date and place of birth, mother's maiden name, etc." OMB Circular M-07-16, "Safeguarding Against and Responding to the Breach of Personally Identifiable Information," May 22, 2007. Under California law, which is typical of many states, PII "means an individual's first name or first initial and last name in combination with any one or more of the following data elements, when either the name or the data elements are not encrypted: (1) Social security number. (2) Driver's license number or California Identification Card number. (3) Account number, credit or debit card number, in combination with any required security code, access code, or password that would permit access to an individual's financial account. For purposes of this section, 'personal information' does not include publicly available information that is lawfully made available to the general public from federal, state, or local government records." Under EU Directive 95/46/EC, Art. 2a, " 'personal data' shall mean any information relating to an identified or identifiable natural person ('data subject'); an identifiable person is one who can be identified, directly or indirectly, in particular by reference to an identification number or to one or more factors specific to his physical, physiological, mental, economic, cultural or social identity."

31. "The Information That Is Needed to Identify You: 33 Bits," *Wall Street Journal*, August 4, 2010, at http://blogs.wsj.com/digits/2010/08/04/the-information-that-is-needed-to-identify-you -33-bits/, accessed August 4, 2010. A mere 32 bits of information would yield a mere 4.3 billion possibilities, which is fewer than the world's population of about 6.6 billion.

32. The patent application appears at www.faqs.org/patents/app/20100010993, accessed December 11, 2010.

## CHAPTER 2: A PRIMER ON CYBERCRIME

1. Sharon Gaudin, "Federal Prosecutor: Cybercrime is Funding Organized Crime," *Information Week*, July 20, 2007, at www.informationweek.com/news/security/government/ showArticle.jhtml?articleID=201200167, accessed September 27, 2008; Paul Horn, "It's Time to Arrest Cybercrime," *Bloomberg/BusinessWeek*, February 2, 2006, at www .businessweek.com/technology/content/feb2006/tc20060202_832554.htm, accessed December 10, 2010, citing U.S. Treasury officials.

2. Brian Krebs, "Cyber Thieves Steal Nearly $1,000,000 from University of Virginia College," KrebsOnSecurity.com, September 1, 2010, at http://krebsonsecurity.com/2010/09/cyber -thieves-steal-nearly-1000000-from-university-of-virginia-college/, accessed September 2, 2010; Brian Krebs, "Crooks Who Stole $600,000 From Catholic Diocese Said Money Was for Clergy Sex Abuse Victims," KrebsOnSecurity.com, August 30, 2010, at http://krebsonse curity.com/2010/08/crooks-who-stole-600000-from-catholic-diocese-said-money-was-for -clergy-sex-abuse-victims, accessed September 2, 2010. Owen Fletcher, "Report: Russian Gang Linked to Big Citibank Hack," *Computerworld*, December 22, 2009, at www.com

puterworld.com/s/article/9142578/Report_Russian_gang_linked_to_big_Citibank_hack, accessed December 11, 2010. Christopher Williams, "Russian Hacker Avoids Jail for $10M Royal Bank of Scotland Raid," *The Telegraph*, February 10, 2011, at www.telegraph.co.uk/ technology/news/8316246/Russian-hacker-avoids-jail-for-10m-Royal-Bank-of-Scotland -raid.html, accessed March 1, 2011; Siobhan Gorman, August Cole, and Yochi Dreazen, "Computer Spies Breach Fighter-Jet Project," *Wall Street Journal*, April 21, 2009, at http:// online.wsj.com/article/SB124027491029837401.html, accessed March 1, 2011; Andy Greenberg, "For Pentagon Contractors, Cyberspying Escalates," *Forbes*, February 17, 2010, at www.forbes.com/2010/02/17/pentagon-northrop-raytheon-technology-security-cyberspy ing.html, accessed March 1, 2011.

3. Verizon, *2010 Data Breach Investigations Report*, p. 2, at www.verizonbusiness.com/resources/ reports/rp_2010-data-breach-report_en_xg.pdf, accessed December 12, 2010. At about the same time, the Privacy Rights Clearinghouse reported that the number of sensitive data thefts in the United States had shot up to more than five hundred million—and they only started counting in 2005. Privacy Rights Clearinghouse, "500 Million Sensitive Records Breached Since 2005," August 26, 2010, at www.privacyrights.org/500-million -records-breached, accessed December 12, 2010. This is a series of annual reports. Starting with 2010 (reporting 2009 data), Verizon began producing it in cooperation with the U.S. Secret Service. Meanwhile the Identity Theft Resource Center reported more than 222 million personal records were exposed—not necessarily stolen—in 2009 alone. "Affinion Security Center Updates BreachShield, Targets Medical Industry," *Security Week News*, April 19, 2010, at http://s1.securityweek.com/content/affinion-security -center-updates-breachshield-targets-medical-industry, accessed December 12, 2010.

4. Verizon, *2010 Data Breach Investigations Report*.

5. Kroll International, "Global Fraud Report 2009/2010," at www.kroll.com/about/library/fraud/ Oct2009/downturn_and_fraud.aspx, accessed December 12, 2010.

6. The report also noted that 285 million records were compromised in 2008 alone. Veri- zon, *2009 Data Breach Investigation Report*, pp. 20, 22, at www.verizonbusiness.com/ resources/security/reports/2009_databreach_rp.pdf, accessed April 8, 2010.

7. Jason Franklin and Adrian Perrig, "An Inquiry into the Nature and Causes of the Wealth of Internet Miscreants" (Carnegie Mellon University, 2007), research paper, at www .cs.cmu.edu/~jfrankli/acmccs07/ccs07_franklin_eCrime.pdf, accessed March 31, 2011.

8. "Revealed: 8 Million Victims in the World's Biggest Cyber Heist," *Scotland Sunday Herald*, August 25, 2008, at www.sundayherald.com/news/heraldnews/display.var.2432225.0.0 .php, accessed September 27, 2008.

9. Hospitals may be even more careless than hotels. According to one report, "[P]rotecting patient data is not a priority" for hospitals. Perhaps that will change, because data breaches are costing hospitals serious money in damages and expenses under data breach laws—as much as $2 million annually per organization in the United States. Ponemon Institute, "Benchmark Study on Patient Privacy and Data Security," November 2010, at www2 .idexpertscorp.com/resources/healthcare/healthcare-articles-whitepapers/ponemon -benchmark-study-on-patient-privacy-and-data-security/, accessed December 12, 2010.

10. Zeijka Zorz, "Hotel Systems Breaches and Card Info Stolen All Over the U.S.," *Help Net Security*, September 10, 2010, at www.net-security.org/secworld.php?id=9853, accessed September 10, 2010.

11. Verizon, *2009 Report*, p. 5.

12. This description of Shadowcrew relies chiefly on the indictment, U.S. District Court, D.N.J., No. 2:04-CRr-0076-WJM-1, October 28, 2004, at www.justice.gov/usao/nj/ press/files/pdffiles/firewallindct1028.pdf, accessed January 17, 2010. For more on the unraveling of the group, see Brad Stone, "Global Trail of an Online Crime Ring," *New York Times*, August 12, 2008, at www.nytimes.com/2008/08/12/technology/12theft .html?pagewanted=print, accessed January 17, 2010. For a discussion of the number

of members and amount of damage created by this group, see Wikipedia, "Shadow-crew," at http://en.wikipedia.org/wiki/ShadowCrew, accessed January 18, 2010. Other details come from James Verini, "The Hacker Who Went Into the Cold," *New York Times Magazine*, November 14, 2010, p. 44, at www.nytimes.com/2010/11/14/magazine/14Hacker-t.html?scp=1&sq=The+Hacker+Who+Went+Into+the+Cold&st=nyt, accessed November 14, 2010. One of the Shadowcrew founders, Andrew Mantovani, was sentenced to thirty-two months in prison. Charles Harman, "Online Identity Theft Ring Out of the 'Shadows,'" ABC News, June 29, 2006, at http://abcnews.go.com/Technology/story?id=2136453&page=1, accessed March 22, 2011.

13. Stone, "Global Trail," *New York Times*, August 12, 2008.

14. Ibid.

15. Joseph Menn and Francesco Guerrera, "Cyber-thieves Linked to Citibank ATM Breach," *Financial Times*, August 24, 2009.

16. Kim Zetter, "TJX Hacker Gets 20 Years in Prison," *Wired*, March 25, 2010, at www.wired.com/threatlevel/2010/03/tjx-sentencing/, accessed March 22, 2011.

17. Trend Micro, "2010 in Review: No Recession for Cybercrime," December 23, 2010, at http://blog.trendmicro.com/2010-in-review-no-recession-for-cybercrime/, accessed December 31, 2010; Verizon, *2010 Data Breach Investigations Report*, p. 2; "Norton Cybercrime Report: The Human Impact," August 2010, at http://us.norton.com/content/en/us/home_homeoffice/media/pdf/cybercrime_report/Norton_USA-Human%20Impact-A4_Aug4-2.pdf, accessed December 31, 2010.

18. Kim Zetter, "Big-Box Breach: The Inside Story of Wal-Mart's Hacker Attack," *Wired*, October 13, 2009, at www.wired.com/threatlevel/2009/10/walmart-hack/, accessed October 30, 2009.

19. Brian Bergstein, "Wards Didn't Tell Customers About Credit Card Hack," *USA Today*, June 27, 2008, at www.usatoday.com/tech/news/computersecurity/infotheft/2008-06-27-wards-data-theft_N.htm, accessed December 16, 2010.

20. Help Net Security, "Every Week 57,000 Fake Web Addresses to Try to Infect Users," September 6, 2010, at www.net-security.org/malware_news.php?id=1456, accessed September 6, 2010.

21. Fletcher, "Report: Big Citibank hack," December 22, 2009.

22. Rhys Blakely et al., "Cybergang Raises Fear of New Crime Wave," *The Times* (London), November 10, 2007, at http://technology.timesonline.co.uk/tol/news/tech_and_web/the_web/article2844031.ece, accessed November 18, 2010.

23. Help Net Security "Twitter Accounts Spreading Malicious Code," December 3, 2010, at www.net-security.org/malware_news.php?id=1554, accessed December 3, 2010; "The Rise of Crimeware," October 6, 2010, at www.net-security.org/malware_news.php?id=1488, accessed October 6, 2010. Al-Qaeda is also busy making friends on Facebook. Jane Winter, "Al Qaeda Looks to Make New 'Friends'—on Facebook," Fox News, December 9, 2010, at www.foxnews.com/scitech/2010/12/09/facebook-friends-terror/, accessed December 10, 2010.

24. Darren Waters, "Spam Overwhelms E-Mail Messages," BBC News, April 8, 2009, at http://news.bbc.co.uk/2/hi/technology/7988579.stm, accessed December 12, 2010.

25. Help Net Security, "420,000 Scam E-Mails Sent Every Hour," June 16, 2010, at www.net-security.org/secworld.php?id=9421, accessed August 24, 2010.

26. According to UK law enforcement officials I spoke with, some of these attacks were carried out by simply entering a shop and swapping out a "straight" device for one that had been doctored. See also Henry Samuel, "Chip and Pin Scam Has Netted Millions From British Shoppers," *Daily Telegraph*, at www.telegraph.co.uk/news/newstopics/politics/lawandorder/3173346/Chip-and-pin-scam-has-netted-millions-from-British-shoppers.html, accessed October 12, 2008; Siobhan Gorman, "Fraud Ring Funnels Data from Cards to Pakistan," *Wall Street Journal*, October 11, 2008, at http://online.wsj.com/

article/SB122366999999723871.html, accessed October 12, 2008. Unlike the one-time big heist, which is usually discovered quickly, the long-term slow pilfering of relatively small amounts from many accounts can generate greater returns. One wealthy investor lost $300,000 this way from an account at JPMorgan Chase over a fifteen-month period. Dana B. Hernriques, "The Bank Account that Sprang a Leak," *New York Times*, August 30, 2008, at www.nytimes.com/2008/08/30/business/yourmoney/30theft.html?ei=5070&emc=etal&p, accessed September 6, 2008.

27. For perhaps the best inside account of a criminal cyberoperation, see Kevin Poulson, "One Hacker's Audacious Plan to Rule the Black Market in Stolen Credit Cards," *Wired*, December 22, 2008, at www.wired.com/print/techbiz/people/magazine/17-01/ff_max_butler, accessed January 17, 2010.

28. Internet Crime Complaint Center, *2010 Internet Crime Report*, p. 7, at www.ic3.gov/media/annualreport/2010_ic3report.pdf, accessed March 1, 2011. The Internet Crime Complaint center is a joint project of the Justice Department, the FBI, and the National Crime Complaint Center. Government statistics on Internet crime are difficult to fathom. It is not clear, for example, whether arrests or convictions reported in any year arise from investigations opened in that year, or from those opened in prior years. The mismatch between convictions and crimes is clear, however. The hundreds of thousands of complaints reviewed by the FBI and referred to law enforcement in 2010 appear to have resulted in only thirty-one arrests and six convictions. Internet Crime Complaint Center, *2010 Internet Crime Report*, p. 5, at www.ic3.gov/media/annualreport/2010_ic3 report.pdf, accessed March 1, 2011.

29. Byron Acohido, "Theft of Personal Data More Than Triples This Year," *USA Today*, December 10, 2007, at www.usatoday.com/money/industries/technology/2007-12-09-data-theft_N.htm, accessed March 31, 2011.

30. Verizon, *2009 Report*, p. 13.

31. In early 2011, for example, the NASDAQ Stock Market confirmed that its network had been breached—not its trading platform but an electronic service on which corporate leaders post confidential documents. Devlin Barrett, Jenny Strasburg, and Jacob Bunge, "Nasdaq Confirms Breach in Network," *Wall Street Journal*, February 7, 2011, at http://online.wsj.com/article/SB10001424052748703989504576128632568802332.html, accessed February 7, 2011. As of March 2011, the investigation was ongoing, and the full extent and consequences of the breach were far from clear. Trial of this case has been delayed. Mark Ballard, "Zeus Fraud Gang Trial Hits Another Delay," *ZDNet UK*, accessed March 21, 2011.

32. "[I]n 2009, there were 25 million new strains of malware. That equals a new strain of malware every 0.79 seconds." Kevin Coleman, "Stronger Measures Necessary to Address More Frequent and Sophisticated Attacks," *Defense Systems*, April 22, 2010, at www.defensesystems.com/Articles/2010/04/26/Digital-Conflict-Cyber-Defense.aspx, accessed May 15, 2011. As to the lack of trained cyberinvestigators, see Pete Yost, "Many FBI Agents Said Lack Ability in Cyber Cases," Associated Press, April 28, 2011, at http://news.yahoo.com/s/ap/20110429/ap_on_go_ca_st_pe/us_fbi_cybersecruity, accessed May 15, 2011. For recent law enforcement successes, see Gregg Keizer, "Court Order Cripples Coreflood Botnet, Says FBI," *Computerworld*, April 26, 2011, at www.computerworld.com/s/article/9216190/Court_order_cripples_Coreflood_botnet_says_FBI, accessed April 28, 2011; Nick Wingfield, "Spam Network Shut Down," *Wall Street Journal*, March 18, 2011, at http://online.wsj.com/article/SB10001424052748703328404576207173861008758.html, accessed April 13, 2011; Internet Law Resource Center, "Jury Convicts Last of Defendants in Massive Bank Fraud Phishing Scheme," Bureau of National Affairs, March 30, 2011, at www.alacrastore.com/storecontent/BNA_Banking_Daily-Jury_Convicts_Last_of_Defendants_In_Massive_Bank_Fraud_Phishing_Scheme-2101-3939, accessed March 30, 2011; Kim Zetter, "Carder Pleads Guilty to Fraud Involving $26

Million in Losses," *Wired*, April 21, 2011, at www.wired.com/threatlever/2011/04/rogelio-hackett-guilty, accessed April 25, 2011.

33. Jaikumar Vijayan, "Poughkeepsie, N.Y., Slams Bank for $378,000 Online Theft," *Computerworld*, February 8, 2010, at www.computerworld.com/s/article/9153598/Poughkeepsie_N.Y._slams_bank_for_378_000_online_theft, accessed February 10, 2010.

34. A Web address is called a URL, for "uniform resource locator." This is the plain English tag for an Internet Protocol, or IP, address that tells your computer where to look for information, or how to find your correspondent. The Internet works because everyone on it uses this consistent method of addressing. An IP address looks like this: 100.148.0.11. A URL is a lot easier to remember than an IP address, which is why we use them.

35. Internet Crime Complaint Center, *2010 Internet Crime Report*, p. 10, at www.ic3.gov/media/annualreport/2010_ic3report.pdf, accessed March 31, 2011.

36. Help Net Security "Sensitive Information Retrieved from P2P Networks," February 8, 2010, at www.net-security.org/secworld.php?id=8841, accessed February 8, 2010.

37. Bill Brubaker, "Online Records May Aid ID Theft," *Washington Post*, January 2, 2008, A1, at http://pqasb.pqarchiver.com/washingtonpost/access/1406254921.html?FMT=ABS&FMTS=ABS:FT&date=Jan+2%2C+2008&author=Bill+Brubaker+-+Washington+Post+Staff+Writer&pub=The+Washington+Post&edition=&startpage=A.1&desc=Online+Records+May+Aid+ID+Theft%3B+Government+Sites+Post+Personal+Data, accessed January 4, 2008.

38. Brian Krebs, "Justice Breyer Is Among Victims in Data Breach Caused by File Sharing," *Washington Post*, July 9, 2008, at www.washingtonpost.com/wp-dyn/content/article/2008/07/08/AR2008070802997.html, accessed September 26, 2008. As of this writing (mid-2011), LimeWire has effectively been shut down by a federal injunction after a finding that it was engaging in copyright enfringement. Joseph Plambeck, "Court Rules That File-Sharing Service Infringed Copyrights," *New York Times*, May 12, 2010, at www.nytimes.com/2010/05/13/technology/13lime.html, accessed December 13, 2010. According to LimeWire's Web site, the injunction remained in effect as of this writing. See www.limewire.com, accessed March 22, 2011. For more on P2P, see "Classified U.S. Military Info, Corporate Data Available Over P2P," *Computerworld*, July 25, 2007, at www.computerworld.com/action/article.do?command=viewArticleBasic&articleId=9027949, accessed September 25, 2008. See "P2P Increasingly Favored by Malware Attackers," Help Net Security, July 27, 2010, at www.net-security.org/secworld.php?id=9641, accessed August 24, 2010, citing Cisco, *2010 Global Threat Report*.

39. See, e.g., Zelijka Zorz, "A Lesson to Learn from the HPGary Breach," Help Net Security, February 18, 2011, at www.net-security.org/article.php?id=1559, accessed February 19, 2011.

40. Mark Clayton, "How the FBI and Interpol Trapped the World's Biggest Butterfly Botnet," *Christian Science Monitor*, June 30, 2011, at http://news.yahoo.com/fbi-interpol-trapped-worlds-biggest-butterfly-botnet-221210285.html, accessed June 30, 2011; Help Net Security, "Large Zeus Botnet Used For Financial Fraud," August 4, 2010, at www.net-security.org/malware_news.php?id=1418, accessed August 4, 2010; see also Roger Thompson, "Mumba Botnet Shows the Sophistication of Criminal Gangs," AVG, August 2, 2010, at http://thompson.blog.avg.com/2010/08/todays-battle-with-cyber-criminals-is-a-bit-like-the-old-fashioned-cops-and-robbers-stories-of-years-ago-the-police-were-cons.html, accessed August 25, 2010.

41. Noam Cohen, "Web Attackers Find Cause in WikiLeaks," *The New York Times*, December 9, 2010, at www.nytimes.com/2010/12/10/world/10wiki.html?_r=1, accessed January 6, 2011.

42. Elinor Mills, "Heartland Sued Over Data Breach," CNET News, January 28, 2009, at http://news.cnet.com/8301-1009_3-10151961-83.html, accessed January 19, 2010.

43. *In re Heartland Payment Systems, Inc. Securities Litigation*, Civ. No. 09-1043 (D.N.J., December 7, 2009). Opinion at www.huntonfiles.com/files/webupload/PrivacyLaw

_Heartland_Decision.pdf, accessed December 9, 2009. The attack used a "structured query language," or SQL, attack, which injects code where it does not belong in order to take control of a system.

44. *Heartland Payments Systems, Inc. Annual Report on SEC Form 10-K*, March 10, 2011, at www.faqs.org/sec-filings/110310/HEARTLAND-PAYMENT-SYSTEMS-INC_10-K/, accessed March 30, 2011; see also Jaikumar Vijayan, "Heartland Breach Expenses pegged at $140M—so far," *Computerworld*, May 10, 2010, at www.computerworld.com/s/article/9176507/Heartland_breach_expenses_pegged_at_140M_so_far, accessed March 31, 2011.

45. Oscar Wilde, "The Critic as Artist," Part 2, in *The Complete Works of Oscar Wilde* (New York: Wm. H. Wise & Company, 1927), v. 5, p. 203.

46. One of the most ancient propositions of the common law is *Sic utere tuo ut alienam non lædas*, or: Use what is yours so you do not harm others. See Joel F. Brenner, "Nuisance Law and the Industrial Revolution," *J. Legal Studies* (1974)3: 403.

47. *Terry v. Ohio*, 392 U.S. 1 (1968) decided that evidence from such an encounter was admissible in the federal courts.

## CHAPTER 3: BLEEDING WEALTH

1. McAfee, the antivirus company, dubbed the attacks Operation Aurora, and the name stuck. George Kurtz, "Operation 'Aurora' Hit Google, Others," McAfee Security Insights Blog, January 14, 2010, at http://siblog.mcafee.com/cto/operation-"aurora"-hit-google-others/, accessed January 27, 2010. McAfee chose that name—the attackers used it. This operation has nothing to do with another Aurora project, the simulated remote attack on electricity generating equipment described in chapter 5.

2. In its original release, the company stated that the attacks "resulted in the theft of intellectual property," but it did not specify that source code had been stolen. "A New Approach to China," January 12, 2010, at http://googleblog.blogspot.com/2010/01.new-approach-to-china.html, accessed February 22, 2010.

3. The notable exception was Ariana Eunjung Cha and Ellen Naksahima, "Google China Cyberattack Part of Vast Espionage Campaign, Experts Say," *Washington Post*, January 14, 2010, at www.washingtonpost.com/wp-dyn/content/article/2010/01/13/AR2010011300359.html, accessed February 21, 2010.

4. Google, "A New Approach to China," January 12, 2010, at http://googleblog.blogspot.com/2010/01/new-approach-to-china.html, accessed April 4, 2011.

5. Based partly on private sources. McAfee concurs that the attacks targeted intellectual property. Kurtz, "Operation 'Aurora,'" McAfee Blog, January 14, 2010; Kim Zetter, "Google Hackers Targeted Source Code of More than 30 Companies," *Wired*, January 13, 2010, at www.wired.com/threatlevel/2010/01/google-hack-attack/, accessed December 14, 2010.

6. Kim Zetter, "Report Details Hacks Targeting Google, Others," *Wired*, February 3, 2010, at www.wired.com/threatlevel/2010/02/apt-hacks/, accessed December 26, 2010.

7. See Cha and Nakashima, "Google China Cyberattack," January 14, 2010. They name Yahoo, Symantec, Adobe, Northrop Grumman, and Dow Chemical. A day later the *New York Times* added Juniper to the list. Juniper is the second largest manufacturer of network routers in the United States. David E. Sanger and John Markoff, "After Google's Stand on China, U.S. Treads Lightly," *New York Times*, January 15, 2010, at www.nytimes.com/2010/01/15/world/asia/15diplo.html?scp=1&sq=After%20Google's%20Stand%20on%20China,%20U.S.%20Treads%20Lightly&st=cse, accessed February 21, 2010. In its 2009 annual report filed with the SEC, Intel stated that it had been targeted by "sophisticated" attacks during the same time, but did not state what, if anything, had been stolen. Computerworld Security, "Intel Confirms 'Sophisticated' Attacks in January," February 23, 2010, at www.computerworld.com/s/article/9160999/Intel_confirms_sophisticated_attacks_in_January, accessed February 23, 2010. For the attack on

Morgan Stanley, see Zeljka Zorz, "Stolen E-Mails Reveal Morgan Stanley Was Hit by Aurora Attacks," Help Net Security, March 1, 2011, at www.net-security.org/secworld .php?id=10679, accessed March 1, 2011. The attack on Morgan Stanley came to light when the bank's security consultant, HBGary, was in turn penetrated by the group Anonymous.

8. Kurtz, "Operation 'Aurora,'" McAfee Blog, January 14, 2010; McAfee, "Operation Aurora: How to Respond to the Recent Internet Explorer Vulnerability," [n.d.], at www.mcafee .com/us/threat_center/operation_aurora.html, accessed January 26, 2010. The encryption is described in Kim Zetter, "Google Hack Attack Was Ultra Sophisticated, New Details Show," *Wired*, January 14, 2010, at www.wired.com/threatlevel/2010/01/opera tion-aurora/, accessed January 27, 2010.

9. Google cofounder Sergey Brin confirmed the theft of Google's code. Jessica E. Vascellaro, "Brin Drove Google to Pull Back in China," *New York Times*, March 24, 2010.

10. Note to Mr. Li's translator: In English, "top dog" means "big shot." It's not an insult.

11. See James Glanz and John Markoff, "Cables Discuss Vast Hacking by a China Fearful of the Web," *New York Times,* December 4, 2010, at www.nytimes.com/2010/12/05/world/ asia/05wikileaks-china.html, accessed December 4, 2010. Among other things, they cite a cable dated May 18, 2009.

12. Sanger and Markoff, "After Google's Stand," *New York Times*, January 15, 2010; Michael Richardson, "Details on Taiwan connection emerge in Operation Aurora hack of Google," Examiner.com, January 27, 2010, at www.examiner.com/x-34331-Taiwan -Policy-Examiner~y2010m1d25-Details-on-Taiwan-connection-emerge-in-Operation -Aurora-hack-of-Google, accessed January 27, 2010.

13. Ellen Nakashima, "U.S. Plans to Issue Official Protest to China Over Attack on Google," *Washington Post*, January 16, 2010, at www.washingtonpost.com/wp-dyn/content/ article/2010/01/15/AR2010011503917.html, accessed February 21, 2010.

14. John Markoff, "Evidence Found for Chinese Attack on Google," *New York Times*, January 20, 2010, at www.nytimes.com/2010/01/20/technology/20cyber.html?hp, accessed January 20, 2010.

15. Michael Wines, "China Issues Sharp Rebuke to U.S. Calls for an Investigation on Google Attacks," *New York Times*, January 26, 2010, at www.nytimes.com/2010/01/26/world/asia/ 26google.html?scp=1&sq=China%20Issues%20Sharp%20Rebuke%20to%20U.S.%20 Calls%20for%20an%20Investigation%20on%20Google%20Attacks&st=cse, accessed January 26, 2010.

16. John Markoff and David Barboza, "Two Chinese Schools Said to Be Tied to Online Attacks," *New York Times*, February 19, 2010, at www.nytimes.com/2010/02/19/tech nology/19china.html, accessed February 19, 2010.

17. McAfee, "Global Energy Cyberattacks: 'Night Dragon,'" February 10, 2011, at www.mcafee .com/us/resources/white-papers/wp-global-energy-cyberattacks-night-dragon.pdf, accessed February 11, 2011. International organizations have suffered similar attacks. In 2008, cyberspies deeply penetrated the computer networks of the World Bank and for nearly a month had access to sensitive economic information from many nations.

18. Even if an intrusive caller from a phone bank blocks his caller ID, the telephone company can determine its location with certainty and shut it down. This may change as telephone and Internet communications converge.

19. According to officials, countries in Eastern Europe, Africa, and South America—including Nigeria, Brazil, Ukraine, and until recently Romania—have become burgeoning sanctuaries for hackers because of weak law enforcement. "U.S. Takes Fight Against Hackers Overseas," December 9, 2009, at www.msnbc.msn.com/id/34351026/ns/technology _and_science-security/, accessed December 28, 2010; Saleh Sikandar, "FIA Says No Law Now to Check Cyber Crimes," July 15, 2010, at http://propakistani.pk/2010/07/15/ fia-says-no-law-now-to-check-cyber-crimes/, accessed March 1, 2011, see also www

.i-policy.org/2011/02/the-international-convention-on-cybercrime-one-of-the-most
-needed-treaties-of-this-century.html.

20. Major David Willson, U.S. Army, "When Does Electronic Espionage or a Cyber Attack Become an 'Act of War'?" *CyberPro*, National Security Cyberspace Institute, May 2010, at www.nsci-va.org/WhitePapers/2010-05-06-David%20Willson-Electronic%20Espionage-Act%20of%20War.pdf, accessed December 29, 2010; Kim Zetter, "Former NSA Director: Countries Spewing Cyberattacks Should Be Held Responsible," *Wired*, July 29, 2010, at www.wired.com/threatlevel/2010/07/hayden-at-blackhat/, accessed December 29, 2010.

21. "The United States was the top country for malicious activity." See Symantec Intelligence Quarterly Reports for 2010 (up to September 2010), at www.symantec.com/business/theme.jsp?themeid=threatreport, accessed December 29, 2010.

22. Sharon LaFraniere and Jonathan Ansfield, "China Alarmed by Security Threat from Internet," *New York Times*, February 12, 2010, at www.nytimes.com/2010/02/12/world/asia/12cyberchina.html?ref, accessed February 12, 2010.

23. Ellen Nakashima, "Diverse Group of Chinese Hackers Wrote Code in Attacks on Google, U.S. Companies," *Washington Post*, February 20, 2010, at www.washingtonpost.com/wp-dyn/content/article/2010/02/19/AR2010021902643.html, accessed February 23, 2010.

24. Kelly Jackson Higins, "Anatomy of a Targeted, Persistent Attack," *Dark Reading*, January 27, 2010, at www.darkreading.com/shared/printableArticleSrc.jhtml?articleID=222600139, accessed February 5, 2010.

25. "CATIC is a professional state-owned enterprise with aviation products & technology import and export as its core business. With 1 billion' register [*sic*] capital and hundreds of million's [*sic*] property, CATIC has exported fighters, trainers, bombers, helicopters, transporters, general aviation aircraft and associated airborne equipment and ground support equipment as well as various components and spare parts. Through multinational cooperation, CATIC has invested and developed high-performance aircrafts such as K-8 trainer, JF-17 fighter and EC-120 helicopter. CATIC has provided to its customers from home and abroad and to the national key projects with professional value-added services including market surveys and analysis, project development, business planning, program management, investment and financing, technology introduction, international trade and cooperation." See "About CATIC," at www.catic.cn/indexPortal/home/index.do?cmd=goToChannel&cid=754&language=US, accessed December 29, 2010; see also "China National Aero-Technology Import and Export Corporation," at http://en.wikipedia.org/wiki/China_National_Aero-Technology_Import_%26_Export_Corporation, accessed December 29, 2010.

26. Department of Commerce Bureau of Industry and Security, "McDonnell Douglas, China National Aero Technology Import and Export Corporation and Others Indicted on Federal Charges for Making False and Misleading Statements in Connection with Exporting Machinery to the People's Republic of China," October 19, 1999, at www.bis.doc.gov/news/archive99/dojindictmentmcdonneldouglas.html, accessed February 28, 2010; DoC BIS, "People's Republic of China Corporate Entity Waives Soverign Immunity and Enters Plea to Felony Export Violation; Sentenced to Pay $1 Million Criminal Fine and Five Year Term of Corporate Probation," May 11, 2001, at www.bis.doc.gov/news/archive2001/dojreleaseprccase.htm, accessed February 28, 2010.

27. Gerald Posner, "China's Secret Cyberterrorism," TheDailyBeast.com, January 13, 2010, at www.thedailybeast.com/blogs-and-stories/2010-01-13/chinas-secret-cyber-terrorism/p/, accessed February 1, 2010.

28. A 2008 Pew Research Center report found that 86 percent of Chinese citizens were satisfied with the direction of their country and that 65 percent thought the Chinese government was doing a good job addressing critical issues. This statistic inched higher among

wealthy Chinese citizens, 72 percent of whom gave the government a positive review. *The 2008 Pew Global Attitudes Survey in China: The Chinese Celebrate Their Roaring Economy, As They Struggle With its Costs,* July 22, 2008, p. 17, at http://pewglobal.org/reports/pdf/261.pdf, accessed April 4, 2011.

29. Robert Lemos, "Law Firm Suing China Suffers Attack," SecurityFocus, a Semantec-sponsored Web site, January 14, 2010, at www.securityfocus.com/print/brief/1062, accessed January 27, 2010.

30. For a discussion of current U.S. counterespionage strategy, see the *National Counterintelligence Strategy of the United States of America (2008)*, at www.ncix.gov/publications/policy/2008_Strategy.pdf, accessed March 2, 2010.

31. The French have successfully created a widely accepted myth to the contrary, but it's false. See Jacques Isnard, "L'Europe « piégée » par le réseau d'espionnage Echelon," *Le Monde,* October 13, 2000, at www.lemonde.fr/cgi-bin/ACHATS/acheter.cgi?offre=ARCHIVES&type_item=ART_ARCH_30J&objet_id=105523, accessed April 4, 2011; Duncan Campbell and Paul Lashmar, "Revealed: 30 More Nations with Spy Stations," *The Independent,* July 9, 2000, at www.independent.co.uk/news/uk/politics/revealed-30-more-nations-with-spy-stations-707320.html, accessed April 4, 2011.

32. Hedieh Nasheri, *Economic Espionage and Industrial Spying* (Cambridge, UK: Cambridge University Press, 2005), p. 197, n. 14, quoting the *New York Daily News,* September 5, 1994; see also Harvey Rishikof, "Economic and Industrial Espionage: Who Is Eating America's Lunch, and How Do We Stop It?" in Jennifer E. Sims and Burton Gerber, eds., *Vaults, Mirrors and Masks: Rediscovering U.S. Counterintelligence* (Washington, DC: Georgetown University Press, 2009), p. 201.

33. Susan W. Brenner and Anthony C. Crescenzi, "State-Sponsored Crime: The Futility of the Economic Espionage Act," v. 1, n. 28, *Houston Journal of Int'l Law* (January 2006): p. 389, at http://findarticles.com/p/articles/mi_hb3094/is_2_28/ai_n29266288/?tag=content;col11, accessed December 15, 2010; *United States v. Hsu,* 155 F.3d 189, 194 (3d Cir. 1998). ("The end of the cold war sent government spies scurrying to the private sector to perform illicit work for businesses and corporations . . . and by 1996 . . . nearly $24 billion of corporate intellectual property was being stolen each year.")

34. Economic Espionage Act of 1996, Pub. L. No. 104-294, 11, 110 Stat. 3488, 18 U.S.C. § 1831 (1996).

35. Brenner and Crescenzi, "State Sponsored Crime," p. 390, citing S. Rep. No. 104-359, at 11 (1996): "Only by adopting a national scheme to protect U.S. proprietary economic information can we hope to maintain our industrial and economic edge and thus safeguard our national security. Foremost, we believe that the greatest benefit of the Federal statute will be as a powerful deterrent."

36. "The development of the U.S. textile industry in the early 1800s is a direct result of Francis Cabot Lowell visiting England and memorizing the workings of their power looms. Upon returning to New England he recruited a master mechanic to recreate and develop what he had memorized. The Chinese were able to protect their proprietary interests in the silk trade for in excess of two thousand years, further illustrating that economic espionage is not a recent phenomena. The secret was ultimately lost, according to one account, when a Chinese princess married a foreign prince and smuggled silkworm eggs out of China by hiding them in her voluminous hair piece (circa AD 440). A second account credits two Nestorian monks (circa AD 550) with smuggling silkworm eggs in their hollow bamboo staves for delivery to the Byzantine Emperor Justinian. Brenner and Crescenzi, "State Sponsored Crime," p. 395.

37. *The Independent,* January 10, 1997, at http://www.independent.co.uk/news/business/vw-agrees-to-100m-settlement-with-gm-1282486.html, accessed March 21, 2011; "Inaki Lopez's Last Stand," *Newsweek,* August 2, 1993, at www.newsweek.com/1993/08/01/inaki-lopez-s-last-stand.html, accessed March 21, 2011. He was indicted in

Germany but never convicted. By the time he was indicted in the United States, he had gone to Spain, which refused to extradite him. Emma Daly, "Spain Court Refuses to Extradite Man G.M. Says Took Its Secrets," *New York Times*, June 20, 2001, at www .nytimes.com/2001/06/20/business/spain-court-refuses-to-extradite-man-gm-says -took-its-secrets.html, accessed March 21, 2001.

38. See Eamon Javers, *Broker, Trader, Lawyer, Spy: The Secret World of Corporate Espionage* (New York: HarperCollins, 2010).

39. The key allegations appear in Oracle's "Fourth Amended Complaint for Damages and Injunctive Relief," ¶¶ 16, 93, 96–100. SAP admitted liability. The judgment is reported in Cari Tuna, "Jury Rules SAP Owed Oracle $1.3 Billion," *Wall Street Journal*, November 24, 2010, at http://online.wsj.com/article/SB10001424052748704369304575633150256505376.html, accessed November 24, 2010. As of this writing (early 2011), the judgment is under appeal.

40. Mike Lennon, "Former Bristol-Myers Squibb Employee Pleads Guilty to Theft of Trade Secrets," *Security Week News*, November 8, 2010, at www.securityweek.com/former-bristol-myers-squibb-employee-pleads-guilty-theft-trade-secrets, accessed December 15,2010.

41. Robert McMillan, "Former Goldman Sachs Coder Gets 8-year Sentence," *Computerworld*, March 21, 2011, at www.computerworld.com/s/article/9214880/Former_Goldman_Sachs_coder_gets_8_year_sentence?source=CTWNLE_nlt_security _2011-03-22&utm_source=feedburner&utm_medium=feed&utm_campaign=Feed%3A +computerworld%2Fs%2Ffeed%2Ftopic%2F144+%28Computerworld+DRM+and +Legal+Issues+News%29, accessed March 22, 2011.

42. CERT, "Spotlight on: Insider Theft of Intellectual Property Inside the U.S. Involving Foreign Governments or Information," June 2009, available through www.cert.org. CERT is part of the Software Engineering Institute, a federally funded research and development center at Carnegie Mellon University.

43. The State Department's Directorate of Defense Trade administers the International Traffic in Arms Regulations, but violations of these regulations, as well as of the Arms Export Control Act, are enforced by the Homeland Security Department's Immigration and Customs Enforcement agency. For the list of military items prohibited from export, see 15 C.F.R. 774, supp. 1. Other export controls are administered by the Commerce Department. 15 C.F.R. § 736, 50 U.S.C. app §§2401-2420. For the list of dual-use items controlled by the Commerce Department, see 22 CFR 121.

44. Except as otherwise noted, this account is based on the criminal complaint in *United States v. Yang*, case no. MJ10-498 (W.D. Wash.), filed December 2, 2010.

45. See Web site of Xian Space Star Technology (Group) Corporation, at http://nippledrinker .en.alibaba.com/aboutus.html, accessed December 16, 2010.

46. As of late March 2011, this case had not gone to trial.

47. FBI press release, August 31, 2010, at http://indianapolis.fbi.gov/dojpressrel/pressrel10/ ip083110a.htm, accessed December 16, 2010; Christopher Drew, "New Spy Game: Firms' Secrets Sold Overseas," *New York Times*, October 17, 2010, at www.nytimes .com/2010/10/18/business/global/18espionage.html, accessed December 16, 2010. As of early April 2011, this case had not gone to trial.

48. Rhys Blakely, Jonathan Richards, James Rossiter, and Richard Beeston, "MI5 Alert on China's Cyberspace Spy Threat," *The Sunday Times*, December 1, 2007, at http://business.timesonline.co.uk/tol/business/industry_sectors/technology/article2980250.ece, accessed March 1, 2011; "Merkel Tells China to Respect International Rules," Agence France-Presse, August 27, 2007, at http://services.inquirer.net/print/print.php?article _id=20070827-85028, accessed March 1, 2011.

49. David Leppard, "China Bugs and Burgles Britain," *The Sunday Times*, January 31, 2010, at www.timesonline.co.uk/tol/news/uk/crime/article7009749.ece, accessed February 16, 2010.

50. Some examples would be documents that contain a client's strategy and bottom line terms for prospective negotiations with a foreign company or government; discuss a client's plans to invest in oil and gas leases, and bid data; contain client plans for investment options in hot areas such as "clean tech"; analyze a foreign firm's likely merger and acquisition targets and their chances of passing muster with U.S. regulatory authorities; analyze investment options in the United States for a foreign client; relate to a client's physical and electronic security; contain a .pdf file for the entry pass to a restricted conference on export controls or another sensitive topic; or contain a partner's travel plans for a trip to China, including contacts in China and hotel reservations (very useful in making sure he gets a bugged room).

51. Chuck Hawks, "The Best Fighter Aircraft of World War II," at www.chuckhawks.com/best_fighter_planes.htm, accessed February 14, 2010; Larry Dwyer, "Mitsubishi A6M Zero-Sen—Japan," at www.aviation-history.com/mitsubishi/zero.html, accessed April 4, 2011, citing Heiner Emde and Carlo Demand, *Conquerors of the Air* (New York: Viking Press, 1969), and David Mondey, *The Concise Guide to Axis Aircraft of World War II* (New York: Smithmark Publishers, 1996), p. 194.

52. "Ex-espionage Chief Admits France Engaged in Economic Spying," Agence France-Presse, January 10, 1996, quoted in Charles Lathrop, *The Literary Spy: The Ultimate Source for Quotations on Espionage and Intelligence* (New Haven: Yale University Press, 2004), p. 131.

53. "Yugoslavia: Serb Hackers Reportedly Disrupt US Military Computer," Bosnian Serb News Agency SRNA, March 28, 1999 (BBC Monitoring Service, March 30, 1999), cited in Kenneth Geers, "Cyberspace and the Changing Nature of Warfare," NATO [n.d.] note 10, at www.blackhat.com/presentations/bh-jp-08/bh-jp-08-Geers/BlackHat-Japan-08-Geers-Cyber-Warfare-Whitepaper.pdf, accessed April 4, 2011; Michael Dobbs, "The War on the Airwaves," *Washington Post*, April 19, 1999, reported that NATO controlled all four Internet access providers in Yugoslavia and intentionally kept them open to spread disinformation and propaganda.

54. Nathan Hodge, "Defense Mergers Opposed by U.S.," *Wall Street Journal*, February 9, 2011, at http://online.wsj.com/article/SB10001424052748703313304576132522909188468.html, accessed February 9, 2011.

55. Office of the National Counterintelligence Executive, *2008 Annual Report to Congress on Foreign Economic Collection and Industrial Espionage (hereafter, "2008 Economic Espionage Report")*, App. B., at www.ncix.gov/publications/reports/fecie_all/fecie_2008/2008_FECIE_Blue.pdf, accessed April 4, 2011.

56. The NetWitness press release is available at www.netwitness.com/resources/pressreleases/feb182010.aspx, accessed February 28, 2010. The companies were named by Siobhan Gorman, "Broad New Hacking Attack Detected," *Wall Street Journal*, February 18, 2011, at http://online.wsj.com/article/SB10001424052748704398804575071103834150536.html, accessed February 18, 2011.

57. "The Globalist," *The Economist* [n.d.], at www.theglobalist.com/countryoftheweek/sample.htm, accessed February 15, 2010.

58. "It seems likely that average incomes in Japan, China, and parts of southeast Asia were comparable to (or higher than) those in western Europe even in the late eighteenth century." Kenneth Pomeranz, *The Great Divergence: China, Europe, and the Making of the Modern World* (Princeton, Princeton University Press: 2000), p. 49.

59. "The Globalist," *The Economist* [n.d.], at www.theglobalist.com/countryoftheweek/sample.htm, accessed February 15, 2010, citing OECD statistics.

60. Paul Halsall, ed., *Internet Modern History Sourcebook*, a project of the Fordham University Department of History, "Table Illustrating the Spread of Industrialization," Table 1, at www.fordham.edu/halsall/mod/indrevtabs.1.html, accessed February 10, 2010.

61. Adda B. Bozeman, *Strategic Intelligence and Statecraft: Selected Essays* (Washington, DC: Brassey's, 1992), p. 12. These essays deserve to be widely read and studied.

62. Ibid., p. 50.

63. Ibid., pp. 15–16.

64. Cited in ibid.

65. Alan Murray, "Parting Words," *Wall Street Journal*, November 22, 2010, at http://online .wsj.com/article/SB10001424052748703628204575619250079601996.html?KEY WORDS=parting+words, accessed December 15, 2010, quoting Lawrence Summers, outgoing director of the U.S. National Economic Council.

## CHAPTER 4: DEGRADING DEFENSE

1. The Chi Mak chronology is stated in detail in Calland F. Carnes, *Snake Fish: The Chi Mak Spy Ring* (New York: Barraclough, 2008), which provides most of the facts given in this account.

2. *2009 Report to Congress of the U.S.-China Economic and Security Review Commission*, November 2009, pp. 5, 155–56, at www.uscc.gov/annual_report/2009/annual_report_full _09.pdf, accessed March 4, 2009.

3. Ibid., p. 2, at www.uscc.gov/annual_report/2009/annual_report_full_09.pdf, accessed March 4, 2009.

4. *U.S. v. Tai Shen Kuo*, U.S.D.C., E.D. Va., indictment filed February 6, 2008; *U.S. v. Chung*, U.S.D.C., C.D. Cal., indictment filed February 6, 2008.

5. 18 U.S.C. § 793.

6. Chi Mak was convicted of "conspiracy to commit economic espionage, six counts of economic espionage to benefit a foreign country, one count of acting as an agent of the People's Republic of China and one count of making false statements to the FBI." U.S. Department of Justice Press Release, "Former Boeing Engineer Convicted of Economic Espionage in Theft of Space Shuttle Secrets for China," July 16, 2009, at www.justice.gov/opa/pr/2009/ July/09-nsd-688.html, accessed March 21, 2011. See *U.S. v. Chi Mak*, second superseding indictment, SA CR 05-293 (B)-CJC, filed October 26, 2006.

7. H.G. Reza, "10 Years for Man in China Spy Case," *Los Angeles Times,* April 22, 2008, at http:// articles.latimes.com/2008/apr/22/local/me-spies22, accessed March 27, 2011; H.G. Reza, "3-Years Sentence in China Spy Case," *Los Angeles Times*, October 3, 2008, accessed March 27, 2011.

8. *2009 Report to Congress*, pp. 5–6, at www.uscc.gov/annual_report/2009/annual_report_full_ 09.pdf, accessed March 4, 2009.

9. *2008 Economic Espionage Report*, App. B.

10. Migration Information Source, May 2010, at www.migrationinformation.org/USfocus/dis play.cfm?id=781, accessed December 27, 2010.

11. Yu Ran, "Growing Number of Chinese Students Head to US," *China Daily*, December 27, 2010, at www.chinadaily.com.cn/china/2010-02/27/content_9513253.htm, accessed December 27, 2010, quoting a U.S. consular official.

12. Ray Clancy, "US Sees Significant Rise in the Number of Chinese Students," EXPATFO RUM.com, November 24, 2010, at www.expatforum.com/america/us-sees-significant-rise-in-the-number-of-chinese-students.html, accessed December 27, 2010.

13. "1 million: The Number of Chinese Tourists that Visited the US in 2010," *China Economic Review*, December 23, 2010, at www.chinaeconomicreview.com/today-in-china/2010 _12_23/1_million:_The_number_of_Chinese_tourists_that_visited_the_US_in_2010 .html, accessed December 27, 2010.

14. *U.S. v. Chung*, U.S.D.C., C.D. Cal., indictment filed February 6, 2008, ¶ 21.d. Chung was sentenced to nearly sixteen years in prison. U.S. Department of Justice press release, February 8, 2010, at http://losangeles.fbi.gov/dojpressrel/pressrel10/la020810.htm, accessed December 19, 2010.

15. Studies on this subject are appropriately inconclusive and generally lack psychological depth. See, e.g., Katherine L. Herbig and Martin F. Wiskoff, "Espionage Against the United States by American Citizens 1947–2001," Technical Report 02-5, July 2002, based on research conducted by the Defense Personnel Security Research Center, at www.ncix.gov/docs/espionageAgainstUSbyCitizens.pdf, accessed December 19, 2010.

16. Ideologically motivated espionage was common during the 1950s but has reappeared several times in prominent cases in recent years. Apart from Chi Mak and related cases, the most striking example is the Cuban spy Ana Belem Montes. See Scott W. Carmichael, *True Believer: Inside the Investigation and Capture of Ana Montes, Cuba's Master Spy* (Annapolis, MD: Naval Institute Press, 2007).

17. *U.S. v. Tai Shen Kuo*, case no. 1:08mj-98, U.S.D.C., E.D. Va., Affidavit in Support of Criminal Complaint, Three Arrest Warrants, and Three Search Warrants, filed February 6, 2008, at www.justice.gov/opa/pr/2008/February/under-seal-bt-affidavit-edva.pdf, accessed April 18, 2010.

18. Alan Furst, *Dark Star* (New York: Random House, 2002), p. 102.

19. Based on an interview with a former intelligence official.

20. Ed Pilkington, "China Winning Cyber War, Congress Warned," *The Guardian*, November 20, 2008, at www.guardian.co.uk/technology/2008/nov/20/china-us-military-hacking, accessed April 30, 2011; Congressional Research Service, "Terrorist Capabilities for Cyberattack: Overview and Policy Issues," January 22, 2007, p. 17, at www.dtic.mil/cgi-bin/GetTRDoc?AD=ADA463774&Location=U2&doc=GetTRDoc.pdf, accessed February 15, 2010.

21. U.S.-China Economic and Security Review Commission, *2010 Report to Congress* (November 2010), p. 237. For public references to Byzantine Hades, see, e.g., James Glanz and John Markoff, "Vast Hacking by a China Fearful of the Web" *New York Times*, December 4, 2010, at www.nytimes.com/2010/12/05/world/asia/05wikileaks-china.html?scp=1&sq=byzantine%20hades&st=cse, accessed December 4, 2010; "Bush Goes Looking for Cyber Battles," *The Inquirer*, at www.theinquirer.net/inquirer/news/1001456/bush-wants-cyber-war, accessed April 4, 2011.

22. U.S.-China Economic and Security Review Commission, *2009 Report to Congress* (November 2009), p. 168, at www.uscc.gov/annual_report/2009/annual_report_full_09.pdf, accessed April 18, 2010.

23. Ellen Nakashima, "Soldiers' Data Still Being Downloaded Overseas, Firm Says," *Washington Post*, October 2, 2009, at www.washingtonpost.com/wp-dyn/content/article/2009/10/01/AR2009100104947.html, accessed October 2, 2009.

24. The Canadian government is fighting off similar attacks. Clement Sabourin, "China Hackers Behind Cyber Attack on Canada," AFP, *The Ottawa Citizen*, February 17, 2011, at www.ottawacitizen.com/technology/China+hackers+behind+cyber+attack+Canada/4301051/story.html, accessed February 20, 2011.

25. Ibid.

26. Siobhan Gorman, A. Cole, and Y. Dreazen, "Computer Spies Breach Fighter-Jet Project," *Wall Street Journal*, April 21, 2009, at http://online.wsj.com/article/SB124027491029837401.html, accessed August 19, 2009; Jaikumar Vijayan, "Update: Strike Fighter Data Was Leaked on P2P Network in 2005, Security Expert Says," Computerworld Security, May 5, 2009, at www.computerworld.com/s/article/9132571/Update_Strike_Fighter_data_was_leaked_on_P2P_network_in_2005_security_expert_says_, accessed May 28, 2009.

27. *2009 Report to Congress of the U.S.-China Economic and Security Review Commission*, November 2009, p. 167, at www.uscc.gov/annual_report/2009/annual_report_full_09.pdf, accessed March 4, 2009.

28. Paul Watson, "Data Leaks Persist from Afghan Base," *Los Angeles Times*, April 13, 2006, at http://articles.latimes.com/2006/apr/13/world/fg-disks13, accessed April 19, 2010.

29. "Computer Hard Drive Sold on Ebay 'Had Details of Top Secret U.S. Missile Defence System,'" *The Daily Mail*, May 7, 2009, at www.dailymail.co.uk/news/article-1178239/

Computer-hard-drive-sold-eBay-details-secret-U-S-missile-defence-system.html, accessed February 8, 2010.

30. www.nytimes.com/2010/04/20/technology/companies/20apple.html.

31. I'm making this up, but according to the U.S. military, this is how it may actually have happened. See, e.g., Julian Barnes, "Cyber-Attack on Defense Department Computers Raises Concerns," *Los Angeles Times*, November 28, 2008, at www.latimes.com/news/nationworld/iraq/complete/la-na-cyberattack28-2008nov28,0,230046.story, accessed November 29, 2008.

32. Homeland Security Newswire, "Russian Hackers Attacked U.S. Central Command's Networks," December 2, 2008, at http://homelandsecuritynewswire.com/russian-hackers-attacked-us-central-commands-networks, accessed April 4, 2011.

33. "In 2008, the U.S. Department of Defense suffered a significant compromise of its classified military computer networks. It began when an infected flash drive was inserted into a U.S. military laptop at a base in the Middle East. The flash drive's malicious computer code, placed there by a foreign intelligence agency, uploaded itself onto a network run by the U.S. Central Command. That code spread undetected on both classified and unclassified systems, establishing what amounted to a digital beachhead, from which data could be transferred to servers under foreign control. It was a network administrator's worst fear: a rogue program operating silently, poised to deliver operational plans into the hands of an unknown adversary." William J. Lynn III, "Defending a New Domain," *Foreign Affairs*, September/October 2010, at www.foreignaffairs.com/articles/66552/william-j-lynn-iii/defending-a-new-domain, accessed September 30, 2010.

34. Reuters, "U.S. Code-Cracking Agency Works as if Compromised," December 16, 2010, at www.reuters.com/article/idUSTRE6BF6BZ20101217, accessed December 16, 2010.

35. Noah Schachtman, "Under Worm Assault, Military Bans Disks, USB Drives," *Wired*, November 19, 2008, at www.wired.com/dangerroom/2008/11/army-bans-usb-d/comment-page-3/, accessed April 24, 2010.

36. Noah Shachtman, "Hackers, Troops Rejoice: Pentagon Lifts Thumb-Drive Ban (Updated)," *Wired*, February 8, 2010, at www.wired.com/dangerroom/2010/02/hackers-troops-rejoice-pentagon-lifts-thumb-drive-ban/, accessed April 19, 2010.

37. William Matthews, "Pentagon to Allow Thumb Drives with Strict Rules," *Federal Times*, February 19, 2010, at www.federaltimes.com/article/20100219/IT03/2190306/1032/IT, accessed April 19, 2010.

38. Allan Holmes, "Malicious Thumb Drives in Justice," *Nextgov*, August 20, 2008, at http://techinsider.nextgov.com/2008/08/malicious_thumb_drives_in_just.php, accessed April 24, 2009.

39. Gregg Keizer, "1-in-4 Worms Spread Through Infected USB Devices," *Computerworld*, August 26, 2010, at www.computerworld.com/s/article/9182119/1_in_4_worms_spread_through_infected_USB_devices, accessed September 2, 2010.

40. Air Combat Command, U.S. Air Force, "CONCEPT OF OPERATIONS FOR ENDURANCE UNMANNED AERIAL VEHICLES 3 Dec 1996—Version 2," Section 1, ¶ 1.6.4, at www.fas.org/irp/doddir/usaf/conops_uav/index.html, accessed April 26, 2010.

41. Mark Phillips, "Military Surveillance Hack Warning," CBS News, December 17, 2009, at www.cbsnews.com/video/watch/?id=5990213n&tag=api, accessed April 26, 2010.

42. Declan McCullagh, "U.S. Was Warned of Predator Drone Hacking," CBS News, December 17, 2009, at www.cbsnews.com/8301-504383_162-5988978-504383.html, accessed April 26, 2010.

43. Siobhan Gorman, Y. J. Dreazen, and A. Cole, "Insurgents Hack U.S. Drones," *Wall Street Journal*, December 17, 2009, at http://online.wsj.com/article/SB126102247889095011.html, accessed April 26, 2010. For another example of consumer technology with military application, see Jason Lewis, "Phone App That Tracks Planes 'Is Aid to Terrorists Armed with Missiles,'" *The Daily Mail*, October 4, 2010, at www.dailymail.co

.uk/sciencetech/article-1317184/Phone-app-tracks-planes-aid-terrorists-armed-missiles .html, accessed Octo-ber 4, 2010.

44. Barnaby J. Feder, "Peter F. Drucker, a Pioneer in Social and Management Theory, Is Dead at 95," *New York Times*, November 12, 2005, at www.nytimes.com/2005/11/12/busi ness/12drucker.html?pagewanted=1&_r=1&sq=peter%20drucker%20obituary&st =nyt&scp=1, accessed April 26, 2010.

## CHAPTER 5: DANCING IN THE DARK

1. Joseph Weiss, *Protecting Industrial Control Systems from Electronic Threats* (New York: Momentum Press, 2010), pp. 101, 105–6; author interview with Michael Assante, formerly of Idaho National Laboratories and former vice president and chief security officer, North American Electric Reliability Corporation, December 23, 2010.

2. Steve Kroft, "Cyber War: Sabotaging the System," *60 Minutes*, updated June 10, 2010, at www.cbsnews.com/video/watch/? id=6578069n&tag=related;photovideo, accessed June 1, 2011; video also available on YouTube at www.youtube.com/watch?v=rTkXgqK1|9A, accessed June 1, 2011. The AURORA experiment with the generator had nothing to do with the series of intrusions into Google in late 2009–early 2010 that are known by the same name.

3. E.g., Booz Allen Hamilton, "Convergence of Enterprise Security Organizations," November 8, 2005, at www.asisonline.org/newsroom/alliance.pdf, accessed March 28, 2011; Joseph Weiss, *Protecting Industrial Control Systems from Electronic Threats* (New York: Momentum Press, 2010), chapters 3–5.

4. John D. Moteff, "Critical Infrastructure: Background, Policy, and Implementation," Congressional Research Service, March 13, 2007, p. 1, n. 1, at http://assets.opencrs.com/rpts/ RL30153_20081010.pdf, accessed May 9, 2010.

5. Tony Smith, "Hacker Jailed for Revenge Sewage Attacks," *The Register*, October 31, 2001, at www.theregister.co.uk/2001/10/31/hacker_jailed_for_revenge_sewage/, accessed May 9, 2010.

6. Weiss, *Protecting Industrial Control Systems*, p. 8. By "electric grid," I refer to the entire electricity infrastructure.

7. Ibid., p. 35.

8. Ibid., p. 26, describing Federal Energy Regulatory Commission Orders 888 and 889, April 24, 1996.

9. Ibid.

10. U.S.-Canada Power System Outage Task Force, "August 14th Blackout: Causes and Recommendations," ("Blackout Report"), April 2004, p. 133, at https://reports.energy.gov/, accessed July 3, 2010.

11. Stuart Baker et al., "In the Crossfire: Critical Infrastructure in the Age of Cyber War," Center for Strategic and International Studies and McAfee [January 28, 2010], p. 19, at http://img.en25.com/Web/McAfee/NA_CIP_RPT_REG_2840.pdf, accessed January 28, 2010.

12. Ibid. Also "Blackout Report," p. 133; North American Electric Reliability Corporation and U.S. Department of Energy, "High-Impact, Low-Frequency Event Risk to the North American Bulk Power System" (hereafter "High-Impact, Low-Frequency Report"), June 2010, p. 30, at www.nerc.com/files/HILF.pdf, accessed June 22, 2010.

13. See, e.g., Bentek Systems, www.scadalink.com/support/technotesIP.html, accessed November 18, 2010, which says that Internet- and Web-based SCADA systems offer the advantage of "[i]ntegration of IT to Automation and Monitoring Networks," notwithstanding "Security concerns"; Automation.com, at www.automation.com/content/arc -predicts-scada-market-in-water-wastewater-to-exceed-275-million, accessed November 18, 2010 ("Emerging technology is enabling SCADA to be tightly integrated to the domain of business processes, creating an improved value proposition for its usage").

14. Juniper Networks, "Architecture for Secure Scada and Distributed Control System Networks" (2010), p. 1, at www.juniper.net/us/en/local/pdf/whitepapers/2000276-en.pdf, accessed November 18, 2010.

15. E-mail from Joseph Weiss to the author, December 27, 2010, stating, "Industrial control system field devices, whether in electric or any other industry, have minimal cyber security at best. These devices include programmable logic controllers (PLC) such as those targeted by Stuxnet, sensors, drives, chemical analyzers, breakers, etc. Moreover, these devices have minimal cyber forensic capabilities. Consequently, even if they are impacted, it may not be possible to know it was cyber." See Weiss, *Protecting Industrial Control Systems*, Table 5.1, p. 34.

16. Eric Byres, David Leversage, and Nate Kube, "Security Incidents and Trends in SCADA and Process Industries," *The Industrial Ethernet Book* (Symantec and Byres Security, May 2007), p. 16, at www.mtl-inst.com/images/uploads/datasheets/IEBook_May_07_SCADA_Security_Trends.pdf, accessed December 28, 2010. These authors note, "While commonly denied, both the ARC Study and a number of the incidents in the [Industrial Security Incident Database] show that control systems do get connected directly to the Internet. Reasons for this include a desire to download system patches or antivirus updates from vendor web sites, as well as a misguided desire to conduct typical office activities (such as e-mail) from the plant floor."

17. Andy Greenberg, "Electric, Oil Companies Take Almost a Year to Fix Hackable Security Flaws," *Forbes*, July 28, 2010, at http://blogs.forbes.com/firewall/2010/07/28/electric-oil-companies-take-almost-a-year-to-fix-known-security-flaws/, accessed July 29, 2010.

18. "Blackout Report," p. 131.

19. Weiss, *Protecting Industrial Control Systems*, pp. 35–39.

20. Baker et al., "In the Crossfire," p. 22. See Weiss, *Protecting Industrial Control Systems*, who says that patching industrial control systems is often "slow or impossible," p. 34; that much off-the-shelf ICS software has been modified and thus patches are "not applicable," p. 39.

21. Baker et al., "In the Crossfire," p. 10.

22. Quotations from Michael Assante are from my interviews of him, June 25, 2010, and December 23 and 27, 2010, unless otherwise stated.

23. Federal Energy Regulatory Commission, "Mandatory Reliability Standards for the Bulk-Power System," Docket no. RM06-16-000, order no. 693, March 16, 2007, at www.ferc.gov/whats-new/comm-meet/2007/031507/e-13.pdf, accessed November 27, 2010. This order became law when the industry failed to challenge it. In March 2010, after waiting three years for the industry to comply with Order 693, FERC issued a further order directing compliance and setting deadlines. FERC Docket no. RM06-16-009, "Order Setting Deadline for Compliance," March 18, 2010, reported at 130 FERC ¶ 61,200; FERC Docket no. RM06-16-010, "Order Setting Deadline for Compliance," March 18, 2010, reported at 130 FERC ¶ 61,218. With regard to FERC's exercise of its limited power over critical infrastructure standards, see "Mandatory Reliability Standards for Critical Infrastructure Protection," Docket no. RM06-22-000, Order no. 706, January 18, 2008.

24. FERC is powerless to set standards but wields substantial power to punish power generators for failing to comply with standards approved by NERC. In October 2009, for example, FERC fined Florida Power & Light $25 million for a February 2008 blackout during which millions of consumers in South Florida lost power for hours. FERC, "FERC Approves Settlement on FRCC's Role in Florida Blackout," Docket no. IN08-5-000, March 5, 2010, at www.ferc.gov/media/news-releases/2010/2010-1/03-05-10.pdf, accessed November 27, 2010.

25. NERC, "High-Impact, Low-Frequency Report," at www.nerc.com/files/HILF.pdf, accessed June 22, 2010.

26. Ibid., p. 9.

27. NERC, "Glossary of Terms Used in Reliability Standards," April 20, 2009, at www.nerc
.com/files/Glossary_2009April20.pdf, accessed March 28, 2011.

28. The Federal Power Act, section 215 (a)(4), (8), 16 U.S.C. §8240 (a)(4) and (8), includes
"cybersecurity incidents" as an element of electric reliability but does not define "critical."

29. Letter from Michael Assante, vice president and chief security officer, North American
Electric Reliability Corporation, to industry stakeholders, April 7, 2009.

30. John Markoff, "A Code for Chaos," New York Times, October 2, 2010, at www.nytimes.com/
2010/10/03/weekinreview/03markoff.html?scp=7&sq=stuxnet&st=nyt, accessed October
2, 2010.

31. VirusBlokAda, "Rootkit.TmpHider," June 17, 2010, at www.anti-virus.by/en/tempo.shtml,
accessed December 20, 2010.

32. For the Stuxnet timeline, see Symantec, "W32.Stuxnet Dossier," version 1.3, November
2010, p. 4, at www.wired.com/images_blogs/threatlevel/2010/11/w32_stuxnet_dossier
.pdf, accessed November 30, 2010.

33. Kevin J. O'Brien, "Siemens Alerts Customers to Virus in Its Automation Software," New
York Times, July 22, 2010, at www.nytimes.com/2010/07/23/technology/23iht-siemens
.html?scp=2&sq=stuxnet&st=nyt, accessed July 23, 2010.

34. Symantec, "W32.Stuxnet Dossier," p. 2.

35. David E. Sanger, "Iran Fights Malware Attacking Computers," New York Times, September
25, 2010, at www.nytimes.com/2010/09/26/world/middleast/26iran.html?scp=13&sq
=stuxnet&st=nyt, accessed September 25, 2010.

36. Symantec, "W32.Stuxnet Dossier," p. 6.

37. George Kiezer, "Iran Admits Stuxnet Worm Infected PCs at Nuclear Reactor," Computerworld, September 27, 2010, at www.computerworld.com/s/article/9188147/Iran_admits
_Stuxnet_worm_infected_PCs_at_nuclear_reactor, accessed September 27, 2010.

38. William Yong, "Iran Says It Arrested Computer Worm Suspects," New York Times, October
2, 2010, at www.nytimes.com/2010/10/03/world/middleast/03iran.html?scp=14&sq
=stuxnet&st=nyt, accessed December 20, 2010.

39. William J. Broad and David E. Sanger, "Worm Was Perfect for Sabotaging Centrifuges,"
New York Times, November 18, 2010, at www.nytimes.com/2010/11/19/world/middle
east/19stuxnet.html?scp=2&sq=stuxnet&st=nyt, accessed November 18, 2010; John
Markoff, "Worm Can Deal Double Blow to Nuclear Program," New York Times, November 19, 2010, at www.nytimes.com/2010/11/20/world/middleast/20stuxnet.html?scp
=3&sq=stuxnet&st=nyt, accessed November 19, 2010.

40. William J. Broad, "Report Suggests Problems With Iran's Nuclear Effort," New York Times,
November 23, 2010, at www.nytimes.com/2010/11/24/world/middleast/24nuke.html
?scp=4&sq=stuxnet&st=nyt, accessed November 23, 2010.

41. Symantec, "W32.Stuxnet Dossier," description of "Attack Scenario," p. 3.

42. John Markoff and David E. Sanger, "In a Computer Worm, a Possible Biblical Clue," New
York Times, September 29, 2010, at www.nytimes.com/2010/09/30/world/middleast/
30worm.html?scp=6&sq=stuxnet&st=nyt, accessed September 29, 2010.

43. Ibid. Ralph Langner, a German security consultant, originally asserted that Stuxnet had
been "'weaponized' and designed to attack the Iranian centrifuge array," and has argued
that the malware could have been imported by a Russian engineer, as I speculate.

44. See William J. Broad, John Markoff, and David E. Sanger, "Israeli Test on Worm Called
Crucial in Iran Nuclear Delay," New York Times, January 15, 2011, at www.nytimes.com/
2011/01/16/world/middleast/16stuxnet.html, accessed January 18, 2011. For a technical report on Stuxnet, see Symantec, "W32.Stuxnet Dossier," February 2011, at www
.symantec.com/content/en/us/enterprise/media/security_response/whitepapers/w32
_stuxnet_dossier.pdf, accessed March 1, 2011.

45. Brian Krebs, "'Stuxnet' Worm Far More Sophisticated than Previously Thought," Krebs on

*Security*, September 14, 2010, at http://krebsonsecurity.com/2010/09/stuxnet-worm-far-more-sophisticated-than-previously-thought/, accessed September 15, 2010.

46. "Remarks by the President on Securing Our Nation's Cyber Infrastructure," May 29, 2009, at www.whitehouse.gov/the_press_office/Remarks-by-the-President-on-Securing-Our-Nations-Cyber-Infrastructure/, accessed July 3, 2010.

47. Sioban Gorman, "Electricity Grid in U.S. Penetrated By Spies," *Wall Street Journal*, April 8, 2009, at http://online.wsj.com/article/SB123914805204099085.html, accessed July 3, 2010.

48. Steve Kroft, "Cyber War: Sabotaging the System," *60 Minutes*, November 8, 2009, at www.cbsnews.com/stories/2009/11/06/60minutes/main5555565.shtml, accessed July 3, 2010. One of the Brazilian systems involved denied being attacked and attributed the blackout to dirty equipment. Marcelo Suares, "Brazilian Blackout Traced to Sooty Insulators," *Wired*, November 9, 2009, at www.wired.com/threatlevel/2009/11/brazil_blackout/, accessed May 4, 2010. In an example of selective skepticism, some observers took the denial at face value. See, e.g., Ryan Singel, "Richard Clarke's Cyberwar: File Under Fiction," *Wired*, April 22, 2010, at www.wired.com/threatlevel/2010/04/cyberwar-richard-clarke/, accessed May 4, 2010.

49. Gorman, "Electricity Grid in U.S.," April 8, 2009. For a Chinese academic discussion of the feasibility of attacking the U.S. power grid, see Jian-Wei Wang and Li-Li Rong, "Cascade-based Attack Vulnerability on the US Power Grid," v. 47, *Safety Science*, (2009): 1332, at www.millennium-ark.net/NEWS/10_Sci_Tech/100323.CH.US.Power.Grid.pdf, accessed November 19, 2010.

50. John P. Avlon, "The Growing Cyber-Threat," *Forbes*, October 20, 2009, at www.forbes.com/2009/10/20/digital-warfare-cyber-security-opinions-contributors-john-p-avlon.html, accessed October 20, 2009.

51. "These and other foreign and domestic terrorist groups continue to pursue plans to attack the U.S. directly, likely focusing on prominent government, economic, and infrastructure targets." "High-Impact, Low-Frequency Report," p. 29, citing director of National Intelligence, "Annual Threat Assessment," February 2009.

52. "Blackout Report," p. 132.

53. "High-Impact, Low-Frequency Report," pp. 27–28.

54. Weiss, *Protecting Industrial Control Systems*, p. 107.

55. Ibid., p. 106.

56. Joseph Weiss, "Control Systems Cyber Security—The Current Status of Cyber Security of Critical Infrastructures." Testimony before the U.S. Senate Committee on Commerce, Science, and Transportation, 111th Cong., 1st sess., March 19, 2009, p. 7, at www.controlglobal.com/articles/2009/CyberSecurity0903.html, accessed July 8, 2010.

57. Tim Greene, "Experts Hack Power Grid in No Time," *Network World*, April 9, 2008, at www.networkworld.com/news/2008/040908-rsa-hack-power-grid.html, accessed April 30, 2009.

58. NERC, "High-Impact, Low-Frequency Report," p. 30.

59. Ibid., p. 26.

60. Richard A. Clarke and Robert K. Knake, *Cyber War: The Next Threat to National Security and What to Do About It* (New York: HarperCollins, 2010), pp. 56–57.

61. Weiss, *Protecting Industrial Control Systems*, p. 88, discussing NERC's Critical Infrastructure Protection standard 002 (NERC CIP-002).

62. "The Clinton Administration's Policy on Critical Infrastructure Protection," Presidential Decision Directive 63, May 22, 1998, at www.fas.org/irp/offdocs/pdd/pdd-63.htm, accessed July 8, 2010.

63. "The National Infrastructure Protection Plan," approved June 30, 2006, at www.dhs.gov/xprevprot/programs/editorial_0827.shtm, accessed July 8, 2010. For a detailed discussion of public policy on critical infrastructure, see J. D. Moteff, "Critical Infrastructures:

Background, Policy, and Implementation," Congressional Research Service, March 13, 2007, at http://opencrs.com/document/RL30153/, accessed July 8, 2010.

64. U.S. Department of Energy, "DOE Issues National Energy Sector Cyber Organization Notice of Intent," February 11, 2010, at www.oe.energy.gov/DOE_Issues_Energy_Sec tor_Cyber_Organization_NOI.pdf, accessed July 8, 2010; see "Control System Security," at www.oe.energy.gov/controlsecurity.htm, accessed July 8, 2010.

65. "High-Impact, Low-Frequency Report," p. 36.

66. Ibid., pp. 26, 30, where NERC asserts that the system can handle "low and intermediate" threats and ordinary "balancing and regulating."

67. "High-Impact, Low-Frequency Report," p. 10.

68. Ibid., pp. 30, 37. According to information supplied by the U.S. Cyber Consequences Unit (which is funded chiefly with federal money), courtesy of its director and chief economist, Scott Borg, most electric generators come from China (where several Western companies have moved production), India, France, Germany, Japan, and Mexico. The only manufacturer of generators with a U.S. plant is GE, which makes a small part of its output in Schenectady, New York, and Greenville, South Carolina. GE also manufacturers generators in Germany and Mexico.

69. E-mail, Scott Borg to the author, December 27, 2010.

70. Baker, "In the Crossfire," pp. 1, 4.

71. Ibid., p. 7. Another source, which is also dependent on publicly disclosed events, states that most incidents involve "power and utilities," followed by petroleum and transportation. Zach Tudor and Mark Fabro, "What Went Wrong? A Study of Actual Industrial Cyber Security Incidents," SRI International, slide 11, at www.us-cert.gov/control_sys tems/icsjwg/presentations/spring2010/02%20-%20Zach%20Tudor.pdf, accessed April 4, 2011.

72. David Hancock, "Worm-like Infection at CSX Corp. Also Caused Delays for Amtrak," CBS News, August 21, 2003, at www.cbsnews.com/stories/2003/08/21/tech/main569418 .shtml, accessed November 18, 2010.

73. The report by the inspector general of the Department of Transportation was reported on the Web site of Representative John L. Mica, then the ranking Republican on the U.S. House of Representatives Transportation and Infrastructure Committee, May 6, 2009, at http://republicans.transportation.house.gov/News/PRArticle.aspx?NewsID =596, accessed November 18, 2010.

74. Stewart Baker, Natalia Filipiak, and Katrina Timlin, " In the Dark," Center for Strategic and International Studies and McAfee, April 18, 2011, at http://mcafee.com/US/resources/ reports/rp-critical-infrastructure-protection.pdf, accessed May 17, 2011; Baker, "In the Crossfire," p. 7.

75. Ibid., p. 9.

76. Jeanne Meserve, "Sources: Staged Cyber Attack Reveals Vulnerability in Power Grid," CNN, September 26, 2007, at www.cnn.com/2007/US/09/26/power.at.risk/index.html, accessed July 7, 2007.

77. Gregg Keizer, "Jury Convicts Programmer of Planting Fannie Mae Server Bomb," *Computerworld*, October 7, 2010, at www.computerworld.com/s/article/9189939/Jury_convicts _programmer_of_planting_Fannie_Mae_server_bomb, accessed December 16, 2010.

78. U.S. Secret Service and CERT Coordination Center, "Insider Threat Study: Computer System Sabotage in Critical Infrastructure Sectors," May 2005, p. 3, at www.secretser vice.gov/ntac/its_report_050516.pdf, accessed February 15, 2010. The man who did it was found guilty of one count of denying computer services.

79. Robert McMillan, "Update: Terry Childs Found Guilty," *Infoworld*, April 27, 2010, accessed April 29, 2010.

80. Jaikumar Vijayan, "IT Contractor Indicted for Sabotaging Offshore Rig Management System," *Computerworld*, March 18, 2009, at www.computerworld.com/s/article/9129933/IT

_contractor_indicted_for_sabotaging_offshore_rig_management_system_, accessed March 20, 2009.

81. "Total Gridlock," *Jane's Intelligence Review,* p. 26.

82. Baker, "In the Crossfire," p. 22.

## CHAPTER 6: BETWEEN WAR AND PEACE

1. John P. Sullivan, "Gangs, Hooligans, and Anarchists—The Vanguard of Netwar in the Streets," in John Arquilla and David Ronfeldt, eds., *Networks and Netwars: The Future of Terror, Crime, and Militancy* (Arlington, VA: RAND, 2001), quoting Martin van Creveld, *The Transformation of War* (New York: Free Press, 1991).

2. Richard M. Nixon, *The Real Peace* (New York: Little, Brown & Co., 1984), p. 104.

3. Timothy L. Thomas, *Dragon Bytes: Chinese Information-War Theory and Practice* (Ft. Leavenworth, KS: Foreign Military Studies Office, 2004), pp. 44, 45.

4. Mao Tse-tung, "On Protracted War," *Selected Works,* v. II (Peking: Foreign Languages Press, May 1938), pp. 156, 186, available at www.marxists.org/reference/archive/mao/selected-works/volume-2/index.htm, accessed April 4, 2011.

5. Qiao Liang and Wang Xiangsui, *Unrestricted Warfare* (Beijing: PLA Literature and Arts Publishing House, 1999), p. 61.

6. Ibid., p. 4.

7. Ibid., pp. 11–12.

8. Brian Krekel, "Capability of the People's Republic of China to Conduct Cyber Warfare and Computer Network Exploitation," prepared for the U.S.-China Economic and Security Review Commission, October 9, 2009, p. 12.

9. Qiao and Wang, *Unrestricted Warfare*, p. 64.

10. David Briscoe, "Kosovo-Propaganda War," AP, May 17, 1999.

11. Dorothy E. Denning, "Activism, Hacktivism, and Cyberterrorism: The Internet as a Tool for Influencing Foreign Policy," in Arquilla and Ronfeldt, eds., *Networks and Netwars*, pp. 239–40.

12. Ibid., pp. 268–69, citing Rebecca Allison, "Belgrade Hackers Bombard MoD Web site in 'First' Internet War," *PA News*, March 3, 1999; Dorothy E. Denning, "A View of Cyberterrorism Five Years Later," chapter 7 in *Internet Security: Hacking, Counterhacking, and Society*, K. Himma ed. (Sudbury, MA: Jones and Bartlett Publishers, 2007), at www.dtic.mil/cgi-bin/GetTRDoc?AD=ADA484928, p. 7, accessed April 4, 2011.

13. See, e.g., "NATO Bombs Serbian Decoys," at www.youtube.com/watch?v=1lHyKv4IC3c&has_verified=1, accessed December 22, 2010.

14. The Chinese government was not an entirely disinterested party during the Kosovo conflict. On May 7, 1999, U.S. aircraft bombed the Chinese embassy in Belgrade, killing three PRC nationals and creating an international incident. In China there were mass anti-American demonstrations, followed by back-and-forth electronic attacks between American and Chinese hackers. The U.S. apologized and claimed the bombing was a mistake caused by an out-of-date map, though doubt has been cast on that explanation. The controversy is summarized in Wikipedia, "US bombing of the People's Republic of China embassy in Belgrade," at http://en.wikipedia.org/wiki/US_bombing_of_the_People's_Republic_of_China_embassy_in_Belgrade, accessed July 20, 2010.

15. Timothy M. Thomas, *Cyber Silhouettes: Shadows over Information Operations* (Ft. Leavenworth, KS: Foreign Military Studies Office, 2005), pp. 133, 135.

16. Ibid., p. 145, quoting Elaine Grossman, "US Commander in Kosovo Sees Low-Tech Threats to High-Tech Warfare," *Inside the Pentagon*, September 9, 1999, p. 1.

17. See, e.g., Krekel, "Capability of the PRC to Conduct Cyber Warfare," p. 11.

18. The quotation is the title of chapter 2 of Qiao and Wang, *Unrestricted Warfare*.

19. See Qiao and Wang, *Unrestricted Warfare*, FBIS Editor's Note, p. 2.

20. Ibid., p. 7.

21. As of this writing the cover can be seen on the Web site of Powell's Books, at www.pow ells.com/biblio/0971680728?&PID=33157, accessed July 21, 2010. The original English translation, from which I have been quoting, was made by the Foreign Broadcast Information Service, the CIA's former open-source organization, and is available through Cryptome, at www.cryptome.org/cuw.htm, accessed July 17, 2010. A summary is available through the Federation of American Scientists, at www.fas.org/nuke/guide/china/doctrine/unresw1.htm, accessed July 19, 2010.

22. Qiao and Wang, *Unrestricted Warfare*, p. 23.

23. Ibid., pp. 6, 136.

24. Ibid. p. 143.

25. Ibid., pp. 168–69. In this view, every action falls into three types: "a pure war action, a nonwar military action, or a nonmilitary war action."

26. Ibid., p. 2.

27. Ibid., p. 8.

28. Martin Libicki, *Cyber Deterrence and Cyber War* (Santa Monica, CA: RAND, 2009), p. 1.

29. Ibid., p. 2.

30. As Adda Bozeman, a great scholar of statecraft, put it, "'peace' and 'war' are conceived as opposites in the West, and in law as well as in religion—quite in counterpoint to non-Western mind-sets in which these concepts interpenetrate." Adda B. Bozeman, *Strategic Intelligence and Statecraft* (Washington, DC: Brassey's, Inc., 1992), p. 12. When war is declared, important international and national legal results follow under American law. In wartime, for example, the president of the United States has vastly increased power over private resources, and insurance policies do not cover damage from acts of war. Since the Korean War, the United States has waged war several times without a formal war declaration (or its equivalent, a congressional authorization to use military force), but the legal consequences of a declaration are significant. Three of the six justices who rejected President Truman's asserted authority to seize private steel mills in 1950 referred to the lack of a formal state of war. In Korea there was, however, a UN resolution authorizing combat, and it remains in effect. In Vietnam, President Johnson ramped up combat only after obtaining a joint resolution of Congress authorizing the use of conventional military force in Southeast Asia; Pub. Law 88-408, August 7, 1964 (the "Tonkin Bay Resolution").

31. W. Hays Parks, "National Security Law in Practice: The Department of Defense Law of War Manual," address to the American Bar Association Standing Committee on Law and National Security, November 18, 2010, available through www.abanet.org/natsecurity/.

32. See, e.g., Dan Kuehl, "From Cyberspace to Cyberpower: Defining the Problem," paper for the Information Resources Management College/National Defense University [n.d.], p. 14, remarking that "the events in Estonia . . . contributed to the creation of several organizations to support this protection. These included NATO's Computer Incident Response Capability (NCIRC), the Cyber Defence Management Authority (CDMA), and the NATO Cooperative Cyber Defence Centre of Excellence, to be located in Tallinn, the Estonian capital."

33. See generally Scott J. Henderson, *The Dark Visitor: Inside the World of Chinese Hackers* (Fort Leavenworth, KS: Foreign Military Studies Office, 2007), especially p. xiii.

34. Alvin and Heidi Toffler, *War and Anti-War: Survival at the Dawn of the 21st Century* (Boston: Little, Brown and Co.1993), quoted in Qiao and Wang, *Unrestricted Warfare*, p. 59, n. 6.

35. Qiao and Wang, *Unrestricted Warfare*, p. 41.

36. Ibid., p. 43.

37. Ibid., p. 114, quoting a version of Sun Tzu.

38. U.S.-China Economic and Security Review Commission, "2009 Report to Congress," November 2009, p. 5, at www.uscc.gov/annual_report/2009/annual_report_full_09.pdf, accessed March 4, 2009.

39. Thomas, *Dragon Bytes*, p. 45, citing Dennis J. Blasko, "Chinese Strategic Thinking: People's War in the 21st Century," *China Brief*, March 18, 2010, at www.jamestown.org/programs/chinabrief/single/?tx_ttnews%5Btt_news%5D=36166&tx_ttnews%5BbackPid%5D=25&cHash=0fc6f0833f, accessed July 26, 2010.

40. Henderson, *Dark Visitor*, pp. 127–28, quoting Peng Guangqian and Yao Youzhi, *The Science of Military Strategy* (Beijing: Military Publishing House, Academy of Military Science of the Chinese People's Liberation Army, 2005), p. 455.

41. Henderson, *Dark Visitor*, pp. xiii, 5.

42. Whether the bombing was a mistake, as the United States contends, or whether it was done deliberately because the Chinese embassy was transmitting Yugoslav army communications, is a matter of dispute. See Steven Lee Myers, "Chinese Embassy Bombing: A Wide Net of Blame," *New York Times*, April 17, 2000, at http://query.nytimes.com/gst/fullpage.html?res=9801EED91431F934A25757C0A9669C8B63&pagewanted=1, accessed November 18, 2010; John Sweeney et al., "Nato Bombed Chinese Deliberately," *The Guardian*, October 17, 1999, at www.guardian.co.uk/world/1999/oct/17/balkans, accessed November 18, 2010.

43. Henderson, *Dark Visitor*, p. 14.

44. Ibid., pp. 21, 22, 34.

45. Ibid., p. xii, citing Vivien Cui, "'Godfather' of Hackers Fights for Web Security," *Hong Kong Sunday Morning Post*, May 29, 2005, as translated by FBIS, ref. CPP20050530000043.

46. Motivations for hacking may be changing as China prospers, as this story suggests: "One Beijing hacker says two Chinese officials approached him a couple of years ago requesting 'help in obtaining classified information' from foreign governments. He says he refused the 'assignment,' but admits he perused a top U.S. general's personal documents once while scanning for weaknesses in Pentagon information systems 'for fun.' The hacker, who requested anonymity to avoid detection, acknowledges that Chinese companies now hire people like him to conduct industrial espionage. 'It used to be that hackers wouldn't do that because we all had a sense of social responsibility,' says the well-groomed thirtysomething, 'but now people do anything for money.'" Melinda Liu, "High-Tech Hunger," *Newsweek International*, January 16, 2006, at www.msnbc.msn.com/id/10756796/site/newsweek, accessed July 22, 2010.

47. U.S.-China, "2009 Economic Report," p. 175.

48. U.S.-China, "2009 Economic Report," p. 173, citations omitted, at www.uscc.gov/annual_report/2009/annual_report_full_09.pdf, accessed March 4, 2009.

49. Krekel, "Capability of the PRC," pp. 33, and 35, citing *China's National Defense in 2004* (Beijing: Information Office of China's State Council, 2004), at http://english.peopledaily.com.cn/whitepaper/defense2004/defense2004.html; and *China's National Defense in 2006* (Beijing: Information Office of China's State Council, 2006), at http://english.peopledaily.com.cn/whitepaper/defense2006/defense2006.html.

50. U.S.-China, "2009 Economic Report," p. 174.

51. This account is based on Ellen Nakashima, "Diverse Group of Chinese Hackers Wrote Code in Attacks on Google, U.S. Companies," *Washington Post*, February 20, 2010, at www.washingtonpost.com/wp-dyn/content/article/2010/02/19/AR2010021902643.html, accessed February 23, 2010; and Joseph Menn, "US Experts Close in on Google Hackers," *The Financial Times*, February 21, 2010, at www.cnn.com/2010/BUSINESS/02/21/google.hackers/index.html, accessed July 27, 2010.

52. Thomas, *Dragon Bytes*, pp. 52, 81.

53. In examining Chinese doctrine, one must rely on the many publications in official journals, because the PRC does not publish a strategy for computer network operations, whereas the United States does. See, e.g., U.S. Department of Defense, "Information Operations," Joint Publication 3–13 (Washington, DC: February 2006), at www.c4i.org/jp3_13.pdf, accessed July 28, 2010.

54. U.S. Department of Defense, Office of Force Transformation, "The Implementation of Network-Centric Warfare," January 5, 2005, p. 3, at www.au.af.mil/au/awc/awcgate/transformation/oft_implementation_ncw.pdf, accessed November 18, 2010; U.S. Department of Defense, Office of the Secretary of Defense, "Military and Security Developments Involving the People's Republic of China 2010 Annual Report to Congress," pursuant to the National Defense Authorization Act for fiscal year 2010, p. 3, www.defense.gov/pubs/pdfs/2010_CMPR_Final.pdf, accessed November 18, 2010.

55. Thomas, *Silhouettes*, p. 63, quoting *U.S. Army Field Manual 3.0*.

56. Ibid., p. 24, quoting U.S. Air Force Joint Doctrinal Pub. 2-5, January 2005.

57. Timothy L. Thomas, "Human Network Attacks," *Military Review*, September–October 1999, at www.au.af.mil/au/awc/awcgate/fmso/humannet.htm, accessed July 28, 2010.

58. Krekel, "Capability of the PRC," p. 10.

59. Thomas, *Dragon Bytes*, pp. 32–33, citing Shen Weiguang, "Checking Information Warfare-Epoch Mission of Intellectual Military," *Liberation Army Daily*, February 2, 1999, p. 6, as translated and downloaded from FBIS.

60. Thomas, *Dragon Bytes*, pp. 15, 39.

61. Ibid., pp. 36–37; see Krekel, "Capability of the PRC," pp. 26–28.

62. Thomas, *Dragon Bytes*, p. 14, quoting Yuan Banggen, "On IW Battlefields," *Zhongguo Junshi Kexue*, February 20, 1999, pp. 46–51, as translated and downloaded from the FBIS Web site.

63. Krekel, "Capability of the PRC," p. 15.

64. Qiao and Wang, *Unrestricted Warfare*, pp. 145–46.

## CHAPTER 7: JUNE 2017

1. John Pomfret, "U.S. Takes a Tougher Tone with China," *Washington Post*, July 30, 2010, at www.washingtonpost.com/wp-dyn/content/article/2010/07/29/AR2010072906416.html, accessed July 30, 2010.

2. United Nations Office of Legal Affairs, Division for Ocean Affairs and the Law of the Sea, "Oceans and Law of the Sea," updated November 15, 2010, at www.un.org/Depts/los/reference_files/chronological_lists_of_ratifications.htm#The%20United%20Nations%20Convention%20on%20the%20Law%20of%20the%20Sea, accessed April 5, 2011.

3. United Nations Convention on the Law of the Sea of 10 December 1982, Article 301, at www.un.org/Depts/los/convention_agreements/texts/unclos/closindx.htm, accessed April 6, 2011.

4. The phrase "lawfare," meaning the use of law as a weapon in pursuit of political or military objectives, was coined by Col. Charles J. Dunlap, Jr., USAF, in "Law and Military Interventions: Preserving Humanitarian Values in 21st Century Conflicts," prepared for the Humanitarian Challenges in Military Intervention Conference, Carr Center for Human Rights Policy, Kennedy School of Government, Harvard University Washington, D.C., November 29, 2001, at www.duke.edu/~pfeaver/dunlap.pdf, accessed February 27, 2011.

5. Mike McConnell, "Mike McConnell on How to Win the Cyber-War We're Losing," *Washington Post*, February 28, 2010, at www.washingtonpost.com/wp-dyn/content/article/2010/02/25/AR2010022502493.html, accessed February 28, 2010.

6. Ryan Singel, "Cyberwar Hype Intended to Destroy the Open Internet," *Wired*, March 1, 2010, at www.wired.com/threatlevel/2010/03/cyber-war-hype/, accessed July 14, 2010.

7. This account is based on Gus W. Weiss, "The Farewell Dossier: Duping the Soviets," Central Intelligence Agency, updated June 27, 2008, at https://www.cia.gov/library/center-for-the-study-of-intelligence/csi-publications/csi-studies/studies/96unclass/farewell.htm, accessed August 4, 2010; and William Safire, "The Farewell Dossier," *New York Times*, February 2, 2004, at www.nytimes.com/2004/02/02/opinion/02SAFI.html, accessed August 4, 2010.

8. Weiss, "The Farewell Dossier."

9. Safire, "Farewell Dossier."

10. Sally Adee, "The Hunt for the Kill Switch," IEEE Spectrum, Web site of the American Institute of Electrical Engineers, May 2008, at http://spectrum.ieee.org/semiconductors/design/the-hunt-for-the-kill-switch/1, accessed August 4, 2010. This is also an excellent account of the complexity of the challenge of policing the supply chain for computer chips.

11. Jack Goldsmith, "The New Vulnerability," *The New Republic*, June 7, 2010, at www.tnr.com/article/books-and-arts/75262/the-new-vulnerability, accessed July 15, 2010.

12. Richard A. Clarke and Robert K. Knake, *Cyber War: The Next Threat to National Security and What to Do About It* (New York: HarperCollins, 2010), pp. 9–11.

13. Adee, "The Hunt," May 2008; Clarke and Knake, *Cyber War*, pp. 1–8, have an interesting discussion of how the Israelis may have pulled off this feat.

14. Timothy L. Thomas, *Dragon Bytes: Chinese Information-War Theory and Practice* (Ft. Leavenworth, KS: Foreign Military Studies Office, 2004), p. 45, quoting a lecture to the Chinese National Defense University, "New Situation, New Challenges."

15. Dorothy E. Denning, "Activism, Hacktivism, and Cyberterrorism: The Internet as a Tool for Influencing Foreign Policy," in John Arquilla and David Ronfeldt, eds., *Networks and Netwars: The Future of Terror, Crime, and Militancy* (Arlington, VA: RAND, 2001), p. 267. See also Denning's "Hacktivism: An Emerging Threat to Diplomacy," American Foreign Service Association, at www.afsa.org/fsj/sept00/Denning.cfm, accessed August 2, 2010.

16. Stefan Wray, "The Electronic Disturbance Theater and Electronic Civil Disobedience," Web site under the rubric "Electronic Civil Disobedience," dated June 17, 1998, at www.thing.net/~rdom/ecd/EDTECD.html, accessed August 2, 2010.

17. Denning, "Activism, Hacktivism," in Arquilla and Ronfeldt, p. 264.

18. Qiao Liang and Wang Xiangsui, *Unrestricted Warfare* (Beijing: PLA Literature and Arts Publishing House, 1999), p. 47.

19. John Robb, *Brave New War: The Next Stage of Terrorism and the End of Globalization* (New York: Wiley, 2007), p. 150–51, citing David Kaplan, "Paying for Terror," *U.S. News & World Report*, December 5, 2005. A version of Kaplan's article posted November 27, 2005, is available at www.usnews.com/usnews/news/articles/051205/5terror_2.htm, accessed April 5, 2011.

20. Phil Williams, "Transnational Criminal Networks," in Arquilla and Ronfeldt, pp. 64–65.

21. National Intelligence Counsel, *Global Trends 2015*, December 2000, p. 41, at www.dni.gov/nic/PDF_GIF_global/globaltrend2015.pdf, accessed August 2, 2010. The NIC produces the U.S. intelligence community's highest level analyses.

22. *Global Trends 2025: A Transformed World*, November 2008, p. 68, at www.dni.gov/nic/PDF_2025/2025_Global_Trends_Final_Report.pdf, accessed August 2, 2010.

23. The president did not authorize an attack on the Iraqi financial system, however, because of concern that it could not be contained and would spread throughout the world financial system. John Markoff and Thom Shanker, "Halted '03 Iraq Plan Illustrates U.S. Fear of Cyberwar Risk," *New York Times*, August 1, 2009, at www.nytimes.com/2009/08/02/us/politics/02cyber.html?_r=3&partner=rss&emc=rss, accessed November 18, 2010. Cyberweaponry is computer code. It is a form of information, and as we have seen in other contexts, information leaks.

## CHAPTER 8

1. Quoted in Suzanne Spaulding, "No More Secrets: Then What?" HuffingtonPost.com, June 24, 2010, at www.huffingtonpost.com/suzanne-e-spaulding/no-more-secrets-then-what_b_623997.html, accessed June 25, 2010.

2. The primary source for this account of the murder of Mahmoud al-Mabhouh is the Dubai police, who released selected video footage of many of the events described here. I have constructed this account based on those videos and on the following secondary sources:

Dana Harman, "Dubai Assassination Spotlights Top Cop Skills in a Modern-Day Casablanca," *Christian Science Monitor*, March 19, 2010, at www.csmonitor.com/World/Middle-East/2010/0319/Dubai-assassination-spotlights-top-cop-skills-in-a-modern-day-Casablanca, accessed September 12, 2010; Duncan Gardham, "Dubai Hamas Assassination: How It Was Planned," *The Telegraph*, February 17, 2010, at www.telegraph.co.uk/news/worldnews/middleeast/dubai/7251960/Dubai-Hamas-assassination-how-it-was-planned.html, accessed September 12, 2010; Nick McDermott and Kate Loveys, "'Dubai Hit Squad Stole My Identity': British Man's Name Used by Assassins Who Executed Senior Hamas Leader," *The Daily Mail*, February 16, 2010, at www.dailymail.co.uk/news/worldnews/article-1251260/Mahmoud-Al-Mabhouh-Dubai-assassination-Briton-named-hit-squad-speaks-out.html, accessed September 12, 2010; Robert F. Worth and Isabel Kirshner, "Hamas Official Murdered in Dubai Hotel," *New York Times,* January 29, 2010, at www.nytimes.com/2010/01/30/world/middleeast/30dubai.html, accessed September 22, 2010; for video footage, see, e.g., www.youtube.com/watch?v=l9xMkX98VVE, accessed September 11, 2010.

3. This account relies chiefly on: Harman, "Dubai Assassination," March 19, 2010; Gardham, "Dubai Hamas Assassination," February 17, 2010; McDermott and Loveys, "'Dubai Hit Squad,'" Worth and Kirshner, "Hamas Official," January 29, 2010; for video footage, see www.youtube.com/watch?v=l9xMkX98VVE.

4. Harman, "Dubai Assassination," March 19, 2010.

5. Paul Lewis, Julian Borger, and Rory McCarthy, "Dubai Murder: Fake Identities, Disguised Faces and a Clinical Assassination," *The Guardian*, February 16, 2010, at www.guardian.co.uk/world/2010/feb/16/dubai-murder-fake-identities-hamas, accessed September 12, 2010.

6. "Al Mabhouh Was Sedated Before He Was Killed," *Dubai Police News*, February 28, 2010, at www.dubaipolice.gov.ae/dp/english/news/news_show.jsp?Id=857382312&ArticalType=1, accessed September 12, 2010.

7. Harman, "Dubai Assassination," March 19, 2010.

8. Harman, "Dubai Assassination," March 19, 2010, citing an undated report in the London-based Arabic daily *Al-Hayat*.

9. A leaked State Department cable quoted Yuval Diskin, the head of Israel's internal security service, Shin Bet, saying that Fatah shares with Israel "almost all the intelligence it collects." Reuters, "Israel: Cable Cites Cooperation Against Hamas," *New York Times*, December 21, 2010, at www.nytimes.com/2010/12/21/world/middleeast/21briefs-Israel.html?_r=1&scp=1&sq=Israel:%20Cable%20Cites%20Cooperation&st=cse, accessed December 21, 2010.

10. Al Bawaba News, "Dubai Police Chief Insists Al-Mabhouh Was Betrayed from Within Hamas," March 4, 2010, at www1.albawaba.com/en/news/dubai-police-chief-insists-Al-Mabhouh-was-betrayed-within-hamas, accessed September 12, 2010.

11. In the *plus ça change* department, however, the level of hypocrisy in statecraft level of hypocrisy in statecraft remains unchanged. Thus, Britain expelled an Israeli diplomat over the use of forged UK passports in the operation. Ben Quinn, "Israel Diplomat Expelled by Britain over Dubai Assassination Passport Forgery," *Christian Science Monitor*, March 23, 2010, at www.csmonitor.com/world/Europe/2010/0323/Israel-diplomat-expelled-by-Britain-over-Dubai-assassination-passport-forgery, accessed April 30, 2011.

12. I owe this phrase to blogger Kevin Lovelace, "The Grim Facebook Future," posted May 11, 2010, on the Web site *Grinding*, at http://grinding.be/category/post-privacy/, accessed April 5, 2011.

13. Central Intelligence Agency, "Part II: Selected Venona Messages," at https://www.cia.gov/library/center-for-the-study-of-intelligence/csi-publications/books-and-monographs/venona-soviet-espionage-and-the-american-response-1939-1957/part2.htm, accessed September 25, 2010. Decrypted and now declassified, Venona traffic exposed this program. National Security Agency, "Venona Documents," at www.nsa.gov/

public_info/declass/venona/apr_1942.shtml, accessed September 25, 2010. The Soviet, and Russian, practice of using illegals has not ceased, however. Walter Pincus, "Fine Print: Despite Arrests, Russian 'Illegals' Won't Go Away," *Washington Post*, July 13, 2010, at www.washingtonpost.com/wp-dyn/content/article/2010/07/12/AR2010071205341.html, accessed September 25, 2010.

14. See Jeffrey Brown, "Justice Department: Russian Intelligence Officers Served as Illegal Agents," *PBS NewsHour*, June 28, 2010, at www.pbs.org/newshour/bb/law/jan-june10/spies_06-28.html, accessed September 19, 2010.

15. Christopher Andrew, *For the President's Eyes Only: Secret Intelligence and the American Presidency from Washington to Bush* (New York: HarperCollins, 1995), p. 38.

16. "Slim Chance of Finding an Arabic Speaker at the U.S. Embassy in Baghdad," ABC News, June 20, 2007, at http://blogs.abcnews.com/theblotter/2007/06/slim_chance _of_.html, accessed September 20, 2010.

17. See Kelly Jackson Higgins, "'Robin Sage' Profile Duped Military Intelligence, IT Security Pros," *Dark Reading*, July 6, 2010, at www.darkreading.com/insider-threat/167801100/security/privacy/225702468/index.html, accessed July 14, 2010.

18. Zeljka Zorz, "Russian Hacker Offers 1.5m Facebook Credentials for Sale," Help Net Security, April 23, 2010, at www.net-security.org/secworld.php?id=9186, accessed April 23, 2010.

19. See, e.g., "Real Time Satellite Tracking," N2YO.com, at www.n2yo.com/?s=31140, accessed September 20, 2010.

20. See, e.g., the Web site Airliners.Net, at www.airliners.net/search/photo.search?cnsearch =33010/1037&distinct_entry=true, accessed September 16, 2010.

21. See, e.g., "Aircraft Registration Database Lookup," Airframes.org, at www.airframes.org/reg/n126ch, accessed September 16, 2010. The database includes past as well as current registration information.

22. Paul T. Colgan, "No Landing Permission Needed for US Military Jet," *Sunday Business Post* (Dublin), October 17, 2004, at http://archives.tcm.ie/businesspost/2004/10/17/story265175049.asp, accessed September 16, 2010.

23. Intellectual Capital Group, "Gulfstream N379P becomes N8068V: The Price of Carelessness with Flight Logs, or Notoriety, or Just Business Practice," November 4, 2004, at http://spaces.icgpartners.com/index2.asp?nguid=53D0DFB7D3B64B39BE2316DFCB79707E, accessed September 16, 2010.

24. Stephen Grey, "US Accused of 'Torture Flights,'" *The Sunday Times* (London), November 14, 2004, at www.timesonline.co.uk/tol/news/world/article390989.ece, accessed September 16, 2010.

25. Tom Hundley, "Remote Polish Airstrip Holds Clues to Secret CIA Flights," *Chicago Tribune*, February 6, 2007, pp. 1, 14, at http://articles.chicagotribune.com/2007-02-06/news/0702060187_1_cia-flights-poland-and-romania-detention-centers, accessed September 16, 2010.

26. WikiLeaks, "WikiLeaks Submission," at http://wikileaks.org/wiki/WikiLeaks:Submissions, accessed September 23, 2010.

27. Joby Warrick, "WikiLeaks Works to Expose Government Secrets, But Web Site's Sources Are a Mystery," *Washington Post*, May 19, 2010, at www.washingtonpost.com/wp-dyn/content/article/2010/05/19/AR2010051905333.html, accessed September 21, 2010.

28. This last epithet was thrown at WikiLeaks's founder by Tunku Varadarajan, "Blogs & Stories: What Does Julian Assange Want?" *TheDailyBeast*, July 28, 2010, at www.thedailybeast.com/blogs-and-stories/2010-07-28/wikileaks-founder-julian -assange-is-a-criminal/, accessed September 23, 2010.

29. "For an organization dedicated to exposing secrets, WikiLeaks keeps a close hold on its own affairs. Its Web site doesn't list a street address or phone number, or the names of key officers. Officially, it has no employees, headquarters or even a post office box." Warrick, "WikiLeaks Works," May 19, 2010.

30. Ellen Nakashima and Joby Warwick, "Wikileaks Takes New Approach in Latest Release of Documents," *Washington Post*, July 26, 2010, at www.washingtonpost.com/wp-dyn/content/article/2010/07/25/AR2010072503356.html, accessed September 21, 2010.

31. For interesting commentary by an experienced military video analyst on the video and WikiLeaks's presentation of it, see the blog *A Look Inside*, at http://blog.ajmartinez.com/2010/04/05/wikileaks-collateral-murder/, accessed September 21, 2010.

32. Raffi Khatchadourian, "No Secrets," *The New Yorker*, June 7, 2010, at www.newyorker.com/reporting/2010/06/07/100607fa_fact_khatchadourian, accessed September 20, 2010.

33. WikiLeaks, http://wikileaks.org/wiki/Afghan_War_Diary_2004-2010, July 5, 2010, accessed September 22, 2010.

34. Nakashima and Warwick, "Wikileaks Takes New Approach," July 26, 2010.

35. Khatchadourian, "No Secrets," June 7, 2010.

36. John F. Burns and Ravi Somaiya, "WikiLeaks Founder on the Run, Trailed by Notoriety," *New York Times*, October 23, 2010, at www.nytimes.com/2010/10/24/world/24assange.html, accessed October 23, 2010.

37. Quoted in "WikiLeaks 'Bastards,'" *Wall Street Journal*, July 29, 2010, at http://online.wsj.com/article/SB10001424052748703940904575395500694117006.html, accessed September 20, 2010.

38. Burns and Samaiya, "WikiLeaks Founder on the Run," October 23, 2010.

39. "Reporters Without Borders, an international press freedom organisation, regrets the incredible irresponsibility you showed when posting your article 'Afghan War Diary 2004–2010' on the Wikileaks Web site on 25 July together with 92,000 leaked documents disclosing the names of Afghans who have provided information to the international military coalition that has been in Afghanistan since 2001." Open Letter to Assange, August 12, 2010, at http://en.rsf.org/united-states-open-letter-to-wikileaks-founder-12-08-2010,38130.html, accessed September 22, 2010.

40. "WikiLeaks 'Bastards,'" July 29, 2010.

41. Khatchadourian, "No Secrets," June 7, 2010.

42. "WikiLeaks 'Bastards,'" July 29, 2010.

43. Varadarajan in "What Does Julian Assange Want?" July 28, 2010.

44. Khatchadourian, "No Secrets," June 7, 2010.

45. John F. Burns and Ravi Somaiya, "WikiLeaks Founder on the Run, Trailed by Notoriety," *New York Times*, October 23, 2010, at www.nytimes.com/2010/10/24/world/24assange.html, accessed October 23, 2010.

46. The evidence was sufficient for a British court to order his extradition to Sweden to face the charges. As of this writing, that order is on appeal. Michael Holden, "WikiLeaks' Assange Appeals against UK Extradition," Reuters, March 3, 2011, at www.reuters.com/article/2011/03/03/us-britain-assange-appeal-idUSTRE7222LH20110303, accessed March 22, 2011.

47. Kim Zetter, "WikiLeaks Releases Secret List of Critical Infrastructure Sites," *Wired*, December 6, 2010, at www.wired.com/threatlevel/2010/12/critical-infrastructures-cable/, accessed December 7, 2010.

48. Raw Story, "WikiLeaks Accuses US of 'Financial Warfare,'" October 14, 2010, at www.rawstory.com/rs/2010/10/wikileaks-us-financial-warfare/, accessed December 23, 2010; Robert Mackey, "PayPal Suspends WikiLeaks Account," *New York Times*, December 3, 2010, at http://thelede.blogs.nytimes.com/2010/12/04/paypal-suspends-wikileaks-account/?scp=1&sq=wikileaks%20paypal&st=cse, accessed December 3, 2010; Robert Mackey, "WikiLeaks Founder's Statement from Prison," *New York Times*, December 14, 2010, at http://thelede.blogs.nytimes.com/2010/12/14/wikileaks-founders-statement-from-prison/?scp=3&sq=wikileaks%20paypal&st=cse, accessed December 23, 2010.

49. Miguel Helft, "Why Apple Removed a WikiLeaks App From Its Store," *New York Times*, December 21, 2010, at http://bits.blogs.nytimes.com/2010/12/21/why-apple-removed

-wikileaks-app-from-its-store/?scp=9&sq=wikileaks%20paypal&st=cse, accessed December 23, 2010.

50. For an image of the Anonymous threat against PayPal, see the undated posting at https://uloadr.com/u/4.png, accessed March 29, 2011. For accounts of Anonymous's activities in December 2010, see Cassell Bryan-Low and Sven Grundberg, "Hackers Rise for WikiLeaks," *Wall Street Journal*, December 8, 2010, at http://online.wsj.com/article/SB10001424052748703493504576007182352309942.html, accessed March 29, 2011; Daniel Tencer, "Hackers Take Down Website of Bank that Froze WikiLeaks Funds," Raw Story, December 6, 2010, at www.rawstory.com/rs/2010/12/06/hackers-website-bank-froze-wikileaks-funds/, accessed March 29, 2011.

51. WikiLeaks, "About WikiLeaks," at www.wikileaks.org/wiki/Wikileaks:About#What_is_WikiLeaks.3F_How_does_WikiLeaks_operate.3F, accessed September 21, 2010.

52. Ibid. "WikiLeaks believes that the best way to truly determine if a story is authentic, is not just our expertise, but to provide the full source document to the broader community—and particularly the community of interest around the document."

53. Ibid.

54. WikiLeaks criticizes corporations on many grounds. Here are the first two: "1. The right to vote does not exist except for share holders (analogous to land owners) and even there voting power is in proportion to ownership. 2. All power issues from a central committee." This sounds like a New Left manifesto of 1968.

55. Khatchadourian, "No Secrets," June 7, 2010.

56. Jack Goldsmith and Tim Wu, *Who Controls the Internet: Illusions of a Borderless World* (New York: Oxford University Press, 2006).

57. The orders in *Bank Julius Baer & Co., Ltd. v. WikiLeaks*, case no. CV08-0824 JSW (N.D. Cal., issued February 15, 2008), are available through Citizen Media Law Project, at www.citmedialaw.org/threats/julius-baer-bank-and-trust-v-wikileaks, accessed September 23, 2010.

58. Jaikumar Vijayan, "Rights Groups Seek Court OK to Intervene in Wikileaks Case," *New York Times*, February 28, 2008, at www.nytimes.com/idg/IDG_002570DE00740E18002573FD005AB476.html?ref=technology, accessed September 23, 2010.

59. See, e.g., Dan Goodin, "Wikileaks Judge Gets Pirate Bay Treatment," *The Register*, February 21, 2008, at www.theregister.co.uk/2008/02/21/wikileaks_bulletproof_hosting/page2.html, accessed September 23, 2010, who noted that the judge's "lack of internet savvy was in further evidence when he directed that a copy of his order be e-mailed to Wikileaks within 24 hours of the issuance of his order. The only problem there was that the suspending of Wikileaks.org prevented the organization's e-mail system from working."

60. David F. Gallagher, "WikiLeaks Has a Friend in Sweden," *New York Times*, February 20, 2008, at http://bits.blogs.nytimes.com/2008/02/20/wikileaks-site-has-a-friend-in-sweden/, accessed September 23, 2010.

61. "Welcome to PRQ!" at http://prq.se/?intl=1, accessed September 22, 2010.

62. See also Khatchadourian, "No Secrets," June 7, 2010.

63. WikiLeaks, "WikiLeaks Mirrors," at http://213.251.145.96/mirrors.html, accessed December 6, 2010. Later that month a Google search indicated the site was "not found, overloaded or other issues."

64. Goodin, "Wikileaks Judge Gets Pirate Bay Treatment," February 21, 2008.

65. The documents are posted on WikiLeaks, "Bank Julius Baer: Grand Larceny via Grand Cayman," at http://wikileaks.org/wiki/Bank_Julius_Baer:_Grand_Larceny_via_Grand_Cayman, accessed September 23, 2010.

66. Eight charges have been brought in military court against Private Manning alleging espionage and computer fraud under 18 U.S.C. §§793(e) and 1030(a)(1) and (a)(2). The charge sheet is available at http://boingboing.net/images/xeni/100705-Manning-Charge-Sheet.pdf, accessed December 24, 2010.

67. Khatchadourian, "No Secrets," June 7, 2010.

68. The cable in question appears to be available at http://history-political.blogspot.com/2010/02/classified-cable-from-us-embassy.html, dated January 13, 2010, accessed November 19, 2010, dealing with Iceland's economic and financial crisis.

## CHAPTER 9: THINKING ABOUT INTELLIGENCE

1. CIA Web site at https://www.cia.gov/offices-of-cia/index.html, accessed October 3, 2010. The NSA's principal directorates are Information Assurance (network defense), Signals Intelligence (collecting "communications, radars, and weapons systems used by our adversaries," which is to say, electronic theft), and Research. NSA Web site at www.nsa.gov/, and www.nsa.gov/sigint/index.shtml, both accessed October 3, 2010.

2. "*Counterintelligence* means information gathered and activities conducted to identify, deceive, exploit, disrupt, or protect against espionage, other intelligence activities, sabotage, or assassinations conducted for or on behalf of foreign powers, organizations, or persons, or their agents, or international terrorist organizations or activities." Executive Order 12,333, as amended most recently in 2008, §3.5(a).

3. In contrast to a covert operation, a clandestine operation is one whose existence is intended to remain secret.

4. For two valuable and wide-ranging views of the challenges facing the intelligence agencies—but which do not deal broadly with the transparency issue—see Jennifer E. Sims and Burton Gerber, eds., *Transforming U.S. Intelligence* (Washington, DC: Georgetown University Press, 2005); and by the same editors, *Vaults, Mirrors and Masks: Rediscovering U.S. Counterintelligence* (Washington, DC: Georgetown University Press, 2009).

5. In some such cases, classification may still be warranted to protect sources or methods, but in the case posited—where others can obtain the information as easily as the government—the source or method may have become superfluous.

6. Richard K. Betts, *Enemies of Intelligence: Knowledge and Power in American National Security* (New York: Columbia University Press, 2007), p. 157.

7. According to legend, on the basis of this information Rothschild bought huge quantities of long-depressed British consols (government bonds), making a fortune on information he alone possessed, while his bearish colleagues in the exchange still feared defeat at Napoleon's hands. In fact Rothschild did not begin buying consols until July 20, more than a month after the battle. Niall Ferguson, *The Ascent of Money: A Financial History of the World* (London: Penguin Press, 2008), pp. 78–85.

8. OMB Circular A-76, Attachment D, ¶ B.4.b.6.

9. According to its Web site, the Secret Service was created in 1865 and did not begin to provide security for the president until after the assassination of President McKinley in 1901: www.secretservice.gov/history.shtml, accessed December 26, 2010.

10. James Mackay, *Allan Pinkerton: The First Private Eye* (New York: John Wiley & Sons, 1996), pp. 80, 108–10, 155.

11. Ward Churchill, "The Trajectory of Political Policing in the United States, 1870 to the Present," [n.d.], notes 13–14, citing Max Lowenthal, *The Federal Bureau of Investigation* (New York: William Sloan Assoc., 1950), pp. 6–10.

12. Theodore M. Becker, "The Place of Private Police in Society: An Area of Research for the Social Sciences," v. 21, 3 *Social Problems* (1974): 438.

13. See, e.g., ibid., p. 441.

14. *Kline v. 1500 Massachusetts Avenue Apartment Corporation*, 439 F.2d 477 (D.C. Cir. 1970). See 43 A.L.R. 5th 207 (landlord's liability for failure to protect tenant from criminal acts of third person).

15. Becker, "Private Police," p. 443, 444, n. 5. Becker notes that Pinkerton began with ten employees in Chicago in 1850 to protect railroad property.

16. The regulations recognize that an activity may be already carried on privately yet may

classify that activity as inherently governmental anyway. One of the *nonde*terminative factors is "Whether the activity in question is already being performed by the private sector." Federal Acquisition Regulations, subpart 7.3, § 7.302; Office of Management and Budget, circular A-76, attachment D. Either this is illogical or it implies a judgment about the power of government rather than the nature of the activity.

17. "IBM Commercial: The Road: Intelligent Data Management and Analysis for a Smarter Planet," YouTube.com, at www.youtube.com/watch?v=F8EjUYpqCvw, accessed September 15, 2010.

18. U.S. Air Force, College of Aerospace Doctrine, Research and Education, Air and Space Power Course, at www.iwar.org.uk/military/resources/aspc/text/pow/s_p.htm, accessed October 22, 2010.

19. Leaking is often the product of widespread dissent, or a response to dissent, as occurred when the invasion of Iraq in 2004 produced no evidence of weapons of mass destruction. See, e.g., David E. Sanger and David Johnston, "Bush Ordered Declassifiction, Official Says," *New York Times*, April 10, 2006, at www.nytimes.com/2006/04/10/washington/10leak.html?ex=1302321600&en=a822dffc46e8662d&ei=5090&partner=rssuserland&emc=rss, accessed October 21, 2010. Daniel Ellsberg's leaking in 1971 of *United States–Vietnam Relations, 1945–1967: A Study Prepared by the Department of Defense*, better known as *The Pentagon Papers*, remains the most stunning and consequential example of large-scale leaking—including the WikiLeaks disclosures in 2010—but it involved a special study rather than a National Intelligence Estimate.

20. Bob Woodward, *Obama's Wars* (New York: Simon & Schuster, 2010), p. 53.

21. Jane Perlez, "Pakistan Aims Offensive at a Militant Stronghold," *New York Times*, October 17, 2009, at www.nytimes.com/2009/10/18/world/asia/18pstan.html?hp, last visited October 18, 2009.

22. "Scenarios: Alternative Futures the IC Could Face," *Quadrennial Intelligence Community Review*, January 2009, at www.fas.org/irp/dni/qicr.pdf, accessed October 5, 2010, pp. 3, 9. This most recent effort looks forward to 2025 and explores four different strategic developments, each of which involves a disruptive sea change in global relations. What's missing from this review, however, is an examination of how these or any other futuristic scenarios are likely to affect the intelligence business itself. One of the few comments on that topic in the entire *Quadrennial Review* is the assumption that in 2025 "[c]lassified working environments will remain the norm." Is this right? Or more to the point, which part of this complex business did the authors of the review have in mind when they made that assumption?

23. The objection to using foreign contractors will be that they may be influenced by their nation's intelligence services—but so what? Long-term projections don't deal in facts; they propose imaginative future possibilities.

24. The Intelligence Authorization Act for Fiscal Year 1993 included the Intelligence Organization Act and was based on the Senate version of the National Security Act of 1992, S. 2198. The House version (H.R. 4165) provided for an open source office. That office was not included in the final bill.

25. National Commission on Terrorist Attacks Upon the United States, *Final Report* (New York: W.W. Norton, [2004]), p. 413.

26. Commission on the Intelligence Capabilities of the United States Regarding Weapons of Mass Destruction, *Report* (Washington: USGPO, 2005), pp. 395–96.

27. ODNI "ODNI Announces Establishment of Open Source Center," News Release No. 6-05, November 8, 2005. One of the Open Source Center's valuable services is World News Connection. It carries translated news from 1,750 news sources in 130 countries. Barry Newman, "Today's News, Brought to You by Your Friends at the CIA," *Wall Street Journal*, February 28, 2011, at http://online.wsj.com/article/SB10001424052748704629004576136381178584352.html, accessed February 28, 2011.

28. I have omitted from this list of regrettable characteristics the many constraints on communications that are typical of intelligence agencies. They are difficult to adjust to, but in a secret environment most of these constraints are necessary.

29. I believe the CIA official whose epigraph begins chapter 8, Don Burke, is well aware of this and that he was exaggerating to make a point. For more on this issue, see "No More Secrets: National Security Strategies for a Transparent World," report on a workshop convened by Suzanne Spaulding and sponsored by the American Bar Association Standing Committee on Law and National Security, the Office of the National Counterintelligence Executive, and the National Strategy Forum, Washington, D.C., January 10, 2010, at http://nationalstrategy.com/Portals/0/Conference%20Reports/No%20More %20Secrets%20Conference%20Report.pdf, accessed April 6, 2011.

30. I have heard this proverb attributed to Cardinal Richelieu, who combined the functions of prime minister and intelligence chief for Louis XIV of France, but can find no basis for that or any other attribution.

31. U.S. Senate Subcommittee on Reorganization of the Committee on Government Operations Commission on Government Security. Hearings on S.J. Res. 21, a Joint Resolution to Establish a Commission on Government Security, 84th Cong., 1st sess., March 15, 1955, p. 467. Bundy, who was then the dean of the Harvard University Faculty of Arts and Sciences, was quoting a colleague, Dan Van Vleck.

## CHAPTER 10: MANAGING THE MESS

1. President George H. W. Bush, National Security Directive 42, July 5, 1990, redacted for public release, April 1, 1992, at www.fas.org/irp/offdocs/nsd/nsd_42.htm, accessed June 1, 2010. The following year the National Research Council warned that the nation "depends on computers [for] power delivery, communications, aviation, and financial services" and said plainly that these systems were "vulnerable . . . to deliberate attack." It added, "The modern thief can steal more with a computer than with a gun" and that "tomorrow's terrorist may be able to do more damage with a keyboard than with a bomb." National Research Council, *Computers at Risk: Safe Computing in the Information Age* (Washington, D.C.: National Academy Press, 1991).

2. Preface to "Cyberspace Policy Review: Assuring a Trusted and Resilient Information and Communications Infrastructure," May 2009, at www.whitehouse.gov/assets/documents/ Cyberspace_Policy_Review_final.pdf, accessed January 6, 2010.

3. Presidential Decision Directive 63, May 22, 1998, at www.fas.org/irp/offdocs/pdd/pdd -63.htm.

4. The White House, "The National Strategy to Secure Cyberspace," February 2003, at www .us-cert.gov/reading_room/cyberspace_strategy.pdf, accessed April 5, 2011.

5. National Security Telecommunications Advisory Committee, "An Assessment of the Risk to the Cybersecurity of the Public Network," August 2009, p. ES-1. This document is not classified but it is not disseminated electronically.

6. Bill Gertz, "2008 Intrusion of Networks Spurred Combined Units," *Washington Times,* June 3, 2010, at www.washingtontimes.com/news/2010/jun/3/2008-intrusion-of-networks -spurred-combined-units/. Debora Plunkett, head of the NSA's Information Assurance Directorate, said that even the NSA works on the assumption that its systems have been penetrated by sophisticated adversaries. Jim Wolf, "U.S. Code-Cracking Agency Works as if Compromised," Reuters, December 16, 2010, at www.reuters.com/article/idUS TRE6BF6BZ20101217, accessed December 17, 2010.

7. The White House, "Cyberspace Policy Review: Assuring a Trusted and Resilient Information and Communications Infrastructure," May 29, 2009. The principal author of this review was Melissa Hathaway, who served ably under President George W. Bush as well as President Obama.

8. For the full text of the proposal and a section-by-section analysis, see the White House Web site at www.whitehouse.gov/omb/legislative_letters, accessed May 22, 2011. The proposal would strengthen the Federal Information Security Management Act, known as FISMA, which federal agencies must comply with, but FISMA represents the lowest common denominator of cybersecurity.

9. USCYBERCOM is technically a subcommand under U.S. Strategic Command, but it enjoys considerable independence.

10. For a remarkably candid assessment of cybervulnerabilities and proposals for dealing with them, see William J. Lynn III, "Defending a New Domain," *Foreign Affairs*, September/October 2010, p. 97, at www.foreignaffairs.com/articles/66552/william-j-lynn-iii/defending-a-new-domain, accessed February 20, 2011.

11. Whether this capability will extend to preemptive cyberoperations is legally as well as operationally complex. See Ellen Nakashima, "U.S. Eyes Preemptive Cyer-Defense Strategy," *Washington Post*, August 29, 2010, at www.washingtonpost.com/wp-dyn/content/article/2010/08/28/AR2010082803312.html, accessed August 31, 2010.

12. The rationale for this strategy is elaborated in Herbert Lin, "Offensive Aspects of Cybersecurity and Related Concerns," a paper from TTI Vanguard's Cybersecurity Conference, Washington, D.C., May 6–7, 2010.

13. At the Battle of Vicksburg in 1863, for example, Lieutenant General Ulysses Grant was able to secure the cooperation of the navy for operations on the Mississippi only through his personal relations with Acting Rear Adm. David Dixon Porter. "I had no more authority to command Porter than he had to command me." Ulysses S. Grant, *Memoirs and Selected Letters: Personal Memoirs of U.S. Grant, Selected Letters 1839–1865* (New York: Library of America, 1990), p. 306.

14. James R. Locher III, *Victory on the Potomac: The Goldwater-Nichols Act Unifies the Pentagon* (College Station, TX: Texas A&M University Press, 2002), p. 16.

15. Ibid., p. 17.

16. Ibid., p. 18.

17. Ibid., pp. 20–21. President Roosevelt tried to achieve better cooperation by creating the Joint Chiefs of Staff in 1942, but the chiefs were dominated by their separate services and could take no position without unanimity.

18. See, e.g., John Barry, "Deplaned," *Newsweek*, June 6, 2008, discussing the firing of the air force secretary, at www.newsweek.com/2008/06/05/deplaned.html, accessed January 9, 2010.

19. Locher, *Victory on the Potomac*, chapter 7 and pp. 45–48.

20. For the well-told story of this profoundly significant reform by the man with a ringside seat, see Locher, *Victory on the Potomac*. Goldwater-Nichols also turned the Joint Chiefs into a purely advisory body and took them out of the chain of command.

21. Locher, *Victory on the Potomac*, p. 450, quoting General John Wickham, USA.

22. For an account of how the federal emergency and disaster system (created two years before Katrina) is intended to work, see *The Federal Response to Hurricane Katrina: Lessons Learned* (February 23, 2006), pp. 11–19, prepared under the direction of former assistant to the president for homeland security and counterterrorism, Frances Fragos Townsend.

23. Government Accountability Office, "Opportunities to Reduce Potential Duplication in Government Programs, Save Tax Dollars, and Enhance Revenue," GAO Report GAO-11-318SP, March 2011, at www.gao.gov/new.items/d11318sp.pdf, accessed March 1, 2011.

24. The American fondness for the czar analogy is curious. As former CIA director James Woolsey likes to say, five hundred years of rigidity and stupidity followed by seventy-plus years of Bolshevism is not a governance model worth emulating.

25. In 1944, President Roosevelt established the State-War-Navy *Coordinating* Committee. It worked poorly because action required unanimity.

26. National Security Act of 1947, Pub. L. no. 80-253, § 101 (a), 61 Stat. 496(1947) (my ital-
ics). For a concise and valuable study of the NSC, see Cody M. Brown, *The National
Security Council: A Legal History of the President's Most Powerful Advisors* (Washington,
D.C.: Project on National Security Reform, 2008). When the NSC was originally proposed, constitutional objections were raised against any suggestion that it have directive
power, on the ground that it would diminish the president's constitutional powers. Ibid.,
p. 3. It is difficult to understand how creating a more powerful presidential staff would
diminish the president's power. The real objection to such a step is that it would diminish the power of the cabinet secretaries. Art. II, Sec. 2 of the Constitution assumes the
existence of executive departments but does not specify their respective powers.

27. Executive Order 13,228, October 8, 2001, at http://frwebgate.access.gpo.gov/cgi-bin/get
doc.cgi?dbname=2001_register&docid=fr10oc01-144.pdf, accessed March 30, 2011.

28. "[C]ompromise is the soul of interagency discussion. The process is designed to force agencies to make more and more compromises as disputes move up the ladder from assistant to deputy to secretary." Stewart Baker, *Skating on Stilts: Why We Aren't Stopping
Tomorrow's Terrorism* (Stanford: Hoover Institution Press, 2010), p. 128. This volume is
the inside story of how that process really works. See also Roger Z. George and Harvey
Rishikof, *The National Security Enterprise: Navigating the Labyrinth* (Washington, D.C.:
Georgetown University Press, 2011), Part I: "The Interagency Process."

29. National Commission on Terrorist Attacks Upon the United States, *Final Report* (New
York: W. W. Norton, [2004] ), p. 419, stating: "So long as oversight is governed by current congressional rules and resolutions, we believe the American people will not get the
security they want and need. . . . Few things are more difficult to change in Washington
than congressional committee jurisdiction and prerogatives. The American people may
have to insist that these changes occur, or they may well not happen." NOTE: see ch. 9,
n. 25 for previous cite to this document.

30. The NSA is not the only home of world-class cyberexperts in the federal government, but
it has by far the largest group of them. Its red teams use only open-source tools when
testing systems and not their own specially engineered, classified tools.

31. The mismatch also has a budgetary aspect, and I'm not speaking only of the fact that the
resources devoted to network security have been inadequate. As it stands, the NSA's
budget for red teaming is in the Defense ISSP, or Information Systems Security Program. Not surprisingly, DoD wants the defense red-teaming budget applied to DoD systems. Whether NSA red teams test nondefense systems (they may do so now only with
permission) or whether that function moves to the Department of Homeland Security
is not important. But the budget must be aligned with the scope of the problem, and
the function must be exercised without permission from the officials responsible for the
system.

32. Tom Gjelton, "Cyberwarrior Shortage Threatens U.S. Security," NPR, July 19, 2010, at
www.npr.org/templates/story/story.php?storyId=128574055, accessed July 19, 2010.

33. Bureau of National Affairs, "New Defense Authorization Bill Excludes Key Cyber Pro-
visions," Electronic Commerce & Law Report, December 21, 2010, at www.npr.org/
templates/story/story.php?storyId=128574055, accessed January 3, 2011.

34. The Supreme Court understands the risk of creating rigid legal standards in this fast-
moving field—but only by a vote of 5–4. *City of Ontario v. Quon*, 130 S.Ct. 2619, 2629
(2010) (opinion by Justice Kennedy), at www.texascityattorneys.org/2010speakerpapers/
fall-OntariovQuon-case-SGladsone.pdf, accessed April 5, 2011.

The judiciary risks error by elaborating too fully on the Fourth Amendment implications of emerging technology before its role in society has become clear. . . .
Prudence counsels caution before the facts in the instant case are used to

establish far-reaching premises that define the existence, and extent, of privacy expectations enjoyed by employees when using employer-provided communication devices.

35. J. Alex Halderman, "To Strengthen Security, Change Developers' Incentives," *IEEE Security and Privacy*, March/April 2010, p. 79.

36. For a succinct description of how the OMB works, see Gordon Adams, "The Office of Management and Budget: The President's Policy Tool," in Roger Z. George and Harvey Rishikof, *The National Security Enterprise: Navigating the Labyrinth* (Washington, D.C.: Georgetown University Press, 2011).

37. J. Livingood, N. Mody, and M. O'Reirdan, "Recommendations for the Remediation of Bots in ISP Networks," draft no. 10, December 2, 2010, p. 7, available on the Web site of the Internet Engineering Task Force (IETF) at http://tools.ietf.org/html/draft-oreirdan-mody-bot-remediation-10, accessed January 9, 2010. The IETF is an activity of the International Society, is a nonprofit organization founded in 1992 to provide leadership in Internet related standards, education, and policy.

38. Jack Rosenberger, "How Top ISPs Could Reduce Spam," *Communications of the ACM*, August 2010, p. 13, at http://mags.acm.org/communications/201008/?CFID=4949264&CFTOKEN=36226451#pg15, accessed January 9, 2010.

39. Robert McMillan, "Court Order Helps Microsoft Tear Down Waledac Botnet," *Computerworld*, February 25, 2010, at www.computerworld.com/s/article/9162158/Court_order_helps_Microsoft_tear_down_Waledac_botnet, accessed December 13, 2010.

40. 18 U.S.C. §2511.

41. The two ISPs I know of that offer "walled garden" services are Comcast and Cox Communications. See Lolita C. Baldor, "Internet Security Plan Under Review Would Alert Users to Hacker Takeover," *Washington Post*, October 18, 2010, at www.washingtonpost.com/wp-dyn/content/article/2010/10/18/AR2010101800243.html, accessed October 26, 2010.

42. The technical issues involved in disclosure and notice to customers are discussed in Livingood et al., "Recommendations for the Remediation of Bots in ISP Networks."

43. For a discussion of such a project at Microsoft, see James Larus and Galen Hunt, "The Singularity System," *Communications of the ACM*, August 2010, p. 72, at http://mags.acm.org/communications/201008/?CFID=4949264&CFTOKEN=36226451#pg74, accessed January 9, 2010.

44. See "A Virtual Counter-Revolution," *The Economist*, September 2, 2010, at www.economist.com/node/16941635, accessed April 30, 2011.

45. For a learned and engaging statement of another point of view, as well as a superb account of the fundamental technological issues in the development of the Internet, see Jonathan Zittrain, *The Future of the Internet and How to Stop It* (New Haven: Yale University Press, 2008).

46. U.S. Department of Energy, Office of Inspector General, "Federal Energy Regulatory Commission's Monitoring of Power Grid Cyber Security," report no. DOE/IG-0846, January 2011, p. 2.

47. Improving attribution alone will not solve our cyberinsecurity, however. See David D. Clark and Susan Landau, "The Problem Isn't Attribution; It's Multi-Stage Attacks," [2011], research paper available at http://conferences.sigcomm.org/co-next/2010/Workshops/REARCH/ReArch_papers/11-Clark.pdf, accessed January 10, 2011.

48. James R. Gosler, "The Digital Dimension," in J. E. Sims and B. Gerber, eds., *Transforming U.S. Intelligence* (Washington, D.C.: Georgetown University Press, 2005), pp. 96, 104.

49. Ibid., p. 105, text at n. 24, quoting Michael Wynne, acting undersecretary of defense for acquisition, technology, and logistics, "Memorandum for the Chairman, Defense Science Board, Terms of Reference," Defense Science Board Task Force on High Performance Microchip Supply, December 18, 2003.

50. The reverse is also true. For example, the iPhone is assembled in China. Its components and labor have a value of about $179. Our trade statistics assume that the entire device is made in China, even though its components come from Japan, Germany, South Korea, the United States, and various other countries. The Chinese contribution to the value of the device is about $6.50. Andrew Batson, "Not Really 'Made in China,'" *Wall Street Journal*, December 16, 2010, at http://online.wsj.com/article/SB10001424052748704828104576021142902413796.html?mod=WSJ_Tech_LEADTop, accessed December 16, 2010.

51. Joseph Markowitz, "The Enemy Is Us," in papers from the TTI Vanguard Cybersecurity Conference, Washington, DC, May 6–7, 2010.

52. Stewart Baker et al., "In the Crossfire: Critical Infrastructure in the Age of Cyber War," Center for Strategic and International Studies and McAfee, [January 28, 2010], p. 19, at http://img.en25.com/Web/McAfee/NA_CIP_RPT_REG_2840.pdf. See also Paul Kurtz et al., "Virtual Criminology Report 2009: Virtually Here: The Age of Cyber Warfare," McAfee and Good Harbor Consulting, 2009, p. 17, at http://iom.invensys.com/EN/pdfLibrary/McAfee/WP_McAfee_Virtual_Criminology_Report_2009_03-10.pdf.

53. My pessimistic view about the ability of authoritarian regimes to exert some degree of control over networks is shared by Eric Schmidt and Jared Cohen of Google. See their "The Digital Disruption: Connectivity and the Diffusion of Power," *Foreign Affairs*, November/December 2010, p.81, at www.foreignaffairs.com/articles/66781/eric-schmidt-and-jared-cohen/the-digital-disruption, accessed January 9, 2010.

54. James Glanz and John Markoff, "Egypt Leaders Found 'Off' Switch for Internet," *New York Times*, February 15, 2011, at www.nytimes.com/2011/02/16/technology/16internet.html, accessed February 15, 2011.

55. Help Net Security, "73% of Organizations Hacked in the Last 2 Years," February 8, 2011, at www.net-security.org/secworld.php?id=10550, accessed February 10, 2011.

56. Help Net Security, "Half of IT Professionals Leave Mobile Security to Chance," June 22, 2010, at www.net-security.org/secworld.php?id=9453, accessed June 22, 2010.

57. Mobile voice security, or rather insecurity, is another growing problem. When I joined the NSA in 2002 there were very few organizations in the world capable of systematically intercepting this kind of communication. That capability is now available for a few thousand dollars. But most people don't know that and continue to believe incorrectly that they can communicate securely on mobile phones.

58. This technology is commercially available. See, e.g., the Web site of Mobile Armor, Inc., a division of Trend Micro Incorporated, at www.mobilearmor.com/solutions/usb-encryption.html, accessed April 5, 2011.

59. "Imperva: Survey Finds Most Employees Will Leave with Company Data," *Global Security Mag*, November 2010, at www.globalsecuritymag.com/Imperva-Survey-finds-most,20101122,20732.html, accessed December 16, 2010. See also "Industrial Espionage Escalates as 60 Per Cent of Redundant Workers Take Data," PublicTechnology.net (UK), December 29, 2008, at www.publictechnology.net/content/18397, accessed February 15, 2010.

60. Op. cit., chapter 9, note 31.

61. Between 2002 and 2006, for instance, 478 laptops were lost or stolen from the IRS, 112 of them containing sensitive taxpayer information. Privacy Rights Clearinghouse, at www.privacyrights.org, accessed September 24, 2008.

62. Verizon, "2008 Data Breach Investigations Report," p. 15, fig. 12, at www.verizonbusiness.com/resources/security/databreachreport.pdf, accessed April 5, 2011, analyzing more than five hundred cases.

63. Robert McMillan, "How to Steal Corporate Secrets in 20 Minutes: Ask," *Computerworld*, July 30, 2010, at www.networkworld.com/news/2010/073110-how-to-steal-corporate-secrets.html, accessed August 2, 2010. Under the contest's ground rules, the identity of the companies was not reported.

64. See Joel F. Brenner, "Information Oversight: Practical Lessons from Foreign Intelligence," Lecture no. 851, Heritage Foundation, September 39, 2004, at www.heritage.org/Research/Lecture/Information-Oversight-Practical-Lessons-from-Foreign-Intelligence, accessed November 29, 2010.
65. Web site of the national counterintelligence executive, at www.ncix.gov/publications/reports/traveltips.pdf, accessed February 20, 2011.

# A (VERY) SELECT BIBLIOGRAPHY

A comprehensive bibliography covering issues of electronic warfare, intelligence, and government reform, as well as cyber- and physical security, would itself be a large book. On cybersecurity alone, the number of papers and books constantly emerging is daunting. I offer a few suggestions—necessarily subjective—for basic reading for those interested in these areas. Those who wish to plunge deeper will follow the endnotes and the emerging literature. Those interested in technical issues will know to look elsewhere.

## STRATEGIC THINKING ABOUT THE INTERNET

Jack Goldsmith and Tim Wu, *Who Controls the Internet? Illusions of a Borderless World* (New York: Oxford University Press, 2006).

Lawrence Lessig, *Code and Other Laws of Cyberspace* (New York: Basic Books, 1999).

Jonathan Zittrain, *The Future of the Internet and How to Stop It* (New Haven: Yale University Press, 2008).

The White House, "Cyberspace Policy Review: Assuring a Trusted and Resilient Information and Communications Infrastructure," May 29, 2009. The principal author of this study is Melissa Hathaway, who also ran cybersecurity policy under President George W. Bush. This review contains a useful bibliography.

## CYBERCRIME AND SOCIAL DISRUPTION

John Arquilla and David Ronfeldt, *Networks and Netwars: The Future of Terror, Crime, and Militancy* (Santa Monica, CA: RAND Corporation, 2001).

Joseph Menn, *Fatal System Error: The Hunt for the New Crime Lords Who Are Bringing Down the Internet* (New York: Perseus Books, 2010).

## PRIVACY

Whitfield Diffie and Susan Landau, *Privacy on the Line: The Politics of Wiretapping and Encryption*, 2nd ed. (Cambridge, MA: MIT Press, 2007).

Jeffrey Rosen, *The Unwanted Gaze: The Destruction of Privacy in Amercia* (New York: Random House, 2000).

## ELECTRONIC WARFARE AND INTERNATIONAL CONFLICT

Adda B. Bozeman, *Strategic Intelligence and Statecraft: Selected Essays* (Washington, D.C.: Brassey's, Inc., 1992). This erudite volume has nothing to do with electronic networks and everything to do with the profound impact of patterns of thought on international conflict.

Jeffrey Carr, *Inside Cyber Warfare* (Sebastapol, CA: O'Reilly, 2010).

Richard A. Clarke and Robert K. Knake, *Cyber War: The Next Threat to National Security and What to Do About It* (New York: HarperCollins, 2010).

Martin Libicki, *Cyberdeterrence and Cyberwar* (Santa Monica, CA: RAND Corporation, 2009).

Joseph S. Nye Jr., *The Future of Power* (New York: Public Affairs, 2011).

Timothy L. Thomas, *Dragon Bytes: Chinese Information-War Theory and Practice* (Fort Leavenworth, KS: Foreign Military Studies Office, 2004).


## CYBERSECURITY OF THE ELECTRIC GRID

Stewart Baker, Natalia Filipiak, and Ktrina Timlin, "In the Dark," a report by the Center for Strategic and International Studies and McAfee, April 18, 2011, at www.mcafee.com/us/resources/reports/rp-critical-infrastructure-protection.pdf.

U.S. Department of Energy, Office of Inspector General, "Federal Energy Regulatory Commission's Monitoring of Power Grid Cyber Security." Report no. DOE/IG-0846, January 2011, at www.ig.energy.gov/documents/IG-0846.pdf.

Juniper Networks, "Architecture for Secure Scada and Distributed Control System Networks," 2010, at www.juniper.net/us/en/local/pdf/whitepapers/2000276-en.pdfhttp://www.juniper.net/us/en/local/pdf/whitepapers/2000276-en.pdf.

John D. Moteff, "Critical Infrastructure: Background, Policy, and Implementation," Congressional Research Service, March 13, 2007, p. 1, n. 1, at http://assets.opencrs.com/rpts/RL30153_20081010.pdf.

North American Electric Reliability Corporation and U.S. Department of Energy, "High-Impact, Low-Frequency Event Risk to the North American Bulk Power System" ("High-Impact, Low-Frequency Report"), June 2010, p. 30, at www.nerc.com/files/HILF.pdf.

U.S.-Canada Power System Outage Task Force, *August 14th Blackout: Causes and Recommendations*, ("Blackout Report") April 2004, at https://reports.energy.gov/.

Joseph Weiss, *Protecting Industrial Control Systems from Electronic Threats* (New York: Momentum Press, 2010).


## COUNTERINTELLIGENCE AND ECONOMIC ESPIONAGE

James Gosler, "Counterintelligence: Too Narrowly Practiced," in *Vaults, Mirrors, and Masks: Rediscovering U.S. Counterintelligence*, J. E. Sims and B. Gerber, eds. (Washington, D.C.: Georgetown University Press, 2009).

Eamon Javers, *Broker, Trader, Lawyer, Spy: The Secret World of Corporate Espionage* (New York: HarperCollins, 2010).

Harvey Rishikof, "Economic and Industrial Espionage: Who Is Eating America's Lunch, and How Do We Stop It?" in Sims and Gerber, *Vaults.*

U.S.-China Economic and Security Review Commission, 2010 Report to Congress (Washington, D.C.: USGPO, 2010), at www.uscc.gov/annual_report/2010/annual_report_full_10.pdf.

# INDEX